Green Careers
FOR
DUMMIES®

by Carol McClelland, PhD

WILEY

Wiley Publishing, Inc.

Green Careers For Dummies®

Published by
Wiley Publishing, Inc.
111 River St.
Hoboken, NJ 07030-5774
www.wiley.com

For general information on our other products and services, please contact our Customer Care Department within the U.S. at 877-762-2974, outside the U.S. at 317-572-3993, or fax 317-572-4002.

For technical support, please visit www.wiley.com/techsupport.

Wiley also publishes its books in a variety of electronic formats. Some content that appears in print may not be available in electronic books.

Library of Congress Control Number: 2009941922

ISBN: 978-0-470-52960-7

Manufactured in the United States of America. This book is printed on recycled paper.

10 9 8 7 6 5 4 3 2 1

WILEY

3 1558 00260 8990

About the Author

Carol McClelland, PhD, is one of the nation's leading green career experts. As the executive director of Green Career Central, Carol is driven by three passions: guiding people to discover fulfilling careers aligned with their values, learning about innovations that enable people to live, work, and play more sustainably, and marveling at the inspiring wisdom of nature. Founded in March 2007, Green Career Central is an online resource center committed to clarifying the ever-evolving world of green career possibilities. Green Career Central provides career guidance, coaching, and training for:

- Professionals who want to change careers or find a way to use their existing skills within the green economy.

- Students who are committed to starting their careers with a green focus.

- Career development professionals who must become familiar with the new economy to guide their clients and students to their career goals.

Carol's highly acclaimed email newsletter, *Green Career Tip of the Week*, and the *Green Career Central Blog* are valuable resources for those seeking to understand the green economy. She has appeared on *U.S. News* Online, Planet Green's *Focus Earth*, hosted by ABC reporter Bob Woodruff, and radio talk shows throughout the U.S. She is a highly sought-after speaker at leading green industry events including the Good Jobs Green Jobs Conference Job Expo, the Solar Living Institute's Green Career Conference, and career counseling events such as the International Career Development Conference and Career Management Alliance Conference.

Carol received her PhD in Industrial/Organizational Psychology from Purdue University. Her books on career change and life transitions include *Your Dream Career For Dummies* (2005) and *The Seasons of Change* (1998).

The green economy is evolving. To stay up-to-date explore these links.

- Discover the latest industry trends and updated book links: www.green careercentral.com/updates

- Sign up for the *Green Career Tip of the Week*, a free email newsletter, and receive your copy of Carol's *7 Steps to Your Green Career* audio: www. greencareercentral.com/7stepsaudio

- Explore options for career development professionals who are working solo or in a career center: www.greencareercentral.com/ counselors

- Contact Carol: www.greencareercentral.com/contactus

Dedication

To my parents and my brother, Tom, for the times we shared as a family: camping throughout California, road trips to National Parks in the western U.S. and Canada, cross-country camping trip for the Bicentennial, time in the woods of Dover, New Jersey, and Fourth Lake in upstate New York. I will never forget the ad hoc biology labs and physics discussions!

To Kent Fields, my husband and co-founder of Green Career Central, for our shared passion for nature: trips to Yosemite, Glacier National Park for our engagement, Northern California coast for our wedding, Death Valley for the big bloom, and the Rocky Mountains of Colorado and Canada. Where shall we go next to experience and savor 360 degrees of natural beauty?

Author's Acknowledgments

Every conversation I have about the green economy, whether with a Green Career Central member, a green career colleague, a career counselor, a workshop participant, or a member of the media, inspires me to continue clarifying the unfolding green economy. I'm honored to have the opportunity.

My acquisitions editor, Lindsay Lefevere, had impeccable timing! I started writing soon after the 2009 stimulus package was enacted. Thanks go to my agent, Carol Susan Roth, and Marty Nemko for the roles they played as well.

I thoroughly enjoyed working with Corbin Collins, my Wiley project editor, and Jeana Wirtenberg, our technical editor, to create the book you now hold. I'm indebted to Rebecca Kieler, Richard Hewitt, Christine Hertzog and Lauren Delp for their contributions. A huge thank you goes to the Wiley team for work in transforming my manuscript into a book in the marketplace.

So many names, so little space! I'm incredibly grateful to my team for keeping Green Career Central growing while I wrote: Susan Sullivan, Tessa Valle, Donna Gunter, Angela Giffin, Lauren Delp, Ellen Silva, and Kent Fields. I'm also blessed by colleagues and friends who have offered compelling ideas and heartfelt support since the early days of Green Career Central: Lauren Sullivan, Susan Reid, Kristi Breisch, Cheryl Esposito, Samantha Hartley, Laurie Taylor, Lisa Morrison, Karin Marcus, Lynn Strand Marks, Linda Lenore, Janice Summers, Mudge Kennedy, and Mitch Slomiak.

Kent and I started dating the week I signed my first *For Dummies* deal, so he's a veteran. I so appreciate his dedication to keeping me at the top of my game while also tending to our household, our young goldendoodle, Aspen, and tasks associated with our business. I'm incredibly grateful. I love you!

Publisher's Acknowledgments

We're proud of this book; please send us your comments at http://dummies.custhelp.com. For other comments, please contact our Customer Care Department within the U.S. at 877-762-2974, outside the U.S. at 317-572-3993, or fax 317-572-4002.

Some of the people who helped bring this book to market include the following:

Acquisitions, Editorial, and Media Development

Editor: Corbin Collins

Acquisitions Editor: Lindsay Lefevere

Assistant Editor: Erin Calligan Mooney

Editorial Program Coordinator: Joe Niesen

Technical Editor: Jeana Wirtenberg

Senior Editorial Manager: Jennifer Ehrlich

Editorial Supervisor and Reprint Editor: Carmen Krikorian

Editorial Assistant: Jennette ElNaggar

Cover Photos: ©iStock

Cartoons: Rich Tennant (www.the5thwave.com)

Composition Services

Project Coordinator: Katherine Crocker

Layout and Graphics: Ashley Chamberlain, Joyce Haughey

Proofreaders: Melissa Cossell, Bonnie Mikkelson

Indexer: Claudia Bourbeau

Publishing and Editorial for Consumer Dummies

>   **Diane Graves Steele,** Vice President and Publisher, Consumer Dummies

>   **Kristin Ferguson-Wagstaffe,** Product Development Director, Consumer Dummies

>   **Ensley Eikenburg,** Associate Publisher, Travel

>   **Kelly Regan,** Editorial Director, Travel

Publishing for Technology Dummies

>   **Andy Cummings,** Vice President and Publisher, Dummies Technology/General User

Composition Services

>   **Debbie Stailey,** Director of Composition Services

Contents at a Glance

Table of Contents

Introduction

. . . .

*W*elcome to *Green Careers For Dummies*! You've probably seen news reports that a wave of green jobs is coming. This trend is drawing you to explore whether the green economy has something to offer you.

Whether you're committed to finding a career that will have a positive impact on the planet or you see that there's ample opportunity to make a difference in your own pocketbook, you're ready to discover what it takes to land a job in this new economy. You'll be happy to know that there are plenty of ways to make a good living while doing your part to help the Earth.

By picking up this book, you are already an early adopter, a pioneer at an exciting time in history. The cornerstones of the green economy are still being put in place. Key policies, funding, and technological advances are unfolding and will continue to do so for some time. It's too early to know exactly what these change will mean to our world and the economy in the years ahead.

The green economy is in its infancy and growing fast. Not everything is known yet. What we do know may be obsolete if new technologies or policies are put in place. To succeed in this transformative environment, you must be comfortable with an evolving unknown, changing conditions, and moving beyond the status quo to find innovative ways to do what needs to be done.

The practical suggestions and tactics I give you throughout this book work as long as *you* put them to work. To make the most of these strategies, you need to take what I give you and figure out the best way to apply it to your target industry and your local area. If you do that, you will tap into the opportunities that are best for you. One glimmer of insight leads to a new connection that opens a door you didn't even know existed.

About This Book

If you've been paying any attention to the media, you know the green economy has gotten a fair amount of press since President Obama took office in early 2009. Talk of the power of the green economy to bring jobs back to America had a dreamlike quality there for a while. It seemed the green economy was going to cure all ills from the tanking economy to the overtaxed environment, saving us from high-priced fuel and bolstering national security.

A solid, well-thought-out transition to a clean, non-carbon based economy will likely put more people to work, help the environment, and protect us from high-priced fuel — over time. Reporting about stimulus money made it sound like it would be an overnight transformation, when in fact that money is planned to be distributed through 2012. If you are looking for a magic bullet, a quick fix, or a crystal ball, you've found the wrong book.

I can tell you that my team and I have been studying the green economy from the moment I launched my green career business in March of 2007. We scan our sources every day to discover what we can about developing trends and opportunities. In this book, my job is to give you the straight scoop, as I know it today. By the time you read the pages I've written, some factors may have changed. You need to keep that in mind and use the strategies I show you to build your own knowledge of your target field.

Keep in mind that there is always some risk involved. I can't promise you that your career path will always be straight and clear. What I can predict is that your search for your green career is going to be a roller coaster ride like no other. It's likely to be both exhilarating and a bit hair-raising at times.

Are you up for the challenge? If so, enjoy the ride!

Conventions Used in This Book

To make this book as usable as possible, I use the following conventions.

- ✔ *Italics* are used to emphasize important terms and to illustrate keywords you can use in Web searches.

- ✔ **Boldface** words and phrases in bulleted lists and numbered steps help you pick out the keywords at a glance.

- ✔ All Web addresses are in a special `monofont` typeface. Often the link I provide is only one page of a very interesting Web site. When you find something that grabs your attention, take your time exploring the entire site for other information that may be of interest to you.

  In my search for resources and information to help you understand the green economy, I found a lot of very long Web addresses. Often they are so long they run longer than the width of this page. When you find one of these Web addresses, just ignore the break in the text when you enter the address in your Web browser.

- ✔ When I use the word *companies* in this book, I'm really referring to any kind of organization you might want to work for. You may see yourself working for a public or private company or you might prefer to work for a government agency, a nonprofit, an educational institution, a small business, or a consulting firm. Although green job opportunities are available in all these settings, it would be cumbersome to refer to all of them every time. And besides, if it's really going to be a green economy, there are going to have to be a lot of companies in it.

What You're Not to Read

Whether you're currently employed and exploring your green career options or need to find a job now, chances are you don't have a lot of time. If you need to skip over sections of the book, here's what I suggest you jump over.

- ✔ Sidebars provide descriptions of concepts unique to the green economy and industries that are just beginning to gain traction. These sections are shaded in gray and stand apart from the text.

- ✔ The industry profiles in Chapters 7 through 13 are meant to be scanned for relevance. If the topic isn't interesting to you, feel free to skip it.

- ✔ If you aren't employed at the moment, you can leap right over Chapters 20 and 22 that help you take your green career to the next level or help you green your current job.

Foolish Assumptions

Now that you are reading this book, I assume

- ✔ You want a green career. You may be moving in this direction because you're concerned about the state of the environment or because you recognize the green economy is the next big wave of economic growth. Either way, you are a player in this unfolding story that is going to color our future for some time to come.

- ✔ You're committed to making a difference in your pocketbook. Sure, changing the world is a great goal. I assure you that this book describes real career options that pay.

- ✔ You're not attached to the status quo. You're ready for change in your professional life and the world.

- ✔ You have an inquiring mind. You want to discover more about what you don't know. You're reading this book to expand your thinking about your career options and the green economy.

- ✔ You're willing to put some legwork and elbow grease into your own job search. As much as I'd like to, I can't give you your green career on a silver platter. I give you all the tips and shortcuts I know of, but you've got to take the initiative to put them to work.

How This Book Is Organized

The chapters in this book are organized into six parts.

Part I: Discovering the Green Frontier

The green economy is a broad, far-ranging sea of opportunity. You have to figure out what you're getting into, gain a sense of the factors shaping the green economy, and understand why the green economy is still a work in progress. Grasping the unique features of the new economy provides you with new insights about the possibilities for you. The chapters here help you discover where the opportunities are within the green economy. Better yet, you can find out what's available for someone with your education, background, and salary needs. Getting a sense of why it's a bit challenging to find a green career helps you counteract these unknowns.

Part II: Finding Your Green Focus

The most effective way to shorten your path to your green career is to define the green focus that allows you to leverage your existing skills, experiences, and interests. When you know where you are heading, it's far easier to know what actions you need to take to get there. These chapters get you to explore your interests. Not just within the green/sustainability arena, but in all areas of your life. You also take a look at your favorite skills. Claiming what you enjoy and do well gives you the building blocks for your future career. Finally, this part helps you pull together potential career ideas by combining your interests and skills in creative ways. By the end of this part you have an idea of your green career goal.

Part III: Exploring Careers in Green Industries

One of the most challenging aspects of the green economy is knowing what green careers actually exist. In this part you find seven chapters filled to the brim with profiles of the most advanced green industries. Scan the different industry categories in the table of contents to decide which chapters you're most drawn to explore. Then review each industry profile to identify the industries you want to target.

The industry profiles can serve as a starting point for your own research. Use the industry description and current and future trends to get a sense of the industry. Then explore the associations, resources, and sample job functions to discover what you might want to do in the field.

Part IV: Using Green Job Search 2.0 Techniques

Whether you launched your last job search a year ago or more than a decade ago, in this part you discover up-to-the minute strategies to structure your job search. Discover online and in-person methods for gaining valuable information about your target industry and build a strong, responsive network. Explore the most effective ways to strengthen your knowledge and skills in the green/sustainability world. Bring all your discoveries together as you prepare your resume to articulate your value to green employers.

Part V: Activating Your Green Job Search

When you're ready to launch your job search, here you can identify companies that match your green career goals and figure out how to find job openings in the evolving green economy. After you've landed your green career, use these chapters to find out strategies you can use to develop your green career over the long term.

Part VI: The Part of Tens

In a series of short and sweet tips, these two chapters offer a collection of green career resources you can use to move your job search forward. And while you're searching for your next job, consider ways to green your current job as a way to bolster your resume for your next move.

Icons Used in This Book

Ideas next to this icon help you move your green job search forward.

Paying attention to the tidbits next to this icon saves you time, money, and perhaps even some heartache. With this icon, I warn you about possible problems or glitches you can encounter on the way to your green career.

This icon flags information that you should keep in mind in the long term as you explore your green career options.

Throughout the book I use concrete examples to illustrate important concepts. Seeing the idea in action gives you a better idea about how to apply it in your own job search.

Where to Go from Here

Are you ready to get started? Although you can start with any chapter, let me offer a few suggestions to get you off to a good start.

If you're wondering how to use your skills in the green economy, check out Chapters 4 through 6 to identify your green focus — or explore the green industry profiles in Chapters 7 through 13.

If you're ready to launch your green job search, focus on the second half of the book. Chapters 14 through 17 help you set the stage for your job search.

If you'd like to start at the beginning, heck, turn the page to Chapter 1 to start understanding how the green economy is evolving with opportunities.

Part I
Discovering the Green Frontier

"They're solar panels. We're hoping to generate enough power to run our tanning beds."

In this part . . .

The emerging green economy is this generation's new frontier. Understanding the new economy opens up opportunities for a wide range of professions. In this part you discover the factors that shape the green economy and what jobs qualify as green. Find out what it takes to thrive within the new economy and what mindset you need to hold to find your place in the green economy.

Chapter 1

The New World of Green Careers

In This Chapter
▶ Making sense of where it all stands
▶ Understanding what the green economy really is
▶ Getting a handle on the opportunities within the green economy
▶ Discovering tactics you can use to find a green position

*T*his is a very exciting time. We're in the earliest stages of a new economic era, and the first paths into this future are just beginning to be defined. Many more paths will emerge as new industries take form over time. To risk a metaphor, it's a bit like the Old West, with nascent opportunities beckoning those with the courage to strike out for them. Think of yourself as a pioneer in the first wave of many who will take this journey. As with any frontier situation, you must keep your wits about you as you find the right path through uncertainty to your chosen destination.

Transforming business-as-usual into a new green/clean/sustainable economy is likely to take decades, as new technologies are invented, tested, and adopted, as new policies are shaped and implemented, and as new behaviors become second nature. Each new element of the economy will become a stepping stone for the next level of innovation, just as the inventions of textile machines, steam engines, and ironmaking techniques led to a series of innovations during the Industrial Revolution. The economic landscape of the green future will be defined and shaped by the goals and actions put in place now that can turn our unsustainable way of life into a sustainable one.

Welcome, then, to the new Wild West of the career world. To understand why this world is different from the one you're familiar with, let's look at where we've been and how we got to where we are.

Taking a Step Back in Time

The Industrial Revolution brought incredible progress with an amazing number of breakthrough inventions, mechanized production methods, more-effective transportation methods, and newfangled contraptions. If you scan the inventions that have come on the scene since the Industrial Revolution, you notice that our lives have been forever changed by the advent of consumer goods, synthetic materials such as plastics and polyester, and electronic gadgets. Progress!

What we didn't know at the time, and haven't known for certain until recently, is that the factories that manufactured all the stuff we've come to love and need were also spewing out more human-generated carbon dioxide and other greenhouse gases in a shorter span of time than the planet had ever seen before. These emissions have created an unintended problem for our entire planet. With more emissions in the atmosphere, more solar heat is trapped, creating slowly rising global temperatures. (For more details on global warming, see Chapter 2.)

Looking back, we can also see that the Industrial Revolution set us on a path of pulling a tremendous amount of minerals, materials, and natural resources from our surrounding environment. Over time the United States and other industrialized countries turned to importing resources from other countries without regard to how our harvesting impacted the natural systems of their country or ours.

The modern economy's fuel habit is another part of the problem. We've grown accustomed to using as much fuel as we need to live very cushy lifestyles. In fact, the Center for Environment and Population (www.cepnet.org) notes in its recent U.S. Population Energy and Climate Change Report, that "while the U.S. represents about 5% of the global population, it consumes about 25% of the world's energy, and generates 5 times the world average of CO_2 emissions."

Where does this leave us? With the unpleasant knowledge that our lifestyle is utterly unsustainable. If we continue living the way we've been living, we'll run out of oil, forests, animals, and land at some point in the future. You might not live to see that day, but your kids and their kids might.

Thomas Friedman, in his book *Hot, Flat, and Crowded*, notes that the world's population is growing dramatically (the crowded part), with a larger and larger percentage of people around the world making enough money to strive for a decidedly American lifestyle (flat), in a world that's been heating up since the Industrial Revolution (hot).

It all adds up to a serious problem.

Understanding the Green/Clean/ Sustainable Economy

We're now being called upon to take bold new actions to solve this problem that has the potential to cause catastrophic harm. The good news is that we have the technology and know-how to solve this problem. What we seem to lack is the political and personal will to make the necessary changes to bring our world back into a sustainable balance.

As this book outlines, innovative thinking and groundbreaking actions are occurring right now in many of the industries we depend on. Of course, the transformation we're likely to experience is not going to take us back to the lifestyles of past centuries. Instead, innovations will move us forward to a new way of living that has a much lighter *footprint* (impact) on the planet.

Before we proceed, let's take a look at a few key terms:

✔ **Green:** You've no doubt noticed that it's a word that gets thrown around a lot by the media, activists, and politicians. With the exception of companies that are *green-washing* (leading you to believe that their product or service is beneficial to the planet even though it's not), the people committed to solving this problem use *green* as shorthand for something that improves the state of the environment in a discernable way. It might refer to a product, industry, company, job, process, or organization that conserves energy and resources, generates clean, renewable energy, minimizes waste, eliminates hazardous materials, or restores the environment and biodiversity.

As new trends take hold, it's common for words to evolve quickly and fluidly, so keep these things in mind:

- No industry, company, or job is 100 percent green, though some are making impressive strides in the right direction. Making anything greener is a process that occurs over time.

- Some companies or initiatives may be described as light green (more casual, cursory, and surface attempts) or dark green (very serious, dedicated, and taking real action).

- Look not only at the final product, but delve into its entire life cycle. We must review the materials and processes that went into creating the product, how the product is used, and how it's disposed of at the end of its life.

- Our definition of *green* will evolve with new technology and regulations. As the definition becomes more stringent, the bar will be raised, motivating us to push for better results.

- As green ways become integrated and common, it's likely that the term *green* will fade away. Right now the term distinguishes new innovation from traditional ways. When green policies are standard, we won't need to call attention to them.

✔ **Clean:** Products, processes, and services that depend on renewable energy sources, minimize waste, and use natural resources judiciously are deemed to be clean. You'll often hear this term used to refer to clean energy or *cleantech*. If you look at the fine print on some cleantech Web sites you may find emphatic declarations that they are *not* green. Apparently they are attempting to distance themselves from a previous iteration of *green,* when green groups focused on advocacy or addressed issues of pollution control. Times have changed.

✔ **Sustainable:** Humans in industrialized cultures tend to live in ways that are unsustainable. In other words, we take far more from the Earththan it can regenerate in a reasonable amount of time. As a result, we're making it harder for future generations to have the same standard of living. To become sustainable we need to change our ways: We must find energy sources that are naturally renewable and create effective ways to handle our own waste so we don't foul the planet. One way to become sustainable is the triple bottom line approach — attending to the economic *and* social *and* environmental impacts of our choices.

In this book I use all three terms because the situation calls for all three. That said, it's not always feasible to include all three terms in every discussion. I may also use the word *green* as shorthand for the multi-faceted concepts that create green, clean, and sustainable ways of doing business.

The *green economy* refers to the industries that are producing greener products, using cleaner processes, and offering more sustainable services in an effort to move us toward a new standard. Some industries are farther along the trail than others. You'll be amazed at the activity in this new economy that some experts are already calling the New Industrial Revolution (http://en.wikipedia.org/wiki/New_Industrial_Revolution).

Thar's Green in Them Thar Hills

Are you depressed now? Does all that sound hopeless and impossible? Well, recall that the United States was built by people who took risks during challenging times under seemingly impossible circumstances.

✔ Colonists crossed oceans to settle in a land of opportunity.

✔ Pioneers traversed the plains and clamored over mountain ranges to reach the West Coast for the promise of gold.

✔ Inventors and businesses transformed the economic landscape by implementing innovations to create the industrial revolution.

✔ In just 15 years people overcame the incredible hardships of the Great Depression and won World War II.

✔ In less than a decade scientists set and reached the unbelievable goal of putting a man on the moon.

✔ The Internet, a geeky obscurity just 20 years ago, has completely transformed how we all do business, communicate, and live.

Innovative thinking has always led us to achieve amazing goals, reap astounding profits, and gain personal satisfaction and fulfillment along the way. Just as in previous eras, the opportunities that accompany our huge challenges are enormous, the innovations are inspiring, and the potential benefits are incredible.

Clarifying Your Place in the Green Economy

The transition from where we are now to where we need to be will require a large number of people playing a variety of roles. There are so many opportunities in this transformative process that it's impossible to track them all. The green economy experts I know say that tracking the entire green economy is like drinking from a fire hose.

To find your green career, you have to identify where your skills fit early in your quest. Although it may feel as though it's adding time to your journey, knowing your focus actually shortens your path to your green career. With a clear vision of your target industry and profession, you have a rudder you can use to steer your actions as you prepare for your job search. You'll know what information to read, what meetings to attend, what training to obtain, and who to contact to discover more about your chosen green career. Having this clarity saves you time, frustration, and missed opportunities.

Use the steps outlined in Chapters 4 through 6 to review your interests and skills from various parts of your life. That helps you identify the best way to apply your talents in the green economy. Don't worry if you aren't sure what's possible — you'll find a collection of industry profiles to explore to help you identify the industries that are likely to be the best fit for you.

Opportunities Are Everywhere

Some industries that contribute to the green economy are obvious: Renewable energy, green building, ecotourism, and natural resources are no doubt industries you've heard of. Others are not so obvious. In fact, I've made new green industry discoveries just while researching this book:

- Green ports
- Environmental education
- Waste-to-energy
- Green medical practice
- Organic/green textiles and fashion

The green industries that are likely to have the most impact are those that touch the parts of our lives that are so familiar to us that we take them for granted.

- Look at electricity. As you live now, you probably don't know exactly where your electricity comes from, how it was generated, or how it reaches your house to power your appliances. All you know is that when you flip that switch you have power. As our electric grid is redesigned and smart components are added that enable us to assess our power usage in real time, we'll develop a more conscious relationship with the power we use at home and at work. We'll know how much power we are using and which appliances are costing us the most money. With this knowledge we'll be in a much better position to conserve energy and save money.

- Another example is how we handle waste. When you put your trash on the curb, it disappears, never to be thought of again. In actuality, trash is taking up more and more landfill and polluting our world with toxins and materials that don't biodegrade. What we know about waste and how we handle it is likely to change dramatically as we move to a more sustainable world. New innovations will transform packaging to reduce waste at the front end, while new technologies will allow us to reuse and recycle more and more of the products we use at home and at work.

To grasp the range of industries that are becoming more sustainable and green, scan the industry profiles in Chapters 7 through 13.

The green economy is changing quickly. For nearly half the industries I researched, I found key announcements that had been made within the previous week or month. Even with the final last-minute check on the status of fast-changing industries, I know that the minute I turn in my final manuscript, the green economy will continue moving forward. It's the nature of the beast! But don't worry, I've got you covered. My Web site, Green Career Central, has

been tracking industry developments since this book was published. Visit
www.greencareercentral.com/updates to discover what continues to
unfold in your target industry.

Taking the Initiative: It's Up to You

Although every career change and job search takes commitment and dedication, finding a green career takes a bit more initiative. Given that the green
economy is just now forming, the tools you may be accustomed to using for a
job search may not be very effective. The resources you use to research your
target industry may not have any information about cutting-edge industries,
companies, and jobs. Your usual networking methods may not produce the
leads you need.

The tactics included in this book give you insider tips to help you move your
green job search forward faster. Although plugging into the resources I discuss
gives you advantages other green job seekers may not have, it's impossible
to predict exactly how long your job search will take. Your journey will
depend on how your target industry is developing, as well as your target
position and how many other people are searching for that job.

The key to success is starting your preparations for your green career as
soon as possible, even while you're working in the traditional economy. The
deeper your network, the more you know about your target industry; and
the better you've developed your skills, the more likely you are to attract the
attention of those who will hire you.

Finding Green Job Opportunities

Finding job openings in any economy is challenging. Within the green
economy you have a few more challenges that can hinder your progress.

The first thing you must know about finding potential green job openings is
that, just like in the traditional economy, *the vast majority of the jobs are not
posted on job boards or even on company Web sites*. Sorry. I know that makes it
harder, but it's true. It's up to you to ferret them out.

The people in your target green industry are the ones you need to connect
with to hear about job openings. They also know the inside story of what's
happening in various green companies. Having a strong green network and
being in close contact with those in your network are the most effective ways
to find potential green opportunities. Chapter 15 spells out the best ways to
build your green network.

To make the most of your network connections, you must be able to articulate in crystal clear terms what kind of position you are looking for. Your network can't help you if you haven't figured it out or you don't know how to describe it so others understand you. (For tips on this, see Chapter 17.)

If you can tell your contacts about the companies you're targeting, all the better — but how do you know which companies to target? Unfortunately, at this early stage, there aren't many lists of green companies you can count on. If you do find a list with the top companies in a particular industry, bookmark it, print it out, tape it to your fridge, and use it as a starting point for your own research.

Three factors make finding green jobs challenging (for tactics to help you counteract these challenges, check out Chapter 18):

- ✔ Most likely you want to work in a company in a particular geographic area. You aren't interested in just any solar company — you want to work in one in your city or another city you've already targeted.

- ✔ You also need to discern whether the companies that look appealing to you hire people with your skills and talents. You need some way to get inside these companies to understand them.

- ✔ You also need to determine whether the companies are green/clean/sustainable. Not easy to do, but there are ways.

The Green Economy Is Your Oyster

There is — or will be — a place in the green economy for everyone. Your skills, passions, talents, and education make you uniquely suited to fill a particular position. The trick is finding it. This book gives you the information and resources you need to find your place in the green economy.

If you don't see a place to apply your skills right now, don't despair. New positions are evolving as new technologies emerge, policies are enacted, and goals are defined. While you wait for the perfect fit, continue to build your network, develop your talents, and track movements within your target green industry. Consider applying what you discover to your current position or taking an active role in moving your industry into the new sustainable age.

Ultimately, the opportunities of the green economy are going to be what you make of them. It's up to you to find what part you'll play in designing and implementing a green, clean, sustainable world.

Chapter 2

Inside the Green Economy

· ·

In This Chapter

▶ Taking a quick look at issues related to climate change

▶ Discovering the forces that are defining the green economy

▶ Uncovering how the green economy differs from the traditional economy

▶ Judging where the journey toward the full green economy stands

· ·

*I*n a well-known parable from India, blind men are asked to examine an elephant and report their findings. The man who was at the tail describes a rope, the man at the trunk recalls a snake, the man who felt the tusk is reminded of a spear, the ones at the legs report a treelike being, and so on.

The green economy is like the elephant. As each specialist, politician, business owner, and worker scans their part of the new economy, they develop a picture based on their experience. Because the green economy is a huge, ever-changing, amorphous form at the moment, it's nearly impossible for any one individual to make a thorough, accurate assessment of it. (That includes me, though I use examples from a wide range of experts and companies throughout the book to try to weave together a picture of the green economy for you.)

In truth, the green economy is the sum of many people's impressions. Everyone must contribute knowledge and experience to unlock the best way to move toward an economy that treads lightly on the environment. To participate in defining the problem and searching for the solution, you must gain a solid understanding of why climate change is spurring on the move to a new economy, how the green economy is being formed, and why it's different from the traditional economy.

As you consider the issues in this chapter, don't get bogged down in the magnitude of the problem. Instead, keep your eye out for areas where you may be able to use your talents and skills to be part of the solution. The clues you gather about your interests and skills will help you define your green career focus in Chapters 4 through 6.

Making Sense of Climate Change

By now you have no doubt heard of climate change. You may have read about the subject in detail (if so, you can skip to the next heading) or you may just know vaguely that it's bad without fully understanding the problem and its ramifications. Use this very short explanation to get up to speed.

Scientific definition

As the Earth receives light from the sun, it absorbs that energy and converts it into heat. The gases in our atmosphere, such as carbon dioxide, methane, nitrous oxide, and ozone, hold that heat in, much as a greenhouse retains heat. Scientists have known about this naturally occurring effect since 1824 when Joseph Fourier discovered that our temperatures would be a lot cooler if we didn't have the atmospheric layer surrounding our planet.

So far, so good. The problem is that the carbon dioxide emitted during the Industrial Revolution of the 19th and 20th centuries has changed the quality of our atmosphere such that it holds more of the sun's heat in than it used to. Although scientific finding do show fluctuations in the Earth's temperatures throughout its history, those changes generally take place over thousands of years rather than tens of years. For more details, visit `http://environment.nationalgeographic.com/environment/global-warming`.

Skeptics and deniers

There are those who have questions and doubts about the scientific evidence regarding global warming and climate change. Deniers flat out deny the data regarding climate change. Skeptics are scientists who have reviewed the data and have questions about the conclusions. Generally speaking, there are two issues that attract attention:

- Are temperatures really rising?
- If so, are the increasing temperatures the result of human activity?

The Intergovernmental Panel on Climate Change was founded to review published scientific literature throughout the world to ascertain the impact of climate change. In its most recent report released in 2007, the IPCC's work group on the scientific basis of global warming (`www.ipcc.ch`) concluded that, "Global atmospheric concentrations of carbon dioxide, methane and nitrous oxide have increased markedly as a result of human activities since 1750 and now far exceed pre-industrial values determined from ice cores spanning many thousands of years. The global increases in carbon dioxide concentration are due primarily to fossil fuel use and land use change, while those of methane and nitrous oxide are primarily due to agriculture."

Environmental ramifications

If average temperatures on the planet rise, even by a degree or two, that's enough to shift weather patterns around the globe. Some regions become warmer, and others become cooler. Some areas receive more precipitation and others less. As glacial ice melts due to hotter temperatures in the mountains and the poles, sea levels are likely to rise, threatening coastal areas where a large part of Earth's population lives.

Because the Earth is a natural system, even a seemingly subtle climate change has the potential to trigger a domino effect. For instance, if animals can no longer find food in their traditional range, they search for a new place to live. They may need to adjust their eating habits to fit their new range. As a result of these seemingly innocuous changes, the ecosystem in their original range begins to change as does the balance in their new range.

If these changes occur over a period of thousands of years, the animals adapt over a number of generations (or in the end never adapt). Unfortunately the climate changes we are experiencing now are happening far too quickly for many animals to even have a chance at adapting. As a result, extinctions are likely to follow. To get a glimpse of how climate change will influence the rate of extinctions, read http://news.mongabay.com/2007/0326-extinction.html.

If you think climate change is some far-off, abstract effect, think again. Rising temperatures are already impacting our world in visible ways. Take a look at the interactive map by *National Geographic* to get a sense of the range of changes we may experience on our planet: http://environment.national geographic.com/environment/global-warming/gw-impacts-interactive.html.

Economic impact

As increasing temperatures impact the natural environment, we can also expect to see disruptions in our economic world as well. The Center for Integrative Environmental Research (www.cier.umd.edu/climate adaptation) conducts regional research on the economic impact of climate change and the costs of inaction. Based on its findings, it's clear that we will feel the impact on the economy itself, on the infrastructure we are accustomed to, and on the natural resources we depend on for food, water, food, and building materials.

Although forecasts like these are never very pleasant to read or consider, knowing the problems facing your region can help you see potential ways you can make a difference in your community. Go to www.cier.umd.edu/climate adaptation and scroll down to the map. From there, click on a region to access a concise, easy-to-read two-page report on the economic impact of climate change in that region.

Political fallout

As natural resources become scarce, crops fail, and natural disasters take their toll on various regions of the world, nations have two options: Work together to find solutions to pressing problems or develop strained relationships that make it difficult to collaborate.

Factions in the U.S. are already focusing on preserving traditional industries and resources. Although this strategy may have a short-term payoff, continuing to invest in technologies and resources that cannot take us into the new, clean economy isn't going to pay off in the long run. Some politicians, decision makers, and business owners continue to deny that climate change is worth worrying about.

Just as previous revolutions (the Internet) and economic shifts (the Great Depression) needed an extra boost from the government in the form of funding, incentives, and projects, the green economy will more likely take root and build a strong foundation with similar kinds of support.

Global solutions

Climate change is not just happening in one country or one region. It's happening around the world. Every village and neighborhood is going to feel the impact now or in the future.

To succeed in turning the tide, we must approach climate change with a global focus. Solutions must be based on cooperation, collaboration, and the pollination of ideas. There's no time for each region or town to re-create or build solutions from scratch. When people find something that works, they must share that far and wide so others can reap the same benefits in their local area.

The United Nations Environment Programme's Green Economy Initiative is paving the way for collaboration through three projects: a green jobs report on global employment trends, an economic valuation of ecological services and biodiversity to demonstrate how critical it is to nurture biodiversity throughout the world, and a green economy report to show how policymaking can move the green economy forward worldwide. For more details, see www. unep.org/greeneconomy.

The Green Economy Is a Work in Progress

The move to a green economy was born out of the need to reduce global warming by decreasing the amount of greenhouse gases we are emitting into the atmosphere. Among those who believe climate change is real, there's general agreement that people must make changes in the way they live and do business. Experts say that we must transition from a carbon-based economy to one based on clean, renewable energy, but there's little consensus as to the best strategies to achieve that goal.

There seem to be more good questions than solid answers: What are the steps we need to take? Which steps should come first? How long will it take? What will give us the biggest reduction of greenhouse gases for the investment? How much should the government be involved? What's the best to way to spur this transition to the new economy? The list goes on and on.

Although media reports may have you wondering why the green economy isn't in full swing yet, the reality is that the cornerstones of the green economy are still being put in place. As each feature of the green economy is defined, the business community becomes clearer about the actions it can take to receive a return on investment. Knowing the rules of the road enables companies to be willing to invest in what will be in demand in the green economy.

As it stands now, the green economy is constantly evolving. Each of the following sections discusses a factor that has the potential to change the definition of the green economy. By tracking these factors yourself, you'll be able to watch as the defining features of the green economy continue to unfold.

Goals and mandates

One of the most effective ways to change behavior is to create policies and regulations that encourage green actions and discourage actions that are inconsistent with the goals of the green economy. Over the years some local governments and states have put policies and regulations in place to move their regions in a green direction. The result has been a patchwork of policies that has made it difficult for the business community to fully embrace the stated goals and act. With the new Obama Administration, a more nationally focused set of policies and regulations are under discussion. Although details are not all nailed down, it is clear that the administration intends to encourage investments, innovations, and business development in the green economy. Only time will tell exactly what all the key policies will look like.

In May 2009, the White House announced a new National Fuel Efficiency Policy that requires automobile manufacturers to produce vehicles that have "an average fuel economy standard of 35.5 mpg by 2016." The details of the policy outline various milestones for model years between 2012 and 2016. With this policy in place, auto manufacturers now know exactly what's expected of them. For more details about this policy read the press release, `www.whitehouse.gov/the_press_office/President-Obama-Announces-National-Fuel-Efficiency-Policy`.

One potential policy to watch for is a National Renewable Energy Standard. Currently more than half the states in the U.S. have a policy that encourages or mandates electricity companies to include a certain percentage of their electricity from renewable energy sources (see page 8 of `www.nrel.gov/docs/fy08osti/41409.pdf`). This kind of policy opens up opportunities for renewable energy companies because investors can fund these companies knowing that there is a built-in customer base waiting for the power produced. A national standard would do even more to open up this market.

Incentives and disincentives

Some laws put incentives and disincentives in place to influence the behaviors of consumers, businesses, or investors. Implementing the right incentive program can literally create a marketplace overnight.

But what goes up often comes down. When existing incentive programs expire after a designated period of time, industries may falter as their guaranteed customer base vanishes. The hope is that the corresponding industry has reached a level of stability so that the expiration doesn't cause the industry to contract.

In the past, the wind industry has depended on a production tax credit (PTC) as a vehicle to encourage investors to provide capital for new installations. Unfortunately, the PTC system was often in place for a year and then it would expire. Then it would be reinstated again and expire again. Without a reliable tax credit, investors won't invest because they don't have a guaranteed return through the tax credit system. This graph tells the story even more clearly: `www.ucsusa.org/assets/images/ce/AWEA-wind-capacity-graph.png`. When tax credits are extended, the industry flourishes, but the minute those tax credits lapse, there's been serious trouble for the wind industry. Thankfully, the American Recovery and Reinvestment Act of 2009 extended the current PTC through 2012.

A couple of programs to watch as they work their way through the national or local political system include the cap and trade system to encourage companies to reduce their greenhouse gas emissions (`www.epa.gov/captrade`) and a solar feed-in tariff to motivate home owners to install solar panels so they can sell their extra energy to their local utility (`http://earth2tech.com/2009/03/02/florida-utility-kicks-off-solar-feed-in-tariff-a-first-for-the-us/`). Both of these programs, if put in place, have the potential to stimulate the green economy.

Treaties and agreements

In 1997, a number of industrialized nations came together to agree to reduce six greenhouse gases in the Kyoto Protocol, an addition to the United Nations Framework Convention on Climate Change (UNFCCC), an international treaty originally signed by 192 countries in 1994. Although the United States signed the Kyoto Protocol, it was never ratified by the Senate, so the U.S. is not legally bound by the agreement. In 2005 the Kyoto Protocol was officially put in place for the more than 140 other countries who had ratified it.

Nevertheless, the Kyoto Protocol has continued to play a part in forming the green economy through the world. Under President George W. Bush, the United States chose to address the problem independently through voluntary measures that would reduce the *greenhouse gas intensity*, which is the "ratio of greenhouse gas emissions to economic output." Although this is not the same as reducing greenhouse gas emissions, it was the step the Bush Administration was willing to commit to. For a full description of the Kyoto Protocol process and U.S. policy, check out this entry on the Encyclopedia of Earth: www.eoearth.org/article/Kyoto_Protocol_and_the_United_States.

When Mayor Greg Nickels of Seattle, Washington, realized that the United States was not on board with the Kyoto Protocol, he created the U.S. Conference of Mayors Climate Protection Agreement, which enabled mayors to commit to the same Kyoto reductions in greenhouse gas emissions for their cities. As of 2009, more than 1,000 mayors had signed the agreement and used it to guide their actions locally. For more information and to see whether your mayor has signed, visit http://usmayors.org/climateprotection/agreement.htm.

By the time this book is published, another meeting will have been held in Copenhagen to figure out what to do when the Kyoto Protocol expires in 2012. As I write this section, it's clear that it's too early in the pre-treaty discussions to predict what strategy the Obama Administration will take on the world stage. For more on this meeting, take a look at http://en.cop15.dk.

Research funding

With the green economy comes the need for new innovations and new knowledge. As you've no doubt noticed, a number of interlocking problems need exploration and out-of-the-box thinking. Unfortunately, research, thinking, and innovation requires quite a bit of funding — that is, money. Most universities, think tanks, and research labs have been stretched in recent years by decreasing funding and tight budgets.

The American Recovery and Reinvestment Act provided a much needed boon for many research facilities around the country. Entering *research* into the search field on `www.recovery.gov` yields many announcements on research funding. The following are three that I found. If you try it, you're likely to find even more announcements by the time this book is published.

- ✔ The National Science Foundation committed $300 million dollars to research instrumentation and $200 million for repairs and renovations of academic research facilities.

- ✔ The Department of Energy is providing more than $786.5 million to fund biofuel research and development and a demonstration biorefinery and $2.4 billion to explore carbon capture and storage technology.

- ✔ The Department of Interior is dedicating $140 million to over 300 projects at the U.S. Geological Survey.

Capital investments

Money makes the world go around. Start-up companies need money. Period. Without funds, companies promoting innovations that could change the world can fail quickly. Funds for the green economy come from three main sources:

- ✔ **Venture capitalists** continue to fund green companies. Investment trends are a good way to see how and where the green economy is growing. See the list of blogs on `www.dummies.com/cheatsheet/greencareers` for ones that track investments in key green industries.

- ✔ **Large capitalized companies**, such as Google, GE, IBM, and Cisco Systems, are moving into the green space by investing in other companies or partnering with other companies on joint projects.

- ✔ **Contracts, grants, and loans** from the American Recovery and Reinvestment Act funds are also proving to be a welcome revenue source through 2012. Companies that fit the criteria announced by various governmental agencies may be in a good position to receive funding for certain kinds of projects. For a map of funds see `www.recovery.gov`.

Innovations

Although climate change is unlikely to be reversed through innovation alone, technological advances are likely to play a significant role in determining how the green economy develops over time. As new technologies come on the scene, don't be surprised if they knock previous technological darlings off the map. It's entirely possible that innovations within emerging industries such as algae biofuels, cellulosic biofuels, and lithium ion batteries could change the future by opening up new avenues for even further development.

The smart grid, an emerging sector, has the potential to transform how electricity and information are handled from power generation, transmission, and distribution to energy storage and real-time energy management technology. The Gridwise Alliance (www.gridwise.org) believes that developments in this sector are likely to spawn entirely new industries yet to be imagined. See Chapter 10 for more information about the smart grid.

Scientific findings

Watching *An Inconvenient Truth* was the first time many people thought about global warming. By putting scientific findings in engaging contexts, Al Gore woke many up to the issues. Unfortunately, knowing about global warming isn't enough. We must continue to turn to scientific findings to assess the current impact on the planet and to forecast how higher temperatures, shifts in ecosystems, and higher sea levels will impact our lives.

Unique Qualities of the Green Economy

Although the form of the green economy is still being shaped and defined, early adopters are already showing how that economy may look. Over the last two decades, innovative thinkers have shared new business strategies and philosophies that transform business-as-usual. By looking at these new business models, you can get a sense of how the green economy is going to differ from the traditional industrial economy we've had.

Don't worry about understanding every nuance of these new strategies. I cover them in more detail throughout the book and point you to other resources where you can dive into details when you're ready. For now, focus on how changing our energy philosophy can have an impact on the planet.

Putting a value on natural resources

For several centuries we've been taking resources from the planet without paying the bill. We use these resources — such as water, minerals, trees, and energy — without concern or consideration. We don't recognize the role the natural environment plays in providing clean air, clean water, building materials, and a place to grow food. We take it for granted that those services will always be there. If we don't acknowledge the value of these eco-services, we may find ourselves in a very compromised position in the near future.

Natural capitalism, a concept developed by Paul Hawken, Amory Lovins, and Hunter Lovins in their book by the same name, shows businesses the importance of incorporating the cost of natural resources when making business decisions. And by redesigning business processes by using inspiration from nature, resources can be used much more efficiently and economically.

Shifting to sustainable business practices

Companies that take on a green philosophy shift the dynamic within the company. Suddenly, doing business is about more than making products to make money. It's about using and valuing natural resources and human resources to create innovative ways of doing business that do no harm to the environment, the people who are touched by the company (such as employees, suppliers, customers, or neighbors), or the financial status of the company. This *triple bottom line*, as it is called, engages the workforce and the customer base in ways that stimulate creativity and innovation.

One way to implement this approach to business is through *sustainable business practices*, which means finding ways to do business that don't compromise future generations' ability to live healthy, full lives on the planet. To accomplish sustainability goals, companies must look at all aspects of their business to discover new ways to generate power, identify eco-friendly raw materials, handle waste, and rethink transportation and distribution.

Interface, Inc., manufactures carpet tiles under several brand names. In 1994, CEO Ray Anderson, had an insight that changed the course of his business. Determined to re-create the company with an eye toward sustainability, he and his employees spent the next 15 years transforming the processes, materials, and systems of their business to reduce their impact on the environment. Interface strives to create a restorative company, one that gives back more to the environment than it takes. Read about it at www.interfaceglobal.com/Sustainability/Our-Journey.aspx.

Rethinking manufacturing

For most of the industrial age manufacturing has been a linear process: take-make-waste. Industry has had little regard for the planet as it extracts more materials to make more things. At the end of the cycle, we *throw away* those same things with no regard for where they go, their continued impact on the planet, or the fact that we are throwing away materials that still have value.

Several scientists in the 1990s discovered that there *is* no such thing as waste in nature. What decays in nature becomes food for the next cycle of life. Applying this concept to manufacturing, waste and used-up, unwanted products are revealed as resources that can be reused to create new products. Called the *cradle to cradle* process, this shift in thinking opens up a new cyclical form of manufacturing that minimizes the amount of raw materials we extract from the planet and the amount of discarded waste at the end.

Companies who want to rely on cradle to cradle design concepts to produce products that are sustainably built can work with McDonough Braungart Design Chemistry (MBDC), a company founded by William McDonough and Michael Braungart, the authors of a book called, not surprisingly, *Cradle to Cradle*. They certify that companies using the term "Cradle to Cradle" are implementing the concepts thoroughly. Visit www.c2ccertified.com and click through to the certified products to discover companies that are using this philosophy in their manufacturing plants, including Steelcase, Pendleton Woolen Mills, Aveda, Herman Miller, and the U.S. Postal Service.

Building alliances for the greater good

No one group or individual has all the answers. Coming up with innovations and viable solutions requires looking beyond our own fields, connecting with others who see the world through slightly different lenses, and listening as they bring their own unique set of experiences to the problem at hand. As the saying goes, necessity is the mother of invention. As we face large modern problems, strange bedfellows join to find new solutions. The following are just a few stunning examples of what's possible when we work together.

The Blue Green Alliance (www.bluegreenalliance.org) is a partnership founded in 2006 by the Sierra Club and United Steelworkers to advocate for good-paying jobs in the green economy. Since its inception, additional unions and environmental groups have joined the effort that now brings over six million people together to fight for this important cause.

In the field of *biomimicry* (www.biomimicryguild.com), architects, industrial designers, engineers, manufacturers, business owners, and entrepreneurs join biologists, chemists, and researchers to find design solutions in the wisdom of the natural world. What results from these joint explorations are elegant, sustainable innovations in materials, designs, and processes that leverage the solutions nature has created through billions of years of evolution.

Look beyond your own profession to those with other backgrounds. Sometimes the most informative, inspiring conversations happen between people who have different perspectives and overlapping interests. By talking with others about sustainability and climate change, you may discover new career opportunities you may not have considered before.

Implementing efficiency and creativity

Although the word on the street is that it costs more money to go green, businesses that are making strides toward becoming more sustainable are finding just the opposite to be true. By becoming more mindful of how resources are used, the actual costs of doing business go down — sometimes quite dramatically. In fact, the savings created through these measures can then be used to fund other sustainability initiatives.

In New York City, the Empire State Building is going through an energy retrofit expected to cost $20 million, which is admittedly a large chunk of change. But that retrofit is going to produce an energy cost savings of $4.4 million dollars per year for the owner and the tenants of the building.

Of course, coming up with the cash upfront is the most challenging part of the preceding example. In the case of the Empire State Building, several organizations, including the Clinton Climate Initiative, the Rocky Mountain Institute, Johnson Controls, and Jones Lang LaSalle are funding this project as a model to inspire other building owners and cities to retrofit skyscrapers. In other situations, creative financing options are being invented to make it possible for organizations and homeowners to take action on their desire to be more sustainable. For more information see www.esbsustainability.com.

The city of Berkeley, California, has come up with an innovative financing program called FIRST (Financing Initiative for Energy Efficiency Renewable and Solar Technology), which provides initial capital to homeowners who want to install solar technology or make energy efficiency retrofits. The city sells bonds to raise funds to pay for the installations; the residents pay the city back through property taxes. For more details about this program, visit www.grist.org/article/berkeley-rules. This creative financing option makes solar more attractive and stimulates the solar industry in that region.

Dawning of a Brand-New Era

As the green economy takes shape and people recognize how it differs from the traditional economy, it's important to remember that the very first stages of the transformation may take years to play out. As cornerstones drop into place, we'll gain more insight into the forms of the green economy. There's no guarantee that the growth will be a steady ride. It's likely that specific industries, companies, and technologies will go through ups and downs as the economy matures, markets settle out, and technologies are replaced by newer innovations. There will be difficult transitions as traditional industries lose market share and new ones take the lead.

Eighty-eight percent of 2009 "stimulus package" disbursements were targeted toward health care initiatives, education, and income security, whereas only 12 percent were aimed at transportation, community development, and energy/environment. In 2012, the percentages will shift so that 63 percent of the funds will go toward transportation, community development, and energy/environment projects. In other words, funds for the greening of the economy will continue to be distributed through 2012 from this law alone (see `www.recovery.gov/?q=content/report-progress` for more on funding).

Green initiatives such as renewable energy, alternative transportation, smart grid, energy efficiency strategies, and waste management are going to take time to implement. Each industry will develop at a different rate, but it's almost inevitable that we'll continue to see green innovations and developments over the next few decades.

How Durable Is the Green Economy?

Now that this new economy is beginning to roll forward, people I talk to are starting to worry. Is the green economy a fad? Is it a bubble, like the mid-2000s real estate bubble, that's going to burst suddenly and leave us in the dust again? How can we be sure that the green economy is real?

Although I'm not an economist, politician, or psychic, I have been watching developments in the green economy closely since March 2007. Throughout that time my team and I have continued to see promising signs of growth, innovation, and development. True, any particular industry, company, or technology could evaporate in a puff of smoke, but the overall green economy has a broad foundation and reason for existing now. The following are signs that the green economy will gain traction over time:

✔ Many experts see the shift to an energy-efficient, clean-energy economy as the solution to three of the most significant issues facing the world:

- Scientific evidence demonstrates a serious need to change our way of doing business and living. We cannot continue to pull resources from the Earth without regard for the future.

- Foreign affairs experts note that continuing to rely on foreign oil is likely to create more conflicts and much higher prices in the future. Creating a domestic source of energy would allow us to have more control of the pricing and enhance our national security.

- Economic specialists, who look for ways to jumpstart the economy, see that the green economy can stimulate job creation with projects that update and rebuild key elements of the infrastructure.

✔ Previous economic bubbles have been focused on one industry or in a couple of closely related industries. The greening of the economy is touching nearly every industry. Furthermore, green initiatives are being taken up by companies around the world. In fact, all sectors of the economy are involved, including public and private companies, non-profits, government organizations, and joint public-private ventures.

✔ Innovation is occurring from new energy sources, new manufacturing materials and processes, new products, new transportation options, new ways to process waste, and new building materials and methods. Laws, policies, incentives, and disincentives that extend out into the future are being put in place to encourage and support new industries.

✔ Funding for the green economy is coming from multiple sources, including money from the 2009 stimulus package, venture capital companies, major corporations, and grant organizations.

That said, there are no guarantees. And yet there is an underlying sense that we cannot *not* transition to a green economy. Read on to discover how you can help create the solutions that will have a positive impact on our future.

Chapter 3

Staking Out a Green Career

. . . .

In This Chapter

▶ Making sense of what qualifies as a green job

▶ Discovering where your skills are needed in the green economy

▶ Finding the money in the green economy

▶ Understanding how to identify possible paths into your green career

▶ Knowing what it takes to find your green career

. . . .

*D*epending on your news sources, you may be under the impression that green jobs are easy to come by or are scarce. In truth, a lot depends on the kind of green job you are looking for, where you live, and what industry you are targeting. In this chapter you get an overview of where you can look for a green job that fits your needs and interests. A number of factors come into play as you figure out which green jobs may be available for someone with your skills in your geographic region.

 With the green economy being as young as it is, there are no definitive definitions, job titles, job descriptions, or career paths established yet. Even if you ask a green career guru or a career counselor where you should look for this information or that, you may not be very satisfied with the response they provide. It's not that they know and aren't telling you, it's that no one person or organization has the whole green economy cataloged and accessible at the click of a mouse. To succeed, you need to take an active role in understanding the green economy, investigating industries that look intriguing, and identifying the job titles that are good targets for you.

Think of the green economy as a working draft rather than a final report. You may find industry descriptions to be rather vague and future projections to be a bit inconsistent. To get the best possible picture, you need to do your own legwork to fill in what you don't know and connect the dots about what you do know.

Exploring Where Your Skills Fit

Identifying the green job that's best for you is a bit like doing a 3-D puzzle. You have to understand each piece, make your best attempt to solve the puzzle, and then jostle the pieces around a bit to get them all to fit together. The good news is that there are more opportunities in the green economy than you probably know about right now. Before you dive into the process of figuring out the puzzle for yourself, take a few minutes to get the lay of the land.

Defining green jobs

At this point there is no universally agreed upon definition of a "green job." Most will agree that green jobs must improve the environment in some way. While useful, that definition isn't very helpful when you are trying to figure out how you want to contribute to the green economy.

The most helpful definition I've seen was developed in preparation for the first meeting of the Middle Class Task Force headed up by Vice President Biden: www.whitehouse.gov/blog_post/save_the_date_1. In this definition, green jobs are those that provide "products and services that use renewable energy resources, reduce pollution, conserve energy and natural resources, and reconstitute waste."

With specific green goals in the definition, it's easier to discern exactly how green jobs are expected to reduce the impact of humans and industry on the environment.

Not everyone uses any given definition when they talk about green jobs. When you read media stories or read statistics about the green economy, figure out how the author or researcher is defining the term *green job*. If the definition only includes jobs in the renewable energy industry, then the statistics aren't covering the entire green economy, but only one industry.

As the green economy matures and more companies implement sustainability initiatives, it's likely we'll come to a time when all jobs have a green component to them. By then, we may not distinguish between green jobs and traditional jobs because there won't be that much difference between the two. In the meantime, however, it makes sense to focus on jobs that enable you to have the most positive impact on the environment.

Having a direct, positive impact

Most of the green jobs you hear about in the media have a direct impact on the state of the planet. Certainly positions with the goals listed in the definition given in the last section have a direct effect by decreasing the amount of greenhouse gas emissions, waste, and pollution. The people in these jobs see the connection between their work and the state of the environment.

After reviewing the task force definition of a green job, I realized that there were a few more ways to improve the environment. As a result, my definition of green jobs is a bit broader. The bold components are goals I've added:

- ✔ **Generate** and use clean, renewable energy
- ✔ Reduce pollution
- ✔ Conserve energy and natural resources
- ✔ Reconstitute waste
- ✔ **Decrease the use of hazardous materials as inputs and outputs**
- ✔ **Remediate or reverse human impact on the planet**
- ✔ **Promote biodiversity and restore ecosystems**

Do any of these green goals appeal to you? If so, make a note to yourself. You now have a head start for Chapter 4, where you explore your interests.

Having an indirect, positive impact

Not all jobs in the green economy have a direct impact on the environment. Some positions allow people to make their contribution to the planet more indirectly. Rather than hands-on, in-the-lab, on-the-roof, or in-the-forest kind of work, people who hold these jobs have the following roles:

- ✔ Creating and enforcing green laws/policies/regulations
- ✔ Educating, inspiring, motivating, and persuading people/companies to take greener, more sustainable actions
- ✔ Funding or investing in green initiatives/companies

Although these green jobs are rarely mentioned by the media, the work done in these areas has a profound impact on the shape of the green economy. Without updated policies, directed funding, and renewed motivation, the green economy won't develop and grow very effectively.

Knowing There's a Place for Your Skills

At this point, you are probably wondering where your skills fit into the green economy. As the green economy evolves, opportunities will develop for people in all geographic areas, with all skills and education levels, at all pay grades. To get an idea of what you can expect based on your circumstances, take a look at the following descriptions.

Finding trade opportunities

By some accounts you may think every green job is a green collar job, or a blue collar job with a green focus. Certainly the most common jobs referenced in discussions of the green jobs movement are the solar installer who spends his or her time on roof tops and the wind technician who clocks a lot of hours high atop wind turbines.

If you enjoy working with your hands, building things, or making things work more efficiently, you'll find quite a few interesting applications for your skills.

Beyond solar and wind, you might consider green collar jobs in the manufacturing industry, building trade, natural resources management, smart grid infrastructure, or energy efficiency projects. If you don't have the skills needed in these industries, refer to Chapter 16 for information about strengthening your skills through education.

Identifying professional jobs

If you are an individual contributor or manager questioning your green career options, don't give up. The green economy isn't just for green collar workers, it's for everyone.

- **Technical roles:** If you have a scientific or technical background, you are likely to find work in a research capacity, a design role, an engineering function, or a computer modeling position. Nearly every industry category has the need for people who understand how to design spaces, objects, and processes to work efficiently and effectively.

- **Non-technical positions:** If you're accustomed to working in a business setting helping businesses grow, you'll find the same roles in green companies. The one caveat: If you're targeting an emerging industry, you may find that the companies in a research and development mode are not quite ready to hire people in operations, finance, marketing, sales, and human resources. It's possible you can get in on the ground floor if you're willing to be a generalist during this phase. Network in your area to find out about early-stage opportunities as they become available. Another option is to look to established companies that are going green.

- **Management positions:** As a manager, director, or executive, you have a couple options. If you're up for a challenge and have experience working with start-ups, you may find some once-in-a-lifetime opportunities to bring a cutting-edge technology or process to market. If your skills are more suited to working with established companies, your best option is to look for companies that are in the process of transitioning into sustainable businesses.

Scoping out the geographic trends

Green jobs are sprouting up all over the country. For a visual view of the green economy, check out this series of maps created by Earth2Tech, `http://earth2tech.com/maps` . At a glance you see where large solar installations, wind turbine manufacturers, cellulosic ethanol, and cleantech companies are sprouting up around the country. You can also see where coal power plants and ethanol plants are losing ground.

Now — and here's the tricky part — is the green job you want available or likely to be available in your area? Maybe yes, maybe no. It depends on where you live and whether your chosen industry can thrive in your region.

This isn't really a new phenomenon. The U.S. has seen certain industries cluster in particular areas due to natural resources or historical events in the region. If I say *timber*, you'll likely say Northwest. *Financial*, you'll likely think New York City. If I say *automobile manufacturers*, Detroit comes to mind, and for *steel* it's Pennsylvania — *beach tourism*, California, Florida, or Hawaii. You get the idea. Our country is so diverse that each region's industries have developed to take advantage of its resources.

The green economy is no different. Emerging industries are sprouting up in areas that can support the requirements of the industry. Solar, especially the utility-sized arrays, are heating up in the Southwest. Wind farms are blowing through the entire plains area. Biomass, which depends on green and woody growth, is mainly growing in the Mississippi Valley.

Other industries are evolving out of existing hotbeds of talent. Advocacy and lobbying organizations are gaining traction in the Washington, D.C., area and in large cities on the coasts that have a base of passionate donors. Cleantech hubs are becoming the next generation opportunity for a number of high tech centers, such as the Silicon Valley and the Boston area. Manufacturing plants around the country are being converted to produce wind turbines, building supplies, or solar arrays. Large cities with an abundance of outdated, drafty buildings are looking to their unemployed and underemployed to perform energy-efficient retrofits on existing buildings.

One other source of green opportunities in your area may be established companies that are implementing sustainability initiatives or working toward green goals. Watch your local media to see which local companies to track.

Look at the inherent strengths of your area to get a sense of the green industries that are likely to flourish in your area. What is your area known for? What natural resources are abundant in your region? Answers to those two questions will give you a sense of where to start looking for green opportunities in your region.

Understanding the array of industries

Matching up a green industry with your skills, interests, and experience is most likely on your mind as well. Before you hook your green career dreams to a particular industry, take some time to familiarize yourself with the full range of industries that make up the green economy.

You may be surprised by what you discover. The innovation required to reduce greenhouse gases and implement more sustainable processes is astounding. With a little exploration, you can find pioneering actions in emerging industries, governmental agencies, long-standing industries, well-known companies, utilities, and nonprofits. Opportunities abound.

To help you further your exploration, Part III of this book includes seven chapters that profile a number of industries in categories from environmental sciences and natural resources to energy and cleantech. The industry profiles also explore industries and functions that shape the economy, inspire, and motivate. To jump directly to one that interests you, see the table of contents.

Keep in mind that different green industries are developing at different rates. A company that's in a research and development phase won't have a place for someone with marketing and sales experience. That company is going to be allotting its budget to hiring scientists and technical specialists who can help bring a product, service, or process to market as quickly as possible.

While you wait for your target industry or company to be ready to hire people with your background, use the intervening time to gain the knowledge, skills, experience, and connections you need to be their ideal candidate. Spend time networking, talking with people in the industry, and volunteering in ways to develop your skills. Keep your finger on the pulse of the industry so you have a sense of when the doors will begin to open.

Discovering the Earning Power of Green Careers

For years now, those who wanted to do work to improve the state of the environment knew that they'd make less money than their colleagues who worked toward business goals. Many still hold a perception that there's no money in the green economy, that all the work is nonprofit based, and that all the hype about green jobs is just that, hype.

Let me set the record straight. The green jobs of today and tomorrow are not the environmental jobs of the past. There's definitely money flowing into the green economy in the form of venture capital funding and partnerships between established companies and new companies. In addition, funds from the stimulus package (the American Recovery and Reinvestment Act) are flowing to a wide range of recipients from government agencies, states, and cities to established companies and start-ups.

Organizations and companies with money tend to grow their operations by hiring more employees, purchasing equipment (that must be manufactured by someone, somewhere), and investing in new plants or offices (that must be built by someone locally).

A number of organizations, including Green for All (www.greenforall.org), the Apollo Alliance (www.apolloalliance.org), and the Blue Green Alliance (www.bluegreenalliance.org) are doing all they can to lobby for a green economy built on good, well-paying jobs for all. Although their focus is primarily on green collar jobs, their work is acting as a springboard for the entire economy that includes a mix of jobs for people at all levels.

In a *Business Week* piece, the author worked with PayScale (www.payscale.com) to identify the best-paying green jobs of 2009. They include a wide range of positions, from trade to technical, and nonprofit to executive throughout the green economy. For the full scoop, take a few minutes to view the slide show of 23 green jobs, ranging in pay from $39,500 to over $100,000: http://images.businessweek.com/ss/09/07/0721_best_paid_green_jobs/index.htm.

Blazing Your Own Path through the Maze of Green Careers

If you've been in the work world a while or you've listened to how your dad started his career, you may have a vision that you'll get into a green profession and then have a clear career path to follow as your career matures. The idea of this plan no doubt gives you a sense of security. You know where you are headed and what it's going to take to get where you want to go.

Sorry to burst your bubble, but the green economy doesn't yet have that level of structure built into it. Instead of having an established career path that takes you from Job A to Job D, it's far more likely that each person in Job A will embark on their own path to reach their ultimate Job D. It's not that the green economy is disorganized, it's that it's so new and evolving so quickly that there are few established job titles, let alone job paths!

Here are a few suggestions to help you glean as much information as possible about how companies are structured in the green economy:

- Emerging industries are going to be the most difficult to figure out. You'll need to spend time understanding the industry as a whole and then figure out how companies within the industry are structured. In early stage industries, each company is likely to have its own process, job titles, and even department structure. As the industry develops some standard practices, you'll see more continuity across companies in the same industry.

- In industries that are growing and maturing, such as the solar and wind industries, you can begin to see some standardization in their job titles and functions that you didn't see just a few years ago. You'll still need to do your homework, but getting a good picture of one company should help you get a handle on how other companies in the industry are structured. Your industry association or professional association may have some resources to help you.

- If you're looking for a position in one of the more-established industries such as environmental sciences or natural resources management, you'll actually be able to find some job titles on government produced occupation networks such as O*Net (`http://online.onetcenter.org/find`). Be aware, however, that the listings may not include all the latest information about innovations and green trends in your field. Nevertheless, it's a good place to start.

- Established industries that are going green, such as green building or green IT, may have a lot of the same job titles they've always had. The main difference is in what you need to know to excel in the field. It's also possible that a few new job titles will emerge as new positions evolve in the green versions of these industries. Large, existing companies may have a similar strategy. Most of their departments and job titles remain the same with the exception of a few new job titles for special projects or new responsibilities.

Doing a Reality Check

As you consider your green career options, it's possible you'll discover that your green career is more of a long-term goal than a short-term reality. Whether you're currently employed or out of work, you can make significant progress toward your green career while also attending to the realities of your current situation.

If you're employed and can't imagine switching jobs right now, focus on green-ing your current job (see Chapter 22 for strategies you can use), building your green network (see Chapter 15), and strengthening your green training (see Chapter 16). During this period you can also use your time to identify your green focus as I describe in Chapters 4 through 6.

If you're currently out of work or seriously underemployed, consider these strategies to get you back on track.

- **Interim job:** Find a job that allows you to bring money in the door but doesn't take all your energy by the end of the day. A low-stress job that leaves you with energy at the end of the day may be exactly what you need to continue your quest for your green career.

- **Stepping stone job:** Look for a position that helps you build the skills you need to leap into your ultimate position when it becomes available. Be very strategic as you make your decision about which job to take.

- **Bootstrap job:** Do whatever you can to piece together enough income to keep you going. It may not be pretty, but the variable schedule gives you opportunities to volunteer, work on entrepreneurial projects, go to school, and identify your green focus.

Succeeding in Your Quest

Changing your career direction is a significant decision on a good day. Making the choice to enter the green economy ups the ante even more. Use the following tips to stay focused as you step toward your green career:

- **Staying informed:** The green economy is currently in its infancy. Over time, as the economy develops, some industries will thrive, others will change in response to the marketplace and new technologies, and others will fade away into the sunset. The only way you can know where your target industry is heading is to track the factors that are shaping the green economy, your industry, sustainability, your profession, and the technology and processes unique to your field. Instead of being blindsided by these developments, use the changes you see to make strategic decisions about your future.

- **Taking the initiative:** Your green career is not going to be handed to you on a silver platter, you must take an active role in finding your place in the green economy. Throughout this book you find the tips, resources, and action steps I've pulled together from conversations with green career explorers, green job seekers, green career changers, and green career experts. The more of these you can put into action, the more you will see the results you are striving for.

✔ **Becoming an activist:** On occasion, you may find your career hanging in the balance as new laws, regulations, incentives, and disincentives are introduced or reach their expiration date. Stay alert. If you haven't yet subscribed to a newsletter for your profession or industry, it is time to do so. When your industry or profession is galvanizing its members to call for passing or defeating a certain measure, you need to pay attention.

✔ **Demonstrating your commitment to the planet:** Green employers want to hire job candidates who walk their talk. It's not enough to pretend you are green. Employers will know in a heartbeat if you aren't authentic. You must find ways to show prospective employers that you are committed to the environment and sustainability. Check out the Cheat Sheet at the front of the book for tips on how to green your resume.

✔ **Establishing your leadership:** During the early stages of the green economy, everyone must be a leader. Whether your job involves using a new technology, engaging people to take new actions, or encouraging your management team to make a process more sustainable, you must have leadership skills to get the job done. Look for opportunities to develop and demonstrate your leadership skills.

✔ **Navigating a changing world:** If you want to work in the first wave of the green economy, you must be comfortable with uncertainty. To thrive, you must be able to go with the flow when plans change, stay focused, pick up on trends amid the random noise of constant change, and change goals midstream as new circumstances demand it. Are you ready?

If you're just starting out on your quest for a green career, you may feel overwhelmed by all the options and directions you could go. Everything looks so interesting it's hard to narrow down your focus. Begin by keeping track of the topics that interest you. As you collect these clues, you'll begin to see possible themes develop. It's those trends that point you in the right direction for your career. Chapters 4 through 6 give you a step-by-step process you can use to clarify your green focus.

Part II
Finding Your Green Focus

The 5th Wave   By Rich Tennant

"I can tell a lot from your resume.
You're well educated, detail oriented,
and you like to conserve paper."

In this part . . .

Opportunities within the green economy are so numerous you can't possibly investigate each and every one. The key to success is to identify the part of the green economy that best fits your skills, interests, experience, and education. In this part you discover how to identify your green focus. With your green direction in mind, all parts of your green career search become more streamlined and effective.

Chapter 4

Pursuing Your Interests: Finding Green Topics That Engage You

In This Chapter

▶ Building a list of topics to consider

▶ Discovering what fascinates you

▶ Finding topics through everyday activities

▶ Fine-tuning your list of interests

*T*he green economy, as you've probably guessed by now, consists of a vast array of opportunities. Because you're looking for a green career, this may be both good news and bad news. The good news is that you are likely to find a career that matches your interests pretty well within the various green industries and professions. The bad news is that if you don't have well-defined interests to use as starting points, you may become overwhelmed and confused in the land of green opportunity.

The suggestions and activities in this chapter help you identify your own personal interests — the topics that excite you and point you toward your green career. And this process is enriched by taking a little time to devote to thoughtful consideration of many interests in your life. Although you may be drawn to organic food, renewable energy, or green building, for example, it is likely that you have many more interests than the one or two you can identify in the moment.

Throughout this chapter are real-life activities to help you uncover the interests that are clues to your future green career. In Chapter 6 you continue your journey, discovering the strengths you can draw from your education, experience, and talents.

Recognizing and Listing Your Interests

You main goal in this chapter is to create a long list of topics of interest, which you will ultimately narrow down to your top ten. By tapping into activities you do every day, you may be surprised how quickly your list comes together.

How do you know what your interests are? Well, you are what you do. In a nutshell, your favorite topics are pretty much certain to be the subjects you like to discuss, debate with others, read about, and ponder. Nonfiction books, documentary films, magazine and newspaper articles, and even blog posts are generally written about particular topics or sets of related topics. For example, the subjects of this book are green careers and the green economy. The subject of the documentary *An Inconvenient Truth* is global warming. The topic of *Green Eggs and Ham* is green eggs and ham.

The trick to creating your rich list of interests is noticing which topics interest you *most*. As you consider whether to add a topic to your list, take a moment to see if it fits one or more (or all) of the following descriptions:

- ✔ **The topic is like a magnet.** It draws you in. You keep returning to it time and again.

- ✔ **The topic excites you.** You like to think about it, talk about it, read about it, and maybe even dream about it.

- ✔ **The topic keeps you focused.** Time flies when you are thinking about it.

- ✔ **The topic inspires you to make new connections.** You discover new insights when you consider the topic.

- ✔ **The topic engages you.** You want to explore and gain as much new information about it as possible.

Don't set your threshold so high that nothing meets the standard. If you are interested in the topic, record it on your list.

Recognizing when your voice signals your passion

One of the best ways to spot a passion is to pay attention to your voice when you talk about various topics. Your voice is a great tool for judging how excited you are about a particular topic. As you listen, notice the general intensity with which you speak, including the following:

✔ **The speed of your words:** The faster you talk, the more excited you are.

✔ **The insistence in your voice:** If you try to convince, persuade, or educate someone on a topic, you're probably a proponent of the cause you are speaking about.

✔ **The duration of your monologues:** If you talk nonstop for any length of time, you are fascinated by the topic.

If you have a hard time hearing changes in your own voice, recruit your friends and loved ones to point out, in the moment, when you are speaking dynamically. As soon as you realize you are speaking from a passionate place, take a moment to recognize what you are talking about. That topic, whatever it is, is of importance to you. Place it on your list of interests.

Staying open to possibilities

One of the biggest mistakes people make when identifying their interests is getting attached to one, and only one, interest too early in the process. This can lead to the exclusion of others. As you are building your list, keep a broad focus. If a topic strikes your fancy, add it to your list. Don't worry about whether you have the training, education, or experience to incorporate this topic into your work. At this stage of the game, it's all about what fascinates, intrigues, excites, and engages you.

Ultimately, your green career is likely to be a combination of a number of interests identified with the help of this chapter, woven together with the strengths you define in Chapter 5.

Although you may be tempted to focus solely on green topics, I encourage you to keep the door open to all possibilities. Give yourself permission to explore the following:

✔ **Green topics** such as sustainability, environmental, ecology, recycling, socially responsible investing, energy efficiency, renewable energy, cleantech, conservation, organic, waste, mass transit, carbon neutrality, cap and trade, greenhouse gases, carbon emissions

✔ **Non-green** topics such as fashion, travel, business, cars, food, sports, design, home and garden, politics, entertainment, finance, antiques, genealogy, pop culture, building

✔ **Combined topics** such as organic gardening, eco travel, sustainable textiles, green design, green building

Think of your initial list of topics of interest as your first draft. You have an opportunity to edit and refine your list later in this chapter.

Looking at Your Actions

Although you may be able to come up with a list of interests right off the top of your head, don't be surprised if you get stuck. You've heard the phrase *actions speak louder than words.* That phrase is certainly true when you are searching for clues about your interests. Your everyday actions and habits hold a number of clues about your interests.

In this section are a number of activities that can bring your interests to light. Don't feel you need to follow through on every suggested activity. Choose at least one activity from each section. Do a few more if you are getting good results and want to collect more insights.

Each time you take an excursion, virtually or in the real world, take a note pad with you. Jot down the topics you are intrigued by. Although you may think it's safe to wait until you get home to record your discoveries, I encourage you to write topics down as you find them. You don't want to lose any clues, do you?

Studying what you read and watch

What you read can provide an excellent real-time glimpse into your interests. The following are some ideas to get a sense of what your interests are, based on what you read or watch:

- ✔ **Take a tour of your personal bookshelf, local bookstore, or library.** What kinds of books do you own? What books do you pick up at the bookstore or library? What sections of the bookstore or library do you gravitate toward? If you aren't able to go to a location with physical books, take a spin around your favorite online bookstore. Your goal will be the same: to identify the kinds of books you enjoy.

- ✔ **Visit a magazine stand.** Take an excursion to a local store with a wide variety of magazines. Give yourself an hour to browse the magazine racks. What magazines are you drawn to? What articles do you want to read? You may find you are drawn to a number of topics. Record them all on your list.

- ✔ **Scan your favorite Internet bookmarks.** What Web sites are among your favorites? What kinds of sites do you visit over and over again? What topics do they address that fascinate you?

- ✔ **Look for blogs that intrigue you.** Don't have a magazine stand in town? No problem. A virtual magazine stand called Alltop (www.alltop.com) pulls together the top blogs on different topics and shows you links to their articles on particular subjects. For example, entering **green** in the search box brings up a host of links to environmental blogs on all kinds of topics. Visit the site to scan the categories they have listed, enter a keyword for topics you want to read, or explore the alphabetical lists of topics they provide.

✔ **Listen to iTunes or watch YouTube.** If you aren't a reader or you prefer to listen to others read a book, give a presentation, or discuss a topic, you may prefer to look beyond the written word to audio and video. After you listen to or watch a selection, take a moment to determine the main focus of the recording. Include the topic on your list.

   • **iTunes:** To search the iTunes Store podcast directory, click Podcasts and scan the Categories or Featured Providers boxes in the left-hand column for topics that interest you. Or just search iTunes by using keywords and pay attention to the podcast items that your search returns.

   • **YouTube** (www.youtube.com): Click on Videos or Channels to click through on video categories or search by using your keywords.

Tracking what you are drawn to explore

Another source of clues to your interests is your desire to explore various topics. What topics do you want to know more about? What topics are you motivated to spend time delving into?

✔ **Browse course listings.** Pick up a course catalog or browse course listings online for your local university, community college, adult education courses, and recreation center. Imagine you have all the time and money you need. What courses would you like to take? Write down the names of the ones that most interest you.

✔ **Surf the Web.** Give yourself a couple uninterrupted hours to surf the Web. Follow links wherever they take you. Notice which pages interest you and record the topic that each addresses. Add the most interesting sites to your bookmarks so you can go back later for further exploration. File those bookmarks in a new bookmark folder called "Green Careers" or something similar.

Search Google News (news.google.com) for the words **green** or **environment** to return a huge list of current relevant news items.

✔ **Scan groups on social networking sites.** Look at the groups you belong to on your social networking sites. Do you see any themes? Experiment to discover what other groups you might want to add.

   • **Flip through Facebook.** Go to the Info tab on your profile and scroll to the bottom to see the groups you already belong to. Click See All to review your groups. See any themes emerging? At the very bottom of the page, look for a list of group categories or use the search field to explore ideas on your mind. If you prefer, use the search box at the top of any Facebook page to begin your exploration (www.facebook.com).

- **Mine MySpace.** Navigate to the list of groups by hovering over the More tab, and selecting Groups. Play with the categories or enter keywords to delve into a topic of your choice (www.myspace.com).

- **Look through LinkedIn.** Use the group directory (www.linkedin.com/groupsDirectory) to scan groups or search by keyword. You might begin with your current profession and add words such as **green, sustainable, socially responsible.**

- **Search Yahoo!.** On Yahoo! you can also use the search box or browse the existing groups (http://groups.yahoo.com).

Explore Wikipedia

The free online encyclopedia has more than ten million articles and keeps growing. Each article is the collaborative effort of volunteers around the globe. Search by using keywords of your choice or browse listed topics to drill down to explore their various facets.

Consider exploring the following parts of Wikipedia:

- ✔ **Overviews:** http://en.wikipedia.org/wiki/Portal:Contents/Overviews

- ✔ **Lists of topics:** http://en.wikipedia.org/wiki/Portal:Contents/Lists_of_topics

- ✔ **Academic disciplines:** http://en.wikipedia.org/wiki/List_of_academic_disciplines

- ✔ **Current events:** http://en.wikipedia.org/wiki/Portal:Current_events

- ✔ **Annual summary:** http://en.wikipedia.org/wiki/2009 (change the year to see past annual summaries or projected calendars of future years.)

Your goal is not to find out everything about the world in one sitting. Your job, right now, is to notice which topics intrigue you and hold your attention.

Noticing how you spend your time

How you spend your time is another powerful indicator of your interests. Although your former school and work experiences are an obvious source of clues to your next career, you may be surprised to discover what your hobbies and volunteer activities tell you about possible career directions as well.

Take a stroll down memory lane to revisit different phases of your life. Think back to how you spent your time through the years. Notice and record any topics or activities that intrigued you and excited you over the years.

- ✔ **Youth:** What activities did you enjoy as a child? What clubs did you belong to? What hobbies excited you? What subjects did you enjoy in school? What did you dream about doing when you grew up?

- ✔ **School years:** During your middle-school, high-school, college, or trade-school years, what else did you do besides study? Did you volunteer for any causes? What were your favorite courses and your most interesting school projects? What did you argue about with roommates?

- ✔ **Early adult years:** Did your passions run high about any topic in particular? How did your actions contribute to those around you? What groups did you belong to?

- ✔ **Professional years:** If you are a professional who has been in the workforce, what were your favorite positions throughout your career? How did you spend your non-work hours? What causes did you volunteer for?

- ✔ **Retirement years:** If you have already retired and are looking for a new way to make a difference, how have you been spending your time since you left the work world? If you have stayed engaged in work, what projects have kept you coming back for more?

Tapping into Your Dreams

Up until now you've been revisiting your past to excavate clues about your future. Now it's time to turn your attention toward the future. As you look forward, what dreams do you hold for yourself? If you could do what engages you most, what would it be? The triggers in this section help you fill in the details of your dreams.

Are there any dreams you let go of in the past that still come back to you at times? Perhaps reality got in the way of your dreams a while ago. Perhaps your finances or family responsibilities kept you from following through on your dreams. Your interests from the past are still rich sources of potential for your future career. You may, however, find it difficult to pull past dreams into the present time. If you are experiencing this difficulty, give yourself some time. Sit with the questions in this section and allow memories and wisps of your past dreams to return to you.

Identifying those you want to help

Sometimes the core feature of a dream is the kind of people, group, organization, cause, animal, or ecosystem you want to help. By claiming who or what you want to work with, you begin to define your vision.

Even if you haven't ever had a long-term dream, you can still explore these questions to gather clues to create your vision of your future career.

- ✔ If you could work with anyone, who would you be drawn to work with? Who would you like to help?

- ✔ Where would they live or work?

- ✔ Would you rather work with individuals, businesses, governments, organizations, schools, nonprofits, animals, or out in nature?

- ✔ What cause engages the folks you'd like to help?

- ✔ What problem would they need help to solve?

After working in a wildlife sanctuary in Oregon, Laurie Marker became intrigued with the cheetah in her care. She has since dedicated her career to discovering as much as she can about cheetahs. Her passion for the well-being of these animals led her to analyze the genetics of breeding cheetah at the National Zoo. Eventually she decided to leave the United States for Namibia, Africa, to found the Cheetah Conservation Fund (www.cheetah.org). This organization is now an award-winning model for wildlife conservation and management.

Discovering where in the world you want to have an impact

Do you imagine working in a particular location or setting? Sometimes getting a clear picture of where you'd like to work begins to bring your career into focus.

Do you want to work

- ✔ In your home country or abroad?

- ✔ Locally or globally?

- ✔ In person or virtually?

- ✔ In a manufacturing plant, in nature, on the road, or in an office?

- ✔ Within an organization or as a liaison between various groups?

Another way to tackle this question is to consider where you feel most comfortable or most productive. Look to your past experiences to recall where you felt most alive at work or in school. Experiment with how to translate those experiences into your vision of the future.

Highlighting Your Top Interests

At this point, you should know basically what your interests are. In fact, if you haven't simply daydreamed through this chapter, you now likely have a long list of topics that intrigue you. Now the question is: Which of your ideas are most likely to lead you to your future career?

Your list is like a pie, hot and fresh out of the oven. Set it aside for a while — longer than a pie, say, for a day or two. When you return to it, take a new look at your list and notice which interests stand out more than others.

Select the ten interests you would *most* like to address in your work. As you identify your favorite interests, don't concern yourself with what makes sense financially, or what is feasible based on your education and background, or what appears to be fashionable today. Focus instead on *your passions*. Every topic that makes it onto the new, edited version of your list should excite you.

Keep your list in a journal or on your computer where you can access it easily. Feel free to make changes as you discover new interests or notice interests fading over time. Keep this list as fresh and vibrantly alive as possible.

The topics on your list are not your career ideas. They are the subjects you'd like to incorporate into your career in some way. In all likelihood, you'll combine several of your ideas and skills into your future green career.

Chapter 5

Playing to Your Strengths in the Green Careers Arena

In This Chapter
▶ Identifying problems you know how to solve
▶ Finding your favorite skills
▶ Brainstorming possible career ideas
▶ Wrestling with gaps between your vision and reality

*T*o land a new job, you must be able to communicate your ability to solve problems and achieve results. Communicating your track record and your skills effectively and accurately requires you to do a bit of detective work before you even begin your job search.

In the first half of this chapter you discover how to delve into your education, work history, and volunteer work for evidence of your strengths. In some cases you are searching for the skills you've developed through training or experience. In other cases you are looking for evidence of your natural talents or aptitudes — the skills you have by virtue of being you.

What makes you appealing to some employers, and not others, is that your unique combination of skills, training, and natural talents looks likely to help the organization address an issue they are facing. By identifying your strengths, you gain valuable insights about how to position yourself in the green economy. In Chapter 17 you have the opportunity to communicate your strengths in a way that captures the attention of prospective employers.

In the second half of this chapter you use your favorite skills from the first half and your favorite interests from Chapter 4 to brainstorm possible career ideas. From there, you begin to sort out the best way to move from where you are now to where you want to be.

If you want to enjoy your work, use this opportunity to identify the problems you are able to solve by using skills and talents you enjoy most. Then at the end of the day, when you accept the best job offer on the table, you have landed a job that allows you to use the skills and talents that fulfill you.

As you prepare to read this chapter, pull out a piece of paper, grab a notebook, or open a file on your computer. As the questions trigger memories, jot down notes about the projects you've worked on, problems you've solved, and training you've received. About halfway through the chapter, you use the notes to pull together a list of your favorite skills.

Pinpointing the Problems You Have the Training to Solve

One of the best ways to uncover the skills you have is to identify the problems you know how to solve based on your education and your training. Think of a *problem* as something that stands in the way of an organization reaching its goals.

Each company, government agency, nonprofit, educational institution, and start-up, strives to achieve a wide variety of goals. In the following list are a sampling of goals that organizations wrestle with and an example of how an employee might help the organization reach a goal in that arena.

- Green goals:
  - Carbon emissions goals: Finding ways to use renewable energy sources within the company
  - Waste-management goals: Reducing the amount of waste that goes to landfill.
  - Energy efficiency goals: Eliminating leaks in the heating system
  - Time efficiency goals: Streamlining production processes
- Customer service goals:
  - Reducing customer complaints
  - Providing training to increase quality
- Financial goals:
  - Cost goals: Sourcing goods from new suppliers
  - Marketing goals: Increasing the number of people who respond to a special offer

> • Income or sales goals: Up-selling customers to larger packages
>
> • Fundraising goals: Managing campaign to raise funds for organization
>
> ✔ Regulatory goals:
>
> • Compliance goals: Implementing a tracking system to eliminate lapses in compliance
>
> • Hazardous waste goals: Managing federal and state paper work for transportation and disposal of hazardous waste

Review the following questions and write down the problems you are able to solve for organizations as a result of what you know. At first you may be tempted to list the topics you addressed in each of these venues, but taking it a bit deeper allows you to connect what you know with how you can contribute to your future employer.

> ✔ **Coursework:** Think back to your school years. What courses did you take that prepared you to solve problems in the workplace?
>
> ✔ **School projects:** What projects did you work on in school that focused on real-life problems or could be transferred to business issues?
>
> ✔ **Certifications:** Have you completed any certifications or extra coursework that gave you specific knowledge and skills to tackle work-related problems? Think about courses you were required to take by your employer as well as certifications you chose to complete.
>
> ✔ **Conferences:** Review the conferences you've attended over the years for your profession, industry, or region. What did you discover during these conferences that helps you contribute to business goals?
>
> ✔ **Training:** If you received training for your job (perhaps when you were promoted, transferred, or new to the organization) you may have another source of clues to problems you can solve.

Don't be concerned if your list is fairly short at this point. In the next few sections you discover several other sources of clues to add to your list. After working with the next few sections, you may be able to come back to this section with more insight and clarity about what fits on your list.

Searching for What You Have Solved in the Past

The work you have done in full-time positions, contract gigs, part-time jobs and volunteer activities may be a rich source of clues to the way you've solved problems in the past. Activities in your personal life may also provide inspiration in this section.

Take some time to think about the roles you've held. In each case review how the position prepared you to help your next employer break through obstacles to meet their goals.

- ✓ **Work responsibilities:** What are your usual duties on your job? What does your organization expect you to be able to do for them? Think specifically about the ways in which you help your employers reach their goals.

- ✓ **Work projects:** What special projects have you worked on? Perhaps your manager gave you an assignment outside your usual duties because you showed talent or aptitude to fulfill a particular need the organization had. Or you may have volunteered to tackle a particular problem for your organization.

- ✓ **Volunteer projects:** How have you volunteered your talents? Think about the organizations you've volunteered with and the projects you've worked on. Were there any volunteer positions that gave you a feeling of satisfaction and accomplishment?

- ✓ **Personal life experience:** What situations have you faced, and perhaps conquered, in your life? Do any of these experiences give you a special set of skills that you could contribute to your work?

No need to go overboard with this activity. The key is to drill down to the problems and projects you've enjoyed working on through your work and personal activities. If there's a problem you have the skill or talent to resolve, but you are miserable doing that work, it's probably best to keep that problem off your list. Even if you eventually need to fall back on that skill to transition into a new industry, the skill will be there when you need it.

Determining the Dilemmas You Have a Passion to Solve

Sometimes your ability to solve a problem comes from your passion to do so. You may not have previous experience that is directly related or the relevant training, but you have within you a fire the drives you to figure out what must be done to tackle the issue at hand.

- ✓ **Exploring cutting-edge opportunities:** When you look at the green economy, do any new industries and technologies grab your attention? Can you see yourself contributing to a field that is barely on anyone's radar yet? Scan future trends for possible problems you'd like to solve.

- ✓ **Examining what irks you:** What bugs you may actually inspire you to do great things. Are there any issues related to the green movement that make you mad as a hornet? Maybe you don't understand why your family, friends, and colleagues don't get it when the issue is as clear as day to you. Are you fired up about improving energy efficiency, doing away with unnecessary waste, creating greener buildings, or ending dependence on oil? Do you have ideas that could start turning the tide on these issues that are critical to our times?

The issue that weighs me down these days is that Texas-sized collection of plastic garbage swirling in middle of the Pacific ocean (`www.cnn.com/2009/TECH/science/08/04/pacific.garbage.patch/index.html`). I haven't come up with a solution to this problem yet, but I sure wish we could all put our heads together to find a way to eliminate this senseless expression of our overindulgence. Mad as a hornet!

✔ **Revisiting your childhood passions and worries:** Were you concerned about the environment as a youngster or young adult? Did you feel passionately about one or more environmental issues? What you were drawn to explore as a child may point you toward a passion that has been dormant for years. Turn back the clock to see if you can recall issues.

When I was in grade school, I distinctly remember trying to figure out how to capture the water that ran, untouched, down the drain as people brushed their teeth, soaped up their hands, or waited for the hot water to reach the faucet. Although I turned off the water as much as I could during those daily tasks, I knew that others didn't. It bothered me that such a precious resource was literally going down the drain. I got as far as thinking of a two-pipe system, where one set of pipes was for outgoing water that had been used and another set of pipes for outgoing water that was really still clean and useable. The grey water systems of today are a variation of what I used to ponder.

About the same time, my parents were leading a community group to establish a recycling center in our small town. Although we were just gathering glass and cans at the time, the idea of a full-scale recycling plant with dump trucks, conveyor belts, and stations for each kind of waste sparked my imagination. I remember creating a diorama in a bright yellow box with my version of a recycling system, complete with bicycle tire conveyor belts, my brother's matchbox-sized dump truck, and bits of grass, paper, glass, cardboard, and metal I'd collected from around our house. Decades later when I delivered my own recyclables to the local recycling center, I was stunned to see a bright yellow recycling system that was like a full-sized replica of my own diorama.

Although I don't have any direct training to contribute to these issues, I see that I am passionate about the environment and how our daily decisions and actions have a profound impact on the planet. In many ways my passions contribute to my work as I make sense of the green economy for those who want to plug into a green career.

How might your passions and frustrations fuel the greening of your career? Although the connection may not be immediately clear, embrace your present and past passions. By giving them the light of day, you may be surprised how influential they become in defining your green career.

Identifying Your Top Strengths

If you've read up to this point, by now you have scanned your education, your work experience, your volunteer experiences, and your childhood dreams to determine which problems you've solved in the past. The next step is to work backward from these problems and projects to identify the skills you possess that enable you to do the work that you do.

You may notice certain themes repeating through your history or that you have a wide-ranging array of projects and experiences to draw from. Either scenario works; the key is to focus on how your skills allow you to leverage your background as you prepare to enter the green economy.

Take another look at the list of problems, business goals, and dreams you identified as you read this chapter (you have started your list, right?). Use the following tips to identify the skills you had to possess to reach a successful outcome in each scenario:

- Think in terms of words that end in –*ing*. *Gerunds*, as they're called, refer to the name of an action. Thinking in gerunds helps you identify the action that you took to achieve results.

- Be as specific as possible as you describe the action you took to complete your tasks and help your organization reach its intended goal. Play with the wording until the phrase reflects exactly what you did.

- Focus most of your attention on the projects you enjoyed working on. These projects almost always combined the highest concentration of skills you like to use. If you liked a certain part of a project, give special attention to the skills you used in that situation.

- If you have projects that seem to cluster around a particular theme, think of them as a group rather than as individual projects. This big-picture view may illuminate skills you wouldn't see if you looked at each project separately.

- If you have listed a wide variety of projects, keep an open mind as you sort through each one to find the key skills. Your themes may appear when you look at your final list of skills rather than at your list of projects.

- Don't forget to include skills you'd *like* to use more or skills you'd like to develop in a more meaningful way. Perhaps you've always wanted to fly kites. You've never flown kites before, but you know you'd love gaining the skill and using the skill in your work. If this is the case, then by all means add *flying kites* to your list.

- For now don't be overly concerned about how the skills fit together to create a job or whether there's any way to make money with the skill. You'll have an opportunity to wrestle with these realities soon enough.

Heath noticed a theme of event planning in his volunteer and work history as well as his personal life. In addition to throwing some amazing theme parties over the years, he has also organized trade shows and incentive travel for his company's sales team. As he began to list his actions, he came up with this list:

- ✔ Organizing event logistics
- ✔ Designing the theme and decorations
- ✔ Budgeting
- ✔ Project planning

Michelle was surprised to see *building* show up as a theme in her walk through her past. In addition to managing an extensive remodeling project on her home, she was also involved in building out new office space for her company. The actions that seemed most relevant to Michelle included:

- ✔ Evaluating blueprints
- ✔ Choosing appropriate fixtures and coverings for space, function, and aesthetics
- ✔ Researching energy-efficient solutions
- ✔ Designing spaces to resolve workflow issues

As you review your list of skills, identify the ones you consider to be your favorites. Fine-tune your collection of skills until you have a final list of ten you'd like to incorporate into your future career. Don't worry if they don't all fit together in a nice cohesive list; they'll still be useful to you.

Weaving Your Interests and Skills Together

Most career changers try to identify their next career by using their key skill or interest. In fact, your future career, whether green or purple, is likely to be a combination of your skills and interests. In many cases, the most viable career idea comes out of a combination that you have never considered before.

Before you continue with this section, leave your preconceived notions about your future green career at the door. You can always pick them up again later if you care to, but holding onto them right now only limits your ability to think expansively.

Begin your exploration by bringing your list of interests from Chapter 4 and your list of skills from this chapter together. Either lay the two lists out next to each other or combine your list of ten skills and ten interests onto the same piece of paper or screen. As you review your complete lists, consider the following questions.

- ✔ **Do you see any entries that seem to group together naturally?** If so, jot the skills and interests down in clusters. Feel free to reuse the same phrase in multiple clusters. You may discover that all your ideas seem to fall under one general umbrella or that there are two or three groupings that are worth considering.

- ✔ **Do any combinations stand out as particularly intriguing to you?** Perhaps you see a possibility you've never considered before or one that triggers you to think of multiple green career possibilities.

- ✔ **Do any combinations stimulate you to think of innovative ideas?** New thoughts may trigger a series of ideas about a particular field or problem.

- ✔ **Is there a pairing that you are particularly well suited to pursue?** If you see a connection between two seemingly distinct ideas, you may have just identified a skill/interest combination that makes you uniquely qualified to contribute something of substance to a lucky employer.

While giving a presentation at a university green fair recently, I met a young woman who had a distinct combination of skills and interests. On the one hand, she was fascinated by fashion, particularly fashion created from recycled and renewable materials. As we spoke, I could see her booth behind her where she was displaying formal gowns she had designed and constructed from recycled magazine pages and other reused materials. On the other hand, she was working toward her engineering degree. Although these two arenas seem worlds apart, this young woman has a tremendous opportunity to make her mark on the world of eco-textiles as a result of her unique combination of education and interests. Everyone who heard her story was inspired by her combined passion for these two topics.

As you consider possible directions for your green career, keep your lists of skills and interests and your list of potential ideas close at hand. Resist the temptation to run with the first idea that comes to you. Instead, sit with your list for a few days. Let your list incubate as you consider your options, play with possibilities, and explore various angles.

If you keep coming back to the same ideas or constellation of ideas, it's likely you are interested in pursuing a career that falls in that area. As you move through the different phases of exploring your ideas and evaluating your options, don't be alarmed if your target career idea changes. Shifts are natural at this point as you discover new aspects of your target field and as the field itself continues its own evolution.

If you aren't yet clear which direction you want to take, don't be alarmed. It is likely you need more information before you can settle on a career idea. If you have a sense of which green industry you'd like to work in, scan Chapters 7 through 13 to find a profile of that industry and related industries and use the tactics described in Chapter 14 to gain more knowledge about your target industry.

Another option to gain more clarity is to get involved in your local green community to do some hands-on exploration of various green issues. With more experience, you may find that your options come into focus more easily.

Bridging the Gap between Your Vision and Your Reality

Often what we imagine in our minds doesn't look possible in the light of day. If you discover a large gap between your vision of what you'd like to do and what you think you can do, you may feel inclined to stop in your tracks and change direction.

Before you do that, take a look at the gap to identify the true cause of your discomfort. When you know what is standing between you and your ideal green job, you can begin to search for ways to eliminate the blocks that are in your way. There could be several reasons for the gap you see between where you are today and your green dream.

It's no surprise that the strategies to bring your dream into reality take time and personal determination. Keep your goal in sight and celebrate your wins along the way. You may be surprised how opportunities open up for you as you take steps toward your green career goal. Knowing that you are taking the actions necessary to land your green career job brings hope and direction.

Gaining more experience

To succeed in your target field, you may need to develop your skills, especially if your goal is to change careers. Although the prospect of getting experience may look daunting at first, don't let that put your dream on hold. You can do this; it just takes a bit of strategy to put a plan in place.

As soon as your new career goal comes into focus, begin looking at your situation to find ways to build out your resume. The usual catch-22 exists in the green economy. Employers want to hire people who already have experience. People who want to transition into the green economy don't have the experience employers are looking for.

The best strategy is to begin building your green experience base as soon as possible. Look for opportunities to develop skills in your current job through your job responsibilities, committee work, or company-sponsored training opportunities. Search for a volunteer opportunity that is in alignment with your goals or offer to work on a project as an independent contractor for a small business. Evaluate each opportunity to determine whether it will provide you with new skills and résumé-worthy experience.

Getting more training

In some cases, you need more than just experience to make the leap to a new career. You may need to look at training opportunities or education to help you conquer the gap you see. Look for the best way to enhance the skills that are relevant and critical to your target career. What skills do you need to add? What's the best way to gain those skills? What kind of skill-building activities work with your lifestyle?

Don't limit yourself by thinking the only answer is a college or graduate degree. Expand your brainstorming to include online courses, hands-on internships, apprenticeships, a selection of hand-picked courses, or a certificate. Strive to find the solution that truly fits your needs. Chapter 16 has many more ideas on this topic.

In the early stages of evaluating a new career you're likely to base a number of your decisions on assumptions you've made about the industry, profession, and organizations in the field. As you determine where you want to focus your attention, your assumptions are a helpful tool — but as you begin making life-changing choices about training and ultimately employment, it is critical that you move beyond assumption-driven decisions.

As you assess the gaps in your training and how to fill them, you must begin talking with people in your chosen field. Those who work in the profession and industry have the best, most up-to-date information possible.

- ✔ Use your network to connect with these individuals. Check out Chapter 15 for ideas to build your green network.

- ✔ Another valuable source of information about training requirements are professional and industry associations. Check out the Web sites of the associations that are most relevant to your goals (see the industry profiles in Chapter 7 through 13 for links to relevant assocations). You are likely to find overall information about the industry, as well as detailed information about the training required to succeed in the field.

Wrestling with the location of the work

Industries within the green economy tend to be clustered in certain areas of the country due to the availability of renewable energy resources such as wind, solar, or geothermal, or based on the location of existing industries that were a precursor to the green industry. If you don't live in a hotbed of activity for your target industry, you have some decisions to make.

To move or not to move is one key question you must to wrestle with. To wait or not to wait is the corollary to that question. If you wait a while before jumping into the green economy, will other options open up? Will your target industry open up in other areas, or in your area? To answer these questions you must delve into the industry to understand the trends and attempt to forecast the direction of the industry.

If your heart's desire is to work in the wind industry, you most likely need to relocate to one of the wind corridors. Right now, most of the wind industry activity (www.awea.org/projects/) is in the West Coast, New York, and central plains swooping from Texas up to Minnesota. If relocating is not appealing or feasible for your family right now, think outside the box as you consider your options. It's possible the wind corridors will expand to include the East Coast (www.windpoweringamerica.gov/wind_maps. asp) — would that work interest you? Small wind turbines that are appropriate for personal homes and small businesses are showing promise. Is there enough wind in your immediate area to look to this side of the wind industry for employment? Another option would be to look into the manufacturing side of the wind industry, which is primarily located in the Midwest (scroll to the bottom of this Web page for the map of wind manufacturers, www.earth2tech. com/maps).

Feeling limited by family responsibilities

If you have young children at home or are caring for an ailing parent, you may not be able to take on your ideal career at this time. Your best strategy may be to take small steps toward your goal now in preparation for a time when your schedule is more flexible.

Explore simple ways you can make progress for now. Perhaps you can't make the career move you'd like to make, but you can establish a strong network, do some reading, take an online course, or do some volunteering. Any action you take now puts you in a better position to make a move when you are ready.

You may also want to look at your personal responsibilities to get a sense of when they may shift. If your children head to school in three years or your caretaking responsibilities will shift at a certain time, use that information to plot out a tentative timeline. Having a sense of your time horizon helps you stay focused as you prepare for a career change in the future.

Questioning your abilities

If others believe you have what it takes to achieve your vision, but you have your doubts, you may want to take another look at your abilities from a more objective perspective. Sometimes people get in the habit of believing they can't do something when, in fact, they are fully capable of being successful.

Take an inventory of your accomplishments at work and in your life. Make note of the activities, projects, and accomplishments you feel proud of. Then ask friends and colleagues to e-mail you a list of your three biggest accomplishments and your three best strengths from their perspective. Choose people who care about you and whom you trust. If it's uncomfortable to make this request, tell them you are doing an assignment for a career counselor or career coach or because this book told you to. You may be pleasantly surprised at how willing they are to participate in this activity.

As you begin to receive responses, compare how your friends and colleagues view you and how you view yourself. Don't discredit their views; take their perspectives as gifts of insight and perspective. Do what you can to begin to let this new view of yourself in as you move toward your green career.

Waiting for the green economy to catch up

You may also discover that the timing of your transition to a green career doesn't hinge on your experience or education. In fact, your inability to move into a green job may have nothing to do with you at all. It's entirely possible that your target green industry is not ready to hire someone with your skills and talents.

If you long to work in the biofuels industry, creating fuel from algae, switch grass, or sawdust, you may be in just the right place and time if you are a scientist or technician. If, however, your dream job is marketing, sales, or production manager, you may be out of luck, for the time being at least. At this point in time, the entire biofuels industry is in a research and development phase. Every company that exists in this industry is focusingall their time and resources on discovering a way to produce biofuels that is cost effective, efficient, and scalable. In other words, they are still searching for a viable way to produce the product they are in existence to provide. Until they find that formula and know that they can produce the product in mass quantities, they have no business hiring production managers, marketing teams, or a sales force. They have nothing to produce, market, or sell. Yet.

If you find that you've arrived at the party a few months or years too early, acknowledge both your dream and the current state of your target industry and do at least some, if not all, of the following:

- ✔ **Keep tracking your target industry.** Watch for technological break-throughs. Scan for opportunities. Being aware of your industry allows you to follow history in the making. You then know what the industry has tried, what has worked, and what hasn't. Your detailed knowledge means that you are ready to step into any company and be productive from day one.

- ✔ **Gain related experience.** Although you won't be able to gain experience in your target industry, think about related industries that might give you experience in the distribution system your target industry is likely to use, help you build a network of contacts that will be valuable to a future employer from your target industry, or teach you about an analogous technology or process.

- ✔ **Attend industry conferences.** To identify job opportunities in related industries, you need to understand your target industry in as much detail as possible. Although reading blogs, newsletters, and industry association Web sites can help, attending a conference with profession-als who are actively working in the industry is invaluable.

Use the time you have wisely, from when you identify your target green industry to the time that industry is ready to hire you. By staying engaged, you position yourself ahead of all the others who gave up hope of ever find-ing a job in the emerging industry.

Claiming your dreams

You may be a bit discouraged by the amount of time and energy required to plug into the green career of your dreams. Well, don't be. Stay connected to your passion and do what you must to move toward your dream.

The path may not always be straight. You may hit a few bumps along the way. You may even need to take a detour or two before you are able to enter your targeted green field.

As long as you keep your goal in mind, each step you take is moving you closer to your dream. In the end, you may look back and discover that your path has led you to a slightly different, but equally interesting, destination. No harm. As long as you are excited about where you are headed and you feel that you can make a difference, your journey will be worth your investment.

Chapter 6

Setting Your Green Career Goals

. . . .

In This Chapter

▶ Creating a picture of how you want to work

▶ Understanding where you like to work

▶ Defining your green career goal

▶ Stating your goal enthusiastically

▶ Making plans for next steps

. . . .

You know you want a green career, and yet you aren't sure how to describe what you have to offer. Knowing you want a green career is only the first step. Determining exactly where your skills, interests, experience, and education fit into the green economy is a more intricate part of the puzzle. After identifying your favorite interests in Chapter 4 and your favorite skills in Chapter 5, you're now ready to explore the characteristics of the green organization you ultimately want to work for.

Being able to clearly and confidently describe your green career goal is a crucial step in your quest. Toward the end of this chapter you pull together everything you've discovered to create a description of the kind of green work that's the best fit for you.

When you're able to share your goal in a crisp, clear sound bite, you have a powerful tool to guide your exploration, collect resources and referrals from your network, and land a job.

Thinking Through How You Want to Work

As you consider your green career, you're most likely focusing on what you want to do in your job and what green issues you want to resolve through your work. Although it's critical to discover your career focus, there are several other questions that deserve your attention at this point.

The first is: How do you want to work? Most people don't consider this question because they assume that they are looking for a full-time position with benefits. In the emerging green economy, a full-time position may or may not be your first stop. Take some time to expand your vision of what's possible in this section.

As you work through the next few sections, keep your notebook or notes document at the ready. Write down your answers to the following inquiries. Having a written record of your answers makes it easier to see themes and connections.

Looking beyond a full-time job

Although your vision of your next job is a full-time position, the economy and the industry you want to enter may not be able or ready to hire you in that capacity right now. Although it may bring a bit of discomfort to the surface, open yourself to a wider variety of work formats. Looking beyond full-time work allows you to say *yes* to a broader range of opportunities that cross your path.

As you read about work formats you may not have considered before, keep in mind that these options are likely to be short term. Think of them as steppingstones to your ultimate green career. As long as you make strategic decisions about which opportunities to accept, any and all of these options can help you prepare for your ultimate job by building your skills, enhancing your knowledge, building your network, and strengthening your resume.

If you're committed to moving your career forward, don't let the following opportunities pass you by:

- ✔ **Contracting**: The next best thing to a full-time job may be a green contract position. In this arrangement you work full time for a specific period of time. Your pay may be higher than your usual pay rate, but you are responsible for covering your taxes and your benefits. Use your time under contract to gain as much insight as you can about the organization's industry and the unique elements of the business. You never know how the information you glean from this experience will help you land your next position. While in your contract position, leverage your time by building your network, strengthening your own skills, and enhancing your knowledge about the green/sustainable aspects of your work.

- ✔ **Consulting**: If you have an appropriate skill set, you may be able to find green consulting jobs to keep you busy and help you develop additional skills for your target career. You need to spend some time upfront figuring out how to differentiate your skills from others in your profession and then marketing your services. The good news is that you are in control of your schedule. Depending on your workload, you may be able to incorporate some targeted volunteer work as well. Being out in the community is a great way to spread the word about your services and keep your eyes open for your next opportunity.

✔ **Working part time:** If a green part-time position presents itself to you, and the work is right up your alley, take the job! The upside is that you still have time in your schedule to explore the green economy or further your job search. You also get an inside look at a green company in your chosen field. What an opportunity to test the waters. Is the profession what you thought it would be? Is this the right company for you? What do you need to do to improve your position? As you do your job, look for ways to demonstrate your value to the company, in dollars and cents if possible. You never know, you may just set yourself up with a full-time job in the process.

✔ **Interning:** Green internships aren't just for college students and new grads. Some internships are paid (probably not much), and some aren't. If you have the opportunity, step out of your regular life and find an internship that gives you an entirely new experience. If you aren't clear about what you want to do in the green economy, use your internship as an opportunity to explore and experience a broad range of issues.

✔ **Volunteering:** Taking a green volunteer position with a local nonprofit, community group, or start-up can prove to be a very valuable strategy. When you volunteer, your energy is up — you exude excitement, confidence, and passion. These are the qualities that attract people to pay attention to you, whether they are a networking contact or a potential employer.

Jobnob (www.jobnob.com), a Bay Area organization committed to connecting job seekers and companies, sponsored an event that brought 300 people to a San Francisco bar to *volunteer* for start-up companies. The deal was that the start-ups would buy the drinks, and the job seekers would commit to working five hours a week as a volunteer. Jobnob was stunned by the popularity of their event and intends to have monthly events, using this same model. It will be fascinating to hear the success stories that come from these events!

When approached about a position that doesn't match your full-time vision, be open to finding a way to make it work. Be flexible. If necessary, find a creative way to piece together several opportunities to bring in the income you need. Remember, this is the opening you've been waiting for — a first step toward your green career.

If you pass on these opportunities, you miss out on critical skill-building, network-enhancing experiences. In the end, saying *no* to opportunities that align with your ultimate green goal sets you back.

Prospering with multiple streams of income

As you envision your future, you may also want to consider an approach to work that was quite common before the standard workday came into vogue as a result of the Industrial Revolution. In this approach, you create a composite career that allows you to bring together a set of positions that fit your interests and your work style.

With multiple sources of income, you become less dependent on any one company's decisions. Your diversified work life feeds you in ways a single full-time job might not. Time is more fluid as you balance your responsibilities and personal needs.

Over time Grace created a composite career that enables her to use her talents in ways that match her personal and professional needs. In addition to a part-time position at a local, environmental nonprofit, Grace works on several consulting projects and gives presentations several times a month. The part-time position provides a stable baseline income source, while her consulting and speaking allow her some flexibility. At certain times during the year she works more and brings in larger sums of money. As she nears the end of each project, she determines when to start her next contract. Being able to take a couple of weeks between projects helps her manage the rest of her life more effectively.

If you want to explore the idea of having a composite career, create a description of how you want your professional life and your personal life to work. What's most important to you: the freedom of time, stability of your money, a certain work schedule, or a certain kind of project? As you put your picture in place, be aware that your vision may shift and that you may need to find creative ways to fill in the gaps as you are building toward your ultimate plan. Each year or so, reflect on how your composite career is serving you and your needs. If need be, make adjustments by aligning with new opportunities or renegotiating the arrangements you have in place.

Being your own boss

You may also want to consider becoming self-employed. Although consulting is one obvious way to be your own boss, there are other options. With your skills and interests from Chapters 4 and 5 in mind, consider the kind of business that would be best for you.

✔ **Selling a product:** In your industry of choice would it make sense to sell a particular product or collection of products? Perhaps you'd be interested in selling green building supplies, eco-friendly clothing, organic food, or personal wind turbines.

✔ **Providing information:** Another option is to offer a specialized form of information to your customers. You might want to create environmental impact surveys, green market research analysis, or industry trend analysis for investments.

✔ **Performing a service:** In some cases, your best option may be to identify a process you can market. Would you like to have a green printing company, a green dry cleaning company, a eco-friendly bed & breakfast, or an energy efficiency business?

As you identify what you want to offer through a business, you also need to explore the best way to start your business.

✔ **Greening an existing business:** If you already own a business, explore how you might green it. Another option is to purchase a local business that has the potential to become more sustainable. Instead of starting from scratch, you transform a working business into something greener.

✔ **Purchasing a franchise:** If you'd feel more comfortable tapping into a business that already works, consider purchasing a franchise. Currently there are several franchise opportunities that are completely green and many others that have a green element to their offering. The list of green franchise options is likely to grow over time. If you want to explore your options, you might want to contact a company like Frannet (www.frannet.com) for support in making the right decision for you. Consulting and training from a company like this doesn't cost you anything; the company receives payment if and only if you purchase a franchise.

✔ **Starting a green business from the ground up:** Another option is to start your own green business. To succeed, you must come up with your business idea, figure out the best way to offer your product or service, choose your business name, establish your branding, develop your marketing plan, secure funding — and go for it!

Taking over an existing business or starting a new business require thought and planning. Before you take the leap, use the chapters in this book to clarify your direction. When you are confident you are on the right path, look to other resources to build your business. Check out *Green Business Practices For Dummies* by Lisa Swallow (Wiley) and *Small Business For Dummies* by Eric Tyson and Jim Schell (Wiley).

Defining the Work Setting That Fits Your Life

Where you work impacts your sense of satisfaction and your well-being. If you're going to spend 40+ hours a week in a job, don't you want to find the kind of job that's going to be a good fit for you and your life? The best way to uncover where you fit is to look to your past experience for clues about what you liked and what you didn't like about where you worked. You can also tap into your dreams and desires to bring additional clues to light.

Uncovering where you feel at home

Discovering the qualities of the organization where you feel comfortable can be a very valuable source of information when you begin to consider your career options. Use the following categories to trigger your thoughts about how to describe the kind of company you enjoy working for.

- ✔ **Kind of organization:** Working for a nonprofit, educational institution, or governmental agency is likely to be a different experience than working for a start-up or a private company. Working for a small company, whether it is housed in a small office space, home based, or virtual has an even different feel to it. Based on your previous work experience, what setting is the best fit for you?

- ✔ **Size:** Do you have a sense of the size of the organization you want to be a part of? Are you more comfortable in a mega-organization or a small outfit where you know all the players? Do you like to work in an organization that has multiple branches or one location?

- ✔ **Reach:** Another characteristic to consider is the reach of the company. Are you drawn to work with an organization that focuses on making an impact on your local community or on the world? Is your desire to make a difference in your region or in your country as a whole?

- ✔ **Purpose:** Do you have a preference for the overall purpose of the organization that hires you? Do you see yourself working for a manufacturer, a service provider, a research institution, a retail or wholesale organization, an entertainment company, or a provider of information?

As you look at the combination of company qualities you've selected, what kind of organization comes to mind? You may see one obvious answer or several combinations that might work for you. The characteristics that end up on your list can help you narrow your focus within an particular industry or profession.

Patrick is intrigued by all facets of the green building industry, from design to new building construction, building supplies, and retrofitting opportunities. At the moment he's a bit overwhelmed by all the options before him. As he answers the questions in this section, he realizes he's happiest when he works for small, private companies with a regional reach that provide a service. With this information in mind, he's able to narrow his focus to working for a regional construction firm or an energy audit company that services a specific region. Although he's fascinated by the building supply industry, he knows working for a large, multinational manufacturing company or a national service provider is not for him.

Discerning your most productive work environment

As you consider your future career direction, take some time to think through the work environment that is most productive for you. Sure, you could just take whatever work setting comes your way. You would survive, but would you thrive?

Discovering and claiming the work environment that is best for you provides you with valuable clues about your future career. If you know you prefer to work out on the open road, a job sitting a cubicle five days a week might do you in.

Use the following list to pinpoint the kind of work setting you enjoy most. If a combination of several settings appeals to you, make note of that. If you aren't quite sure what you want, think back over the jobs you've held to recall the work stations that worked well for you:

- ✔ Cubicle work environment with a network of offices within close proximity.

- ✔ A small office area with a few desks in a large open space and perhaps an office or two off the main room

- ✔ Being on the road with a local territory

- ✔ Being on the road with a territory that spans an entire region

- ✔ A home office with up-to-date equipment that allows you to work virtually

- ✔ Being outside with fresh air, the wind, and the elements

Stay attuned to your needs. Your desired work setting may change in response to lifestyle changes or changes in your personal needs..

Identifying Your Role within the Green Economy

Having collected a variety of clues about how you want to work and where you want to work, it's time to combine what you know to discover your green career options. To complete this section, have your notebook available with your notes from Chapters 4 and 5 and the first few sections of this chapter.

- ✔ **Focus of your work:** As you reflect on your ten favorite interests, your ten favorite skills, and the career ideas you brainstormed in Chapter 5, what ideas float to the top? At this moment, what two or three green career ideas are most intriguing to you? You don't have to have complete clarity at this point. Rely on your intuition and your gut to tell you which areas you want to explore in more depth.

✔ **Form of work:** Next, take a stab at describing the form of work you want. Do you want a full-time job, a composite career, or a part-time position? Pull together a list of all the options that could work for you in the short term and the long term. For example, you might be willing to take a volunteer position or a short-term project to break into a field and then aim for a full-time position or a consulting project.

✔ **Where you work:** Now consider the kind of organization you want to work for. Pull out the characteristics that are most important to you in terms of the kind, the size, the reach, and the purpose of the organization.

✔ **Your work setting:** And finally, record what you know about your favorite work setting. If you want to work outside or you like to be on the road, this is the place to make that declaration. Knowing you function best when working at home or in a structured environment can be a crucial clue as you pinpoint your green career options.

Don't be alarmed if your green career idea seems to make a U-turn at times. If you change direction, it may be because you discovered, after doing some research, that your original target industry doesn't quite match your interests or needs after all or that the industry itself is changing dramatically.

Before you jump into action to figure out how to narrow down your focus, continue on with this chapter to create a working statement of your *goal*. This goal keeps you focused no matter what your next move is.

Creating a Clear Statement of Your Goal

Now it's time to turn your current green career idea into a clear statement of where you are heading with your green career. As you refine your statement, it will guide you in your research, networking, and job search activities.

You may or may not have enough information and knowledge about your target industry to be able to develop a full statement of your green career goal at this time. But you have to start somewhere. Do the best you can with what you know *right now*. You can always revise and update later. Your green career goal is meant to be a work in progress. During the early stages of your quest, you may update your statement on a daily, weekly, or monthly basis. That's perfect. As you gain more clarity about your interests, the industry, and your direction, your statement naturally evolves.

Defining your ultimate green career goal

Based on the ideas you are considering, how might you describe your ultimate career goal? Perhaps you have a sense of the industry you want to work in. Or you may know what function you want to fulfill for a green organization. You may even dream of working for a particular organization.

Starting with what you know, how might you fill in this question?

I want to _____.

> ✔ I want to work in the green building industry helping homeowners become more energy efficient.
>
> ✔ I want to be actively involved in creating policies that help the country in the transition to renewable energy.
>
> ✔ I want to persuade businesses to take actions that are more sustainable.
>
> ✔ I want to help restore wildlife areas.

Although your statements may feel incredibly vague at first, stick with the process. Draft a handful of these sentences to get your creative juices flowing. You may be surprised with what comes to you in the process.

Choose your two favorite ultimate green career goals and find a way to keep the statements in front of you. Put a sticky note on your computer, include it in your calendar, put it in your wallet, or place it on your bathroom mirror. The more you make this a part of your daily thoughts, the more it will evolve.

As you consider your goal and use it to guide your networking and your research efforts, new thoughts and ideas will come to mind. Incorporate your new discoveries into your statement.

Spelling out your short-term career goal

If you already know you won't be moving right into your dream green career, create a statement to reflect your short-term career goal. The more specific and detailed you can be about your immediate career goal, the more your network will be able to help you find the connections, resources, and contacts you need to find your next job.

As you consider your options for your next position, be as strategic as possible. Do as much research as you can to understand your ultimate career goal so you recognize the skills and qualities required in that career. Then look at your current options to determine which position is the best move for you and your future career.

- ✔ I want to work as a _____ in the _____ industry.

- ✔ I want to work as a _____ for _____ company.

- ✔ I want to use my background in _____ to help _____ industry solve _____ problem.

- ✔ I want to use my background in _____ to help _____ company solve _____ problem.

- ✔ I want to work as a bookkeeper in the solar industry. (By leveraging your bookkeeping skills, an established expertise, you gain access to an industry you want to find out more about.)

- ✔ I want to work as a marketing specialist in XYZ company. (By working as a marketing specialist, you strengthen a skill you know you want to use in the green economy in the future.)

- ✔ I want to use my background in sales to help the energy efficiency industry convert more leads into paying clients. (By leveraging your sales experience in another field, you can help your target industry reach their sales goals while you gain resume-worthy experience in the process.)

- ✔ I want to use my background in design to help ABC Construction save time and add a new income stream to their business. (By leveraging your previous design experience, you can state very clearly and concisely how you would be a valuable asset to a particular company.)

Don't be surprised if your short-term goal continues to evolve as you launch your job search. As you uncover information about your local economy, local industry challenge and opportunities, and your ability to help companies and organizations solve problems, you can tweak your statement to better reflect your value to organizations or companies who are most likely to hire you. To gain more insights about this process, see Chapter 17.

Pinpointing your next step goals

If you've just begun your search for your ideal green career, and you don't need to find a job immediately, you may want to generate a set of goal statements you can use to focus your own exploration. As you research your target industry, having a clear picture in mind of the information you need to move forward helps you use your time more effectively.

Use the following sample goals to create your own personal set of goal statements. If you like, start with one goal and then create your next goal when you are ready to take that action. Or create a series of goal statements to have at the ready as you proceed. These goals statements provide you with the intentions you need to stay focused on your exploration.

- ✔ I am researching _____ industry to get an overview, understand the current trends, and discover future forecasts.

- ✔ I am exploring ways to enhance my skills and knowledge about the topic of _____.

- ✔ I am searching for networking venues that will allow me to meet and interact with people from _____ industry or _____ profession.

- ✔ I am looking for volunteer opportunities that will prepare me to work in the _____ industry.

- ✔ I would like to build my network of contacts in the _____ profession.

See Chapter 14 to discover the best way to use these next-step goal statements to focus your research. Then when you have a general understanding of your target industry, use your goal statements to focus your networking with those who know about your target field. Chapter 15 spells out the do's and don'ts of networking.

Asserting Your Green Career Goal with Confidence, Clarity, and Excitement

How you talk about your employment goals is the best indicator of your readiness to be hired. Your networking contacts and potential employers pick up clues about your credibility, passion, and clarity from your description of your desired career direction.

Use the following guidelines to discover how to share your green career goal in ways that motivate your networking contacts and potential employers:

✔ **State your networking or employment goal clearly and concisely in one or two sentences.**

Jody had a golden opportunity while having lunch with a member of her network. As the conversation started, Jody launched into a description of her green career goals. Unfortunately, she took 20 minutes to explain what she was looking for in a green career. There was no rhyme or reason to her explanation — in fact, she repeated herself a number of times without ever clearly stating her goal. Then Jody asked her colleague what he thought she could do in the green economy with her background.

This one-sided conversation told her colleague several critical things.

1. Jody wasn't at all clear about her direction. He didn't understand her goal well enough to offer suggestions or referrals.

2. She had not done her own homework prior to the meeting. In fact, she was asking him to do her homework for her.

3. He wouldn't be comfortable referring Jody to a company even if he knew of one that was hiring.

In a similar situation, Jane handles the conversation quite differently. Instead of focusing on her confusion and the ups and downs of her journey thus far, Jane focuses on what she does know about her desired direction. Although she's not yet clear about what role she'd play in this industry, she did take the time to research the industry before the meeting. During lunch, Jane asks her colleague questions that help her identify new resources, contacts, and segments of the industry she wants to explore.

1. Jane's colleague is in a much better position to help. He understand where Jane is and, more important, what support she needs.

2. She impressed him with the research she'd already done.

3. When she's ready, he'd be happy to refer her to key contacts in the field.

✔ **State your employment goals with confidence.** In addition to stating your goals clearly and concisely, you also want to infuse your comments with a sense of confidence and excitement about your direction.

If you're just going through the motions because you have to get a job, any job, your lack of connection with your goal will shine through loud and clear to your networking contacts and even to potential employers. If your network picks up that your heart isn't in the game, they can't in good conscience pitch you to their own networks.

✔ **Share your sense of conviction and passion as you talk about your employment goals.** Your network will pick up on your excitement and refer you with more enthusiasm and commitment.

Shirley entered the networking event with a clear statement of what she was looking for. She felt confident that her current goal was a good fit for her skills. Unfortunately, as she spoke to various people around the room, they all noticed one thing: Shirley had no spark, no internal fire, as she described her goal. Her network got the facts clearly and knew she'd technically be a good candidate for the position she was going after, but they didn't sense any passion coming from Shirley.

When Samantha shared her current green career goal, she was fully alive. Her eyes sparkled, her voice expressed her passion about her future career, and she was full of energy as she spoke.

Although both women might be referred to contacts and potential job openings, Samantha's network is more likely to give an enthusiastic, glowing introduction than Shirley's network.

If you don't feel an authentic spark of passion regarding your green career focus, ask yourself if you are heading in the right direction. It's nearly impossible to fake this level of connection with your goal.

If you're focused on a particular direction because you think it's the only option open to you, take another look at your options. Revisit Chapters 4 and 5 to reconnect with your passions. Instead of focusing on your next step, think bigger. If you could do anything, what would that be? Although you may not be able to land your ideal job right now, knowing where you're going will help you make better short-term decisions about your next job.

When you can connect the dots and see that your next job is positioning you for your ideal green career, you will naturally exude the passion you need to show to engage your network in your job search. You may even find that opportunities open up around your ideal green career when you least expect it.

Planning Your Next Steps

With your collection of green career goals, short-term career goals, and your next-step goal statements in hand, along with information about how to share your goals most effectively, it's time to put your goals to good use.

No matter where you are in your quest for your green career, your next step is to research your career options. Your goal is to familiarize yourself with your target industry to discover as much as you can about the field, the trends, the opportunities, and the challenges. You can begin your exploration by reviewing Chapters 7 through 13 to gain more knowledge about your target industry or perhaps to discover industries you didn't know were green. Use the following list to determine which chapters you want to review:

- ✔ Interested in environmental sciences? Take a look at Chapter 7.

- ✔ Attracted by natural resource management? Investigate Chapter 8.

- ✔ Fascinated by renewable energy sources? Check out Chapter 9.

- ✔ Engaged by energy efficiency and sustainability? Explore Chapter 10.

- ✔ Dedicated to building a strong foundation for the green economy? Delve into Chapter 11.

- ✔ Intrigued by inspiring others to go green? Examine Chapter 12.

- ✔ Motivated to provide green services? Consider Chapter 13.

After you review the industries of interest to you, proceed to Chapter 14 to discover the steps to deepening your exploration and Chapter 15 to find out the best way to network in the green economy.

Part III

Exploring Careers in Green Industries

The 5th Wave   By Rich Tennant

"Here's our environmental audit. The numbers are pretty impressive. By the way, you can eat the report after you're done."

In this part . . .

The green economy is a multi-faceted world of opportunity for people in a wide variety of professions. In this part you explore the purpose, current status, and future trends of an array of green industries. Use these chapters to familiarize yourself with the green economy as a whole or to jumpstart your exploration of your target green industry.

Chapter 7

Jobs in Caring for the Earth

• •

In This Chapter

▶ Using sciences to explore the impact of global warming

▶ Applying scientific know-how to turn environmental issues around

▶ Working as part of a team to evaluate environmental impact

• •

*W*hen scientists look at the planet, they see four interwoven spheres: the lithosphere (the outer surface), the hydrosphere (all forms of water on the planet), the atmosphere (the gases surrounding the planet), and the biosphere (the global ecosystem where life thrives). This chapter includes profiles of the sciences and the -*ologies* that focus on these aspects of the Earth.

The most obvious characteristic of this set of profiles is that they are inter-related with no clear demarcations between them. As it turns out, this char-acteristic mirrors the interrelated systems that make up the Earth. Just as it is nearly impossible to talk about a cheetah without mentioning its habitat, prey, and predators (humans), it is just as difficult to talk about zoology with-out also touching on conservation ecology and habitat restoration.

The recent American Recovery and Reinvestment Act of 2009 included the largest infusion of funds ever for basic research projects, instrumentation, and enhancements to research and development facilities. Overall, $151.1 bil-lion is being invested in research and development at the federal level. With many departments receiving more funds than originally requested, the basic sciences at government laboratories and universities are likely to benefit. For a description of the funds allocation prepared by the American Association for the Advancement of Science see www.aaas.org/spp/rd.

As you explore the sciences described in this chapter, keep three things in mind.

> ✔ First, each of these topics is a basic science in which the focus is to understand a portion of the Earth's systems. The knowledge gained through this research is essential to our understanding of global warm-ing and its impact on the planet as a whole and on the species that cur-rently inhabit the Earth.

✔ Second, nearly all these specialties have a sub-discipline that takes the same knowledge and applies it to real-world problems. Some of the real-world applications appear in this chapter, and others become evident in Chapter 8.

✔ Third, you are likely to see the same or similar job titles appearing in profiles within environmental science and natural resource management.

To help you develop a solid grasp of this vast topic, I use the four spheres as the starting point for organizing this chapter. From there, I highlight a few additional topics as they are particularly relevant to issues of global warming and climate change. In some profiles — biology, for example — I keep the focus squarely on environmental issues rather than all the issues addressed by biology.

Environmental Science

Environmental science is an interdisciplinary study of the natural environment from a systems point of view. Often a team of scientists from different fields work together to assess the impact of human actions on the land and water systems of a particular region, with the goal of creating strategies to restore the ecosystem. In many cases the team prepares and presents an Environmental Impact Statement (also called an Environmental Impact Report (EIR) or Environmental Impact Assessment (EIA)) to the local, regional, or national government to describe the potential impact of a project on the surrounding environment.

Environmental scientists also work with planners, designers, and other officials to address a wide range of applied issues such as water quality, groundwater contamination, soil contamination, waste management, air pollution, noise pollution, natural resource management, biodiversity, conservation, and climate change. In addressing these multifaceted issues, environmental science teams may also include experts on economics, law, and social sciences.

Typically, the teams that perform these assessments and prepare the impact reports pull in scientists from a variety of disciplines. The profiles that follow highlight the sciences that are most likely to be included in an environmental science assessment. These same sciences are also likely to study the issues that may arise if climate change is not reversed.

Atmospheric Sciences

According to the American Meteorological Society, meteorologists, also known as atmospheric scientists, use "scientific principles to explain, understand, observe, or forecast the earth's atmospheric phenomena and/or how the atmosphere affects the earth and life on the planet."

Two specialties within atmospheric science are critical to understanding global warming and its effects.

- ✔ **Climatologists** study long-term climate variations by looking at past weather data and using complex computer models and datasets to project how various factors such as greenhouse gases, volcanic activity, and solar flares impact our climate. Climate data is used by architects, land use planners, and industries that are influenced by weather events such as agriculture and insurance companies.

- ✔ **Environmental meteorologists** use their expertise to study and evaluate environmental problems, including climate change, air contaminants, greenhouse gas emissions, fresh water shortages, droughts, and ozone depletion. Environmental meteorologists may be called upon to conduct environmental assessments and prepare environmental impact reports on their findings.

Industry's current status

In a transition document for the new Administration and Congress at the end of 2008 (`www.ucar.edu/td`), several earth-centric organizations noted that more than 75 percent of the world's natural disasters are triggered in some way by weather events from hurricanes, flooding, and tornadoes; to fires, droughts, and severe winter storms. As the climate shifts due to global warming, weather-related disasters are likely to become more intense, cause far more damage, and cost more for recovery.

Furthermore, industries that are highly sensitive to weather and climate events contribute more than 25 percent of the U.S. gross national product. If these industries are damaged or taken offline temporarily, the entire economy will feel the effects.

Although atmospheric scientists and climatologists have been studying and tracking issues related to these natural disasters for several decades, budget cuts and reduced grant money over the years have hindered their ability to upgrade their systems, programs, and technology. Although large-scale modeling has provided broad-brush results, scientists have not had enough detailed information to assess the local and regional impact of weather-related phenomena.

Rating

Atmospheric science is a mature science. Advancing technology is allowing the industry to gain more insights, especially at the regional and local levels.

Future trends (and caveats)

Atmospheric scientists and climatologists should be on the front lines when it comes to research on global warming and climate change. Their knowledge, skills, and technology have played and will continue to play a critical role in our understanding of climate change and global warming. Research results are likely to provide insights to help us mitigate the effects of higher temperatures and changing climate patterns on the Earth.

To fulfill this mission, scientists are clear that they need support from the government in the following ways (`www.ucar.edu/td/transition.pdf`).

✔ Scientists must have the equipment, both satellite and ground instruments, to observe conditions on the Earth. Funding is needed to bring the existing observation system up to current standards.

✔ More computer power is needed to process data for research projects, predictions, and other applications.

✔ Research and computer modeling projects must be undertaken at a much finer scale to provide regional results for decision makers.

✔ Society as a whole must become more literate when it comes to climate issues and the forces that influence our planet. Education and training programs that promote climate literacy are critical. One organization has already created an ebook on climate literacy: `www.climatescience.gov/Library/Literacy/default.php`. See Chapter 12 for more on environmental education.

✔ Systems must be put in place to ensure that investments made toward these endeavors are well managed and serve the nation.

Sample job functions

✔ **Basic and applied research:** Atmospheric scientist, meteorologist, synoptic meteorologist, climatologist, physical meteorologist, research meteorologist, atmospheric measurements and instrumentation designer, manufacturer, technician

✔ **Forecasting:** Broadcast meteorologist, weather analyst, operational meteorologist

✔ **Consulting:** Environmental meteorologist, air quality analyst, air quality controller, forensic meteorologist, tech support for meteorological software, meteorology information services

✔ **Teaching:** Teacher, professor, instructor, administrator

Industry associations

- ✔ International Association of Meteorology and Atmospheric Sciences: www.iamas.org
- ✔ American Meteorology Society: www.ametsoc.org

Continue your exploration

- ✔ National Oceanic and Atmospheric Administration (NOAA): www.noaa.gov and NOAA Research: www.oar.noaa.gov/climate
- ✔ National Center for Atmospheric Research: www.ncar.ucar.edu
- ✔ Careers in Atmospheric Science: www.ametsoc.org/AtmosCareers
- ✔ U.S. Climate Change Science Program: www.climatescience.gov

Biology

Biology is the study of living organisms to determine their structure and function, how they grow, their origins and evolution, and their classification and distribution on the planet. The specialties in biology are determined by the kind of organism being studied.

- ✔ **Microbiologists** examine microorganisms.
- ✔ **Botanists** study plants.
- ✔ **Zoologists** research animals.

The focus of study is generally based on the scale and the method used to research the target organism. Biochemistry, molecular biology, and cellular biology focus on the chemical reactions, systems of molecules, and cellular structures found in organisms. Physiology pinpoints the functions of tissues and organ systems. Ecology looks at the interactions between organisms and their environment. (Also see the section "Ecology" later in this chapter.)

Industry's current status

For much of the 1900s, biological research was compartmentalized according to sub-disciplines, with little discussion or exchange of ideas. In the 1990s the field began to move toward an integrative biology, which takes multiple perspectives and data into account. This transition to a more integrative science continues as it becomes clear that the complex questions of the day require a collaborative approach to research and problem solving.

Although all disciplines within biology contribute to our knowledge of the natural world, several disciplines are likely to play a bigger role in studying and combating climate change. Scientists who study particular animals — such as entomologists (insects), ethologists (animal behavior), herpetologists (reptiles and amphibians), ichthyologists (fish), mammalogists (mammals), and ornithologists (birds) — provide invaluable information about the state of these populations as the climate changes. Other biologists who study the natural world as a whole give us a broader, more integrated view of the situation. (See the later section, "Ecology," for a discussion of this discipline.)

Rating

Biology is a mature science that is extending its reach into a variety of real-world applications.

Future trends (and caveats)

Biologists are contributing their knowledge and expertise to discussions that are unfolding in politics, policy, and economics. It is critical that new policies and programs designed to resolve various environmental problems be based on a solid scientific foundation.

Those with a mathematical background are applying their biological knowledge to solve environmental problems through mathematical applications such as modeling. This technological application allows scientists to uncover trends and findings much more quickly and efficiently than through observation alone.

Biomimicry is an emerging discipline that looks to nature's design and processes to find sustainable solutions to problems in the built environment. When designers, architects, engineers, and builders come together to design an element of the man-made environment sing biomimicry, biologists, ecologists, and other scientists join the conversation. After defining the problem, the entire team then looks to the natural world to discover how nature has solved the same problem in a sustainable manner. With natural models in mind, the team then looks for ways to replicate what nature has accomplished. Biomimicry solutions are innovative, elegant, and often more simplistic than man-made solutions.

Sample job functions

✔ **Research:** Biologists work in in labs and in the field to understand biology and use that knowledge to solve practical problems.

✔ **Environmental management and conservation:** Biologists work in parks systems, zoos, and communities to preserve natural resources, conserve wildlife, and create management plans.

✔ **Education:** Educating students at all levels and the public at natural parks and nature venues is an important role for biologists from all specialties.

Industry associations

✔ American Institute of Biological Sciences: www.aibs.org

✔ Society of Economy Botany: www.econbot.org

✔ More associations: www.aibs.org/careers/mso_career_links.html#13

Continue your exploration

✔ More information about biomimicry: www.biomimicryinstitute.org and www.biomimicryguild.com

✔ Action Bioscience: www.actionbioscience.org

Environmental chemistry versus green chemistry

As you explore the various environmental industries, you are likely to come across references to *environmental chemistry* and *green* or *sustainable chemistry*. At first glance, these two terms may seem to refer to the same field; however, they are actually two distinct specialties within chemistry.

✔ Environmental chemistry strives to understand the chemicals and chemical reactions that take place in nature. By first understanding the natural concentrations and effects of chemicals in the environment, scientists can then discern the impact human activities have on the natural world. In addition, environmental chemists research what happens to the chemicals that are a part of the products we use in our daily lives. In some cases they may discover chemicals that interact within the natural environment to create unforeseen toxic results. Environmental chemists may also apply their knowledge to create solutions to remediate toxic conditions such as water pollution and soil contamination.

✔ Green chemistry is used to eliminate pollutants by designing products and processes that minimize the use and creation of hazardous materials. Green chemistry plays a role at every stage of a product's life cycle, from design and manufacturing through use and disposal. As green chemistry is used more frequently, real-world environmental

(continued)

(continued)

problems such as hazardous waste, energy consumption, pollution, health issues, and damage from raw materials extraction will be addressed upfront through innovation.

Both fields are likely to grow as environmental issues gain status. Whether your focus is understanding the impact of chemicals, creating remediation solutions, or redesigning products and systems to remove pollution, you are likely to have an opportunity to make a difference.

Continue your exploration

✔ Explore the 12 principles of green chemistry: `www.epa.gov/greenchemistry/pubs/principles.html`

✔ Environmental Protection Agency's Green Chemistry Program: `www.epa.gov/greenchemistry`

✔ Description of working as an Environmental Chemist: `http://portal.acs.org` (search for **Environmental Chemist**)

Ecology

Within ecology, scientists study populations of organisms and how those organisms interact with each other and with their physical environment. To put this in context, biology is the study of individual organisms from the molecular and cellular level, to physical systems such as tissues and organs, and to the entire individual (see the earlier "Biology" section). Ecology focuses on the study of the individual organism, populations of like organisms, and the ecosystem the organisms live within.

The ecosystem is the primary unit of investigation for ecologists. Think of an ecosystem as a collection of organisms that share the same habitat. Understanding how the organisms within an ecosystem function and interact provides valuable information about the interdependencies and environmental needs of the organisms under study.

As an applied science, ecology allows scientists to understand the impact of changing environments on organisms and the best ways to conserve and restore the environment to support the ecosystem. The successful management of natural resources such as forests, fish, and wildlife depends on sound ecological research (see Chapter 8 for natural resource management profiles). In addition, ecological science contributes to a wide range of environmental issues, such as ecological restoration, global climate change, reduced biodiversity, habitat destruction, and extinction.

Although it's important to maintain viable ecosystems for wildlife and for our pleasure, keeping the earth in a thriving state is essential to our own well-being. Thriving ecosystems perform essential services that we depend on, including clean air, clean water, food, clothing, fuel, and lumber products. In addition, intact ecosystems regulate floodwaters and keep lands fertile and crops pollinated. Many believe that understanding the true monetary value of these ecological services would bring our economic system into better balance with the needs of the planet. (See the description of natural capitalism in Chapter 2.)

Ecology is a multi-faceted discipline. Each ecological project is defined by a number of factors, including the complexity or scope of interdependencies, the organism, biome, climate, scale, or phenomenon being studied, and the technique used for research. (For more details, see http://en.wikipedia.org/wiki/List_of_basic_ecology_topics.) Furthermore, scientists are guided by the following approaches, depending on the purpose of their work:

- ✔ **Systems ecology** focuses on the influence of humans on ecosystems.

- ✔ **Applied ecology** applies ecological principles to real-world environmental problems.

- ✔ **Conservation ecology** is dedicated to reducing the risk of extinction.

- ✔ **Restoration ecology** uncovers what's needed to repair damaged ecosystems.

- ✔ **Population ecology** is the study of populations of organisms, including how they increase and go extinct.

- ✔ **Environmental biology** studies the natural world, as a whole or in a particular area, especially as affected by human activity.

Industry's current status

The Environmental Protection Agency (EPA) has several programs in motion that incorporate ecology into their planning and programming.

- ✔ In 2008 the EPA released an interactive Report of the Environment that discusses the nation's air, water, land, human health, and ecological conditions. The agency's goal is to track this data over time to create longitudinal trends, which will allow it to compare the conditions at one point in time with conditions at another point in time. This data provides the EPA with objective indicators about the state of the environment that it can use to develop future projects. The first edition of the report highlighted gaps in data reporting that must be resolved before viable conclusions can be drawn. From www.epa.gov/igateway you can also access other reports such as the Air Trends Online and the Inventory of U.S. Greenhouse Gas Emissions and Sinks.

- ✔ The Ecosystem Services Research Program is a five-year project to determine the full value of the services — such as clean water, clean air, land stability — that ecosystems provide. With this knowledge, the EPA, policymakers, and resource managers will be able to make better decisions about programs and projects that protect and enhance ecosystem services. The interactive Web site for this project provides information about the program, about their accomplishments, and ultimately an atlas of all ecological services by geographic area. Go to http://epa.gov/ord/esrp and then click on Frequent Questions and Research Accomplishments for more details.

Rating

Ecology is a mature industry where the focus of this industry is defined and known. Several subsets of the field are emerging and growing. The systems perspective of ecologists is likely to be sought after as more companies, organizations, and communities search for ways to become more sustainable.

Future trends (and caveats)

The Climate Change Science Program (CCSP), the interagency organization responsible for federal climate research, has indicated that its current monitoring systems are not adequate to perform the level of observations needed to track changes from climate change. Scientists believe it is important to understand how climate change impacts the distribution and population of animal and plant species, how the ecosystems are being disturbed by climate change, and how the changes in climate are impacting nutrients in the ecosystem. Although progress has been slow, setting up this monitoring system is one of the CCSP's top priorities.

In a pure sense, ecology is a scientific study rather than an industry. That said, more and more instances of applied ecology are appearing within ecology and in the related disciplines. This trend is likely to continue as sustainability and systems thinking take hold.

In the design world, several industries are emerging that blend ecological principles with aspects of the built environment. Although the names seem similar, each specialty has its own focus and opportunities.

- ✔ **Ecological design** calls upon designers to bring ecological principles into the design projects to conserve energy, reduce toxins, and minimize waste.

- ✔ **Ecological engineering** integrates the two fields of ecology and engineering to design, monitor, restore, and construct aquatic and land-based ecosystems in a way that benefits humans and the environment. Applications include creating ecosystems to handle storm water in urban areas or restore community forests or wetland areas.

- ✔ **Industrial ecology** incorporates ecological principles into the technological world of manufacturing. The goal within this sub-discipline is to create industrial systems that function much like a natural ecosystem. (See Chapter 10 for more information on manufacturing.)

Ecology is also influencing the role humans play in the entire equation of environmental impact. Several fields, including human ecology, environmental psychology, and ecological anthropology have evolved to examine issues related to the interaction between humans, culture, and the planet.

Sample job functions

- **Ecological planning:** Environmental consultant, environmental planner, program manager, environmental analyst, land use planner, landscape architect
- **Ecological management:** Ecologist, naturalist, natural resource manager, wildlife specialist, wildlife biologist, field ecologist, land manager, nature manager, conservation biologist
- **Ecological research:** Research scientist, field technician, research technician, laboratory assistant, research coordinator, research administrator, research assistant, ecosystem modeler, biogeographer, GIS specialist, spatial statistician
- **Teaching:** In universities, schools, museums, and nature centers

Industry associations

- Ecological Society of America: www.esa.org
- United States Regional Association of the International Association of Landscape Ecology: www.usiale.org
- International Society of Chemical Ecology: http://chemecol.org

Continue your exploration

- The Fundamentals of Ecology: A Brief Investigation into the Economy of Nature: www.econguru.com/fundamentals_of_ecology
- Outline of Ecology: http://en.wikipedia.org/wiki/Outline_of_ecology

Geosciences

Geosciences, also known as earth sciences, is an umbrella term for all the sciences that are devoted to studying the planet. Four key disciplines are used in this study, from physics and chemistry to biology and mathematics.

Typically geosciences are divided into four fields:

- ✔ **Geography** is the study of earth, including *human geography,* which refers to the built environment, and *physical geography*, which consists of the natural environment. A new focus is environmental geography, which looks at the interactions between humans and the environment. The focus of study is understanding how the environment is created, managed, and used.

- ✔ **Geology** is the study of the physical properties of the solid and liquid materials that make up the Earth, their history, and the processes that create and change them. Often this field is involved in mineral and hydrocarbon extraction, as well as using the physical aspects of the planet to understand past climates.

- ✔ **Geophysics** looks at the entire Earth as a whole. Using quantitative instruments and the principles of physics, geophysicists explore various parts of the Earth, from the core to tectonic plates. Such observations are used to identify petroleum reservoirs, mineral deposits, and ground-water sources.

- ✔ **Geodesy** is a branch of applied mathematics that specializes in measuring the Earth to determine its shape and size.

According to the American Geological Institute, the field of geosciences is difficult to define because different organizations use different systems to categorize the various elements of the field. For a detailed look at the field, see www.agiweb.org/workforce/reports/2009-AppendixA.pdf.

Industry's current status

The geosciences industry evaluates its status by measuring several key economic metrics, including funding, commodities, gross domestic product, productive activity, and market capitalization. Although the industry has experienced steady growth over the past decade, some changes have occurred due to the recent economic downturn.

Although geosciences contribute to the overall economy in a number of significant ways, many of these contributions aren't necessarily green — oil and gas production and mining, for example. Nevertheless, a few areas that have the potential to be green include environmental remediation, waste management, utilities, professional services, and general industry.

For an in-depth look at the status of the industry, refer to the American Geological Institute's 2009 Status of the Geosciences Workforce (www.agiweb.org/workforce/reports/2009-StatusReportSummary.pdf).

Rating

Geosciences is a mature industry with the potential for growth in areas that address climate change.

Future trends (and caveats)

The geosciences industry is facing a critical time as the workforce ages and the number of new scientists and engineers declines. Referred to as the "Great Crew Change," this challenge concerns those tracking the long-term status of this industry. Read `www.agiweb.org/workforce/reports/2009-StatusReportSummary.pdf` for an overview of employment trends in this field.

To help geosciences and all the sciences stay competitive, the federal government has several programs to encourage students of all ages to become interested, involved, and competent in scientific endeavors:

- ✔ The American Competitiveness Initiative (ACI) provides federal funds toward research and education in the physical sciences. First mentioned by President Bush in his State of the Union Address in 2006, this initiative runs for ten years.

- ✔ The America COMPETES (Creating Opportunities to Meaningfully Promote Excellence in Technology, Education, and Science) Act signed into law by President Bush in 2007 focuses on improving education in science, technology, engineering, and mathematics (STEM).

- ✔ The American Recovery and Reinvestment Act of 2009 contributes $5.2 billion to several organizations committed to doing the work of these initiatives, aligning their budgets with the original vision.

While the industry is contending with negative workforce trends, it also faces considerable changes in the focus of the work done by geoscientists. Two factors are contributing to this shift. First, oil and gas reserves are likely to be more difficult to find as supplies dwindle. To keep up with demand and production goals, geoscientists will turn to technology to help them identify reserves and create new methods to extract energy from these new areas. Second, as the push toward more environmentally sustainable energy sources heats up, geoscientists will apply their skills and knowledge to new areas.

In May 2009, for example, U.S. Secretary of Energy Steven Chu announced $2.4 billion in funding to advance research on carbon capture and develop carbon storage technologies and infrastructure. These funds are intended to go to projects to explore the following:

- ✔ Clean coal that cuts the sulfur, nitrogen, and mercury typically emitted from power plants

- ✔ Carbon capture and storage for industrial plants, including cement plants, chemical plants, refineries, manufacturing facilities, power plants, and steel plants

- ✔ Beneficial ways to reuse carbon dioxide

- ✔ Identification of geologic sites that can be used to store carbon

- ✔ Training programs to bring the new generation of geoscientists up to speed to staff these programs

The goal of these projects is to demonstrate that is it possible to safely, reliably, and affordably contain carbon emissions in an environmentally sound way. Although these projects have been spelled out at a theoretical level, no one has put these concepts to the test yet. With the absence of actual data, it's hard to know whether large-scale carbon capture and sequestration projects are economically feasible or physically possible. To get an overview of this complex topic, see `http://en.wikipedia.org/wiki/Carbon_capture_and_storage`.

Geoscientists are also likely to turn their skills toward finding water, resolving hazardous waste issues, and seeking innovative ways to deal with climate change issues. Although the industry may not look like it does now, the future is full of interesting opportunities for those in this field. Hopefully, the change in focus will motivate more students to work in the field.

Sample job functions

The American Geological Association recently created a working definition of the following functions within the geosciences industry:

- ✔ **Geoscientists** work in a number of subfields, including environmental science, hydrology, oceanography, atmospheric science, geology, geophysics, climate science, geochemistry, and paleontology.

- ✔ **Geoengineers** may work in the environmental area to develop water supplies or remediate hazardous areas, or they may work in exploration to locate and mine various building materials, metals, coal, and oil.

✔ **Geotechnical specialists** focus on understanding the structure of soil and rocks. With this knowledge they design, assess, and inspect building foundations.

✔ **Geomanagers** plan, oversee, and coordinate geoengineering and geoscience projects in the field.

For a more detailed description of each of these functions, see page 15 of their report (www.agiweb.org/workforce/reports/2009-AppendixA.pdf).

Industry associations

✔ The American Geological Institute: www.agiweb.org

✔ Society of Economic Geologists: www.segweb.org

✔ The Geological Society of America: www.geosociety.org

✔ The Environmental and Engineering Geophysical Society (EEGS): www.eegs.org/index.cfm

✔ International Union of Geodesy and Geophysics: www.iugg.org

✔ American Geophysical Union: www.agu.org

Continue your exploration

✔ What is geography? www.aag.org/careers/what_is_geog.html

✔ What is geology? http://geology.com/articles/what-is-geology.shtml

✔ What is geophysics? www.eegs.org/whatis

✔ What is geodesy? www.eoearth.org/article/What_is_Geodesy

✔ Essays by geosciences professionals: http://guide.agiweb.org/employer/Essays.html

Hydrology

Water is essential for life. It covers 71 percent of the Earth's surface in the form of water, ice, and steam. Nearly all the Earth's water is found in large bodies of water such as oceans and lakes. A small percentage is found in underground caverns called aquifers and held in glaciers and the ice caps.

A very slight percentage is seen in the form of clouds and precipitation. Ninety-seven percent of the Earth's water is saltwater and can't be consumed by humans. Of the 3 percent that is fresh water, 70 percent is consumed for agricultural uses. As a result, drinking water in many parts of the world is a scarce, yet essential, resource.

In addition to providing all living organisms, including humans, with life, water is a dissolving agent, a heat transfer fluid, a way to put out fires, a chemical, a location for recreation, a key component of industrial manu-facturing, and a source of power. Water also plays a key role in linking eco-systems across the planet; moving food, organisms, and waste from one ecosystem to the next.

Water evaporates into vapors, which then produce precipitation. Runoff from rain and snow then runs back to the oceans and lakes. This cycle, called the water cycle or the hydrologic cycle, is our main source for naturally occur-ring fresh water.

The science of hydrology assesses the quantity and quality of water by study-ing the movement of water, the quality of water, and how water is distributed over time and space throughout the Earth. The study includes the biologi-cal, chemical, and physical properties of water and how these properties interact with the environment and living organisms during the water cycle. Subspecialties focus on the following areas:

- **Hydrography** researches the distribution of water.
- **Hydrogeology** looks at the movement and distribution of groundwater.
- **Glaciology** focuses on glaciers.
- **Limnology** tracks inland waters.
- **Surface hydrology** studies how water moves on the surface of the earth.
- **Hydrometeorology** examines water as it moves from bodies of water to the atmosphere.
- **Ecohydrology** tackles how organisms interact with water at various stages of the water cycle.
- **Hydroinformatics** investigates how to apply information technology to hydrology.

Industry's current status

In the United States the Environmental Protection Agency (EPA) is respon-sible for protecting, regulating, and improving the water resources within the country. According to its Web site (www.epa.gov/ow/careers), the EPA protects "over 3 million miles of rivers and streams; over 40 million acres of lakes, over 87,000 square miles of estuaries; 95,000 miles of coastal waters; and marine waters."

The EPA's recent Strategic Plan contains several key goals regarding water. Primarily, the Clean and Safe Water Goal strives to keep drinking water safe, protect human health, support economic growth, and promote recreational activity by restoring water systems and aquatic ecosystems.

By 2011, the EPA expects to increase the number of people who have access to safe drinking water through community water systems. In addition, it has plans to rehabilitate and restore rivers, lakes, and streams in watershed areas, coastal areas, and wetlands to protect water quality and improve recreational locations. The EPA is also committed to reducing the toxic nature of fish and shellfish that have been a risk for public health recently.

The Healthy Communities and Ecosystems Goal targets the following estuaries for restoration and rehabilitation: the Mexico Border area, the Gulf of Mexico, the Great Lakes, Chesapeake Bay, the Pacific Island Territories, Long Island Sound, the Puget Sound Basin, and the Columbia River Basin.

To achieve these goals, the EPA plans to implement national programs and partnerships with states to strengthen water standards and reduce pollution. Furthermore, the EPA is committed to creating sustainable and efficient water practices and strengthening the water infrastructure. Through a variety of practices such as water quality trading and watershed permitting, the goal is to use a watershed approach to restore polluted waterways.

Rating

Although the hydrology field is mature, concerns about changes to the natural water cycle as a result of global warming and climate change are requiring new developments in this field.

Future trends (and caveats)

In June 2009, President Obama put forth a Presidential Memorandum to create an interagency task force to develop a national ocean policy to protect the ocean, coastal, and Great Lakes ecosystems. Part of the task force's mission is fitting proposals for offshore energy projects into a cohesive marine spatial plan. Right now these oceanic ecosystems are protected by 140 laws and 20 different agencies that often produce conflicting goals and plans. For the latest updates from this task force, see www.whitehouse.gov/oceans.

Global warming is expected to change the hydraulic cycle, adding more variability to the system. Environmentally sensitive regions may receive too much water, in the form of more frequent and intense storms and flooding, or too little water by way of drought conditions. Understanding the dynamics of these changes is of critical importance for accurate forecasts, proper planning, and adequate policies by the government and private companies.

Freshwater needs will increase due to population growth. Creating adequate supplies of fresh water is a challenge that scientists and engineers are working on. Recycling waste water and creating fresh water through desalinization systems are two strategies. Without consistent ways to produce potable (drinkable) water, conflict may erupt in areas with limited water supplies.

Sample job functions

- **Hydrologists** conduct research with the help of field technicians, research technicians, biologists, foresters, ecologists, and geographers.

- **Some professionals** trained in hydrology teach in higher education.

- **A variety of engineers** plan, analyze, design, construct, and operate projects that control, use, and manage water resources. Job functions include hydraulic engineer, structural engineer, water resources engineer, civil engineer, hydrology engineer, consultant, and engineering hydrologist.

Industry association

American Water Resources Association: www.awra.org

Continue your exploration

- United Nations Educational Scientific and Cultural Organization's (UNESCO) portal for water programs around the world: www.unesco.org/water

- U.S. Geological Survey: http://water.usgs.gov

- U.S. EPA, Office of Water: www.epa.gov/water (scroll down the map to explore information about water in your region)

Chapter 8

Managing Natural Resources

● ●

● ●

*T*he world around us is rich with resources. We are so accustomed to having clean air to breathe and clear water to drink that we don't often realize all that goes into managing our natural resources. For example, on a typical day do you consider that the forests and lands must be effectively managed to supply the wood used to build our houses, the paper used to create this book, and the food we eat?

In addition to the natural resources covered in this chapter, I also provide a couple of resources that may not seem particularly *natural* to you. Although agriculture is considered to be a man-made resource, I include organic agriculture in this chapter because organic farming is as much about the quality of the land and water as it is about the food being produced.

Waste is an abundant resource that has the potential to disrupt the natural world in a number of ways. Waste management experts and those in industry are finding innovative ways to handle waste in a more eco-friendly manner. Although both agriculture and waste management have a ways to go before either field is fully green, there are plenty of opportunities for those who want to help make the transition happen.

Organic agriculture

Although agriculture is technically not a natural resource, organic agriculture is just as concerned with the surrounding ecosystem as it is with producing food and fiber products. According to the USDA National Organic Standards Board (NOSB), "... organic agriculture is an ecological production management system that promotes and enhances biodiversity, biological cycles and soil biological activity. It is based on minimal use of off-farm inputs and on management practices that restore, maintain and enhance ecological harmony."

Demand for organic products continues to grow. According to the Organic Trade Association (www.ota.com), sales of organic food grew from $1 billion in 1990 to $23.6 billion in 2008. Approximately 0.8 percent of the world's farmlands are farmed organically. Organic agriculture is regulated by the International Federation of Organic Agriculture Movements (IFOAM) (www.ifoam.org) as well as national organizations such as USDA's National Organic Program.

Agriculture impacts the environment in a number of ways.

✔ As an overall industry, agriculture is rather a mixed bag when it comes to greenhouse gases. On one hand it produces greenhouse gases through fertilizers, animal waste, and equipment. Then, on the other hand, with proper organic farming techniques it reduces carbon dioxide by eliminating nitrogen rich fertilizers and sequestering carbon in the soil. The degree to which it does either depends on the farming methods used. To find more about how organic farming may be a key solution to global warming, see The Rodale Institute Web site for more information (www.rodaleinstitute.org).

✔ Reducing the use of nitrogen fertilizers not only reduces greenhouse gas emissions, it also reduces toxic runoff that creates dead zones in the oceans, such as the Gulf of Mexico.

✔ Organic agriculture enhances biodiversity and population density in a wide range of species from soil microbes, beetles, and earthworms to birds, butterflies, and mammals.

Sustainable agriculture strives to integrate three goals: environmental stewardship, farm profitability, and thriving farming communities. To close the sustainability loop, the way food is distributed and sold must be factored into the equation as well. Some are exploring the idea of creating vertical farms in urban centers as a way of growing food close to consumers to minimize transportation costs. Others question whether building vertical farming is a cost-effective way to solve the problem. Time will tell.

See also:

✔ Organic Trade Association: www.ota.com

✔ US Department of Agriculture's Natural Agriculture Library: http://afsic.nal.usda.gov

Air

How clean is the air you breathe? The range of factors that influence the quality of the air is astounding when you dig into the details. Factories, utilities, power plants, and vehicles that spew out emissions are just a few of the more obvious culprits. Dry cleaners, wildfires, agriculture, rice cultivation, and cud-chewing animals are a few others you may not have thought about recently. Oh, and don't forget buildings that often emit toxins that pollute the air you breathe indoors.

Poor air quality impacts us all. Our health, crops, animals, buildings, and environment all suffer when the air is difficult or dangerous to breathe. To grasp the scope of air quality issues, see www.epa.gov/ebtpages/air.html and www.4cleanair.org/topicList.asp for lists of issues this industry addresses.

The goal of this industry is to monitor air quality through air measurements or to project air qualityby using computer models. Based on the results, specialists determine the best ways to control and mitigate the offending sources of pollution through technological advances or prevention. If emitters are violating laws, regulators may require that the company add control devices, pay penalties, contribute to air pollution research projects, or, if worse comes to worse, go to jail.

Industry's current status

The move to address air pollution that began in the 1950s and continues to today has made a difference in our air quality. Certainly the most influential legislation was the Clean Air Act of 1970 that allowed states and the Federal government to limit emissions from industrial locations and vehicles. For more information about the historic Clean Air Act, visit www.epa.gov/air/caa/caa_history.html.

Under the auspices of the Clean Air Act, the Environmental Protection Agency (EPA), assesses and monitors air quality in two ways:

- By measuring the concentration of specific sources of pollution, the EPA can determine how pollution levels change over time. Click one of the pollutants on this page, www.epa.gov/airtrends, to review the concentrations over the last few decades and how they compare to the National Ambient Air Quality Standards.

- By tracking the overall amount of pollution in the air, the EPA can provide a real-time assessment of how risky is it to engage in outdoor activities on any given day. To discover the air quality in your area today, take a look at the Air Quality Index map, www.airnow.gov.

Recent developments that have the potential to reduce pollution from vehicles include the National Fuel Efficiency Policy, which raises the average fuel economy standard to 35.5 miles per gallon by 2016. For more details read the official press release, www.whitehouse.gov/the_press_office/President-Obama-Announces-National-Fuel-Efficiency-Policy. In addition, in June 2009 the EPA gave California the long-awaited right to implement a 2002 state law requiring that cars have an average fuel economy standard of 40 miles per gallon by 2016. By granting California's request, the EPA has opened the door to 13 other states who want to strive for this higher standard. To explore this ruling in more depth, see `www.epa.gov/otaq/climate/ca-waiver.htm`.

Rating

Although the air quality management industry is mature, it is also facing new challenges as issues of global warming raise more and more concerns.

Future trends (and caveats)

Although the air quality industry has made great strides over the last few decades, this is no time to rest on their laurels. In fact, air quality experts worldwide must take a very active role in assessing pollutants in the air and combating global warming. Given the projected demographics, economics, and climate of the future, we must find ways to reduce the release of pollutants into the air.

Generally speaking, air quality specialists look for voluntary or mandatory strategies that control a particular pollutant or a specific pollution source. For example, energy efficiency programs, mass transit commute options, renewable energy sources, and cap and trade are all viable strategies that can be implemented to help minimize greenhouse gas emissions (For more on cap and trade, see the nearby "Cap and trade" sidebar.)

According to the National Association of Clean Air Agencies (NACAA), emissions from manufacturing sources and vehicles have been reduced through technological advances. The air pollution control technologies industry is going to play a critical role in the coming years. For a detailed list of the ways in which technology can control various sources of pollution, visit `www.icac.com` and click the Technology tab. From emissions monitoring systems to controls for greenhouse gases, particulates, and mercury, the companies within the Institute of Clean Air Companies are on the cutting edge of this field.

One power tussle that has the potential to be a game changer is the role the EPA has when it comes to monitoring, regulating, and enforcing greenhouse gases. As I write this section, several threads of this story are unfolding, with no clear outcome in sight. To give you a chance of unraveling what may happen after this book has gone to press, let me give you a bit of history.

> ✔ First, during a case between the state of Massachusetts and the EPA in 2007, the Supreme Court found, for the first time, that greenhouse gases fell under the auspices of the Clean Air Act.

✔ Then in April 2009, the EPA filed paperwork with its findings that the combination of the six greenhouse gases is in fact harmful to humans and that the emissions from new vehicles have an effect on global warming. (You can read about this procedure on the EPA site at `http://epa.gov/climatechange/endangerment.html`.) Although these findings do not trigger any new regulations, those who emit greenhouse gases are more than a little nervous by this new state of affairs.

✔ And finally, in June 2009, the American Clean Energy and Security (ACES) bill passed the House of Representatives with an 11th-hour compromise that limits the EPA's ability to regulate carbon dioxide, one of the key greenhouse gases. If this version were to become law, power plants would not have any reason to update old carbon emitting equipment. Here is the best article I've found to explain this rather complex situation: `http://solveclimate.com/blog/20090722/senate-urged-protect-clean-air-act-climate-bill`.

As I write, a grass-roots campaign has started to keep the Clean Air Act from being gutted by this critical bill on climate change. As the drama unfolds, I'll post developments on Green Career Central's updates page, `www.greencareercentral.com/updates`.

Sample job functions

✔ **Monitoring and compliance:** Air quality program manager, air quality managing consultant, air quality chemist, air specialist, environmental testing technician, air quality project manager, air quality permitting specialist, air quality scientist, air quality engineer, air quality planner, air compliance specialist, environmental air specialist, environmental compliance specialist, remediation engineer

✔ **Designing and manufacturing air pollution control technologies:** Environmental engineer, engineering resource manager, product development engineer, process design engineer, software engineer, process maintenance engineer, stress analysis engineer, computer-aided designer

Industry associations

✔ Air & Waste Management Association (A&WMA): `www.awma.org`

✔ Manufacturers of Emission Controls Association: `www.meca.org`

✔ Institute of Clean Air Companies: `www.icac.com`

Continue your exploration

✔ National Association of Clean Air Agencies (NACAA): `www.4cleanair.org/topicList.asp` and `www.4cleanair.org/TopicLinks.asp`

✔ Engineering Careers in the Air Pollution Control Industry: `http://devicac.i4a.com/files/public/APCcareers_AWMA.pdf`

Cap and trade

Cap and trade is a market-based environmental policy used to discourage emissions and encourage early innovation, energy efficiency, and action. Cap and trade systems have been used successfully to manage target pollutants, such as nitrogen oxide and sulfur dioxide, produced by pollution from power plants since 1995. Now cap and trade is being discussed as a way to reduce greenhouse gas emissions such as carbon dioxide and methane.

Although the United States doesn't have a national cap and trade program, it's important to understand the concept. Any national cap and trade system that is put in place is likely to be similar to those already in place. The system must include the following components:

✔ Initially, a cap is set to define the upper limit for greenhouse gases a company or plant can emit.

✔ Greenhouse gas emitters are given allowances to emit a specific amount of emissions. It's likely that the amount of emissions that can be emitted each year will decrease over time. The wording of the final policy will determine which companies and utilities will do business under the cap and trade system.

✔ Each emitter is able to determine how it will comply with the required cap. The emitter can purchase additional allowances from other companies that don't need the allowances for their own emissions. This process is referred to as *trading allowances*. Emitters can also reduce their emissions by implementing efficiency measures, installing controls, or finding less carbon-intensive sources of energy.

✔ At the end of the designated period, the company must turn in allowances equal to the amount of emissions it produced.

For this system to work, each company must accurately measure and report their emissions in a timely manner. New positions, such as carbon accountants, are likely to develop to do this work.

Several regional cap and trade systems are forming throughout the U.S. The Regional Greenhouse Gas Initiative (`www.rggi.org`), a cooperative of ten states in the Northeast and Mid-Atlantic area, is the first mandatory program in the United States. Two other programs, the Western Climate Initiative and the Midwestern Greenhouse Gas Reduction Accord, are in the planning stages.

Continue your exploration:

✔ Cap and Trade 101 online video: `www.epa.gov/captrade/captrade-101.html`

✔ Quick facts about cap and trade: `www.epa.gov/captrade`

✔ Greenhouse Gas Management Institute: `www.ghginstitute.com`

Fish and Wildlife

If you've ever hit a traffic jam in a national park, you know instinctively to look around for large mammals. Whether it's a bear jam or a mountain goat jam, the reason is the same: Humans love to see wildlife up close and personal. Although the enthusiastic response and awe are commendable, most vacationers don't know how to interact with wildlife without endangering themselves and the wildlife.

People who work in this field spend quite a bit of time creating and maintaining the delicate balance that exists between keeping animals wild and people safe. In addition, they use a variety of scientific disciplines to study, manage, and conserve wildlife populations they are there to protect. The strategies they use to achieve positive results for wildlife include protecting endangered species, enhancing biodiversity, tracking migratory birds, and restoring fisheries and other habitats. In addition to educating the public about wildlife conservation and safety, wildlife managers also enforce laws and contribute their expertise to shape Federal and local wildlife policies.

Industry's current status

In the last few decades the focus of wildlife management has shifted from concentrating on a key species to conserving, restoring, and maintaining complete ecosystems and enhancing biodiversity. The impetus for this relatively new focus is the concern about the loss of species that is likely to occur over the next few decades. The broader, more interdependent perspective on wildlife populations makes it easier to restore diversity within ecosystems.

Together the National Park Service and the U.S. Fish and Wildlife Service attend to the needs of the fish and wildlife in parks and refuges throughout the country. To explore the extent of their reach, check out this list of national wildlife programs (www.fws.gov/info/function.html) and this map of refuges in each state (www.fws.gov/refuges). Each state also has several departments that address local conservation issues and manage wildlife issues.

As a result of the American Reinvestment and Recovery Act of 2009, the U.S. Fish and Wildlife Service will receive $280 million over the next few years for construction projects at service facilities, renewable energy projects, habitat restoration, deferred maintenance projects, and road construction on national wildlife refuges.

Rating

The wildlife management industry is mature. Global warming and climate changes are impacting ecosystems and requiring additional efforts to protect and conserve ecosystems and wildlife.

Future trends (and caveats)

A coalition of more than 6,000 organizations, businesses, and agencies have worked together for several years on the Teaming with Wildlife campaign (www.teaming.com) to bring a long-term, stable funding source to state fish and wildlife conservation programs. In May 2009 they announced $61 million in State Wildlife Grants to go toward conservation and restoration of habitats for species in danger of going extinct. These funds are to be distributed through grants into 2010.

The push to develop renewable energy sources, including wind, solar, geothermal, and biomass, is bringing new challenges to wildlife managers throughout the world. Finding the best locations for utility-sized solar arrays, wind farms, and geothermal installations is a challenge on a good day. Unfortunately, no one really knows how these renewable energy systems will impact wildlife and habitats directly, indirectly, or cumulatively. To make the best possible siting decisions, wildlife managers must have a place at the negotiation table.

To get a sense of the scope of this challenge, consider this: The Bureau of Land Management (BLM) has "identified about 21 million acres with wind potential in the 11 western states, 29 million acres with solar energy potential in the six southwestern states and 140 million acres with geothermal resource potential in the West and Alaska." As the renewable portfolio standard is put in place nationally, more and more states will be striving to generate more of their electricity through renewable energy sources.

Several groups are coming together to address this challenge collaboratively. For instance The Wind Energy Subcommittee of the Association of Fish and Wildlife Agencies (www.fishwildlife.org/about_comm_windpower.html) and the American Wind Wildlife Institute (www.awwi.org), a nonprofit organization that includes representatives from conservation organizations, government agencies, and industry, have been created to explore issues related to wind projects. The Audubon Society and the National Resources Defense Council have worked in concert to develop a Google map to highlight areas that are too sensitive for renewable energy developments (www.nrdc.org/media/2009/090401a.asp).

Sample job functions

- ✔ **Wildlife management:** Wildlife biologists, wildlife forester, game warden, wildlife refuge manager, wildlife animal control technician, wildlife keeper, mammalogist, natural resource specialist

- ✔ **Fisheries management:** Fisheries biologist, fisheries technician, hatchery manager, aquatic toxicologist, aquatic ecologist, aquaculturist

- **Law enforcement:** Special agent, wildlife inspector, park ranger, refuge officer, investigator
- **Research and program management:** Scientist, program manager, program analyst, information technology specialist, information technology analyst, information technology programmer, natural resource economist

Industry associations

- Association of Fish and Wildlife Agencies: `www.fishwildlife.org`
- The Wildlife Society: `http://joomla.wildlife.org`

Continue your exploration

- Wildlife Management Institute's Outdoor News Bulletin: `www.wildlife managementinstitute.org` (click on tab for bulletin archives)
- Association of Fish and Wildlife Agencies: `www.fishwildlife.org/ about_comm.html`
- Careers in fish and wildlife management: `http://forestrycareers. org/sub_fish_wildlife_mgmt.html`
- Profiles of jobs at U.S. Fish and Wildlife: `www.fws.gov/jobs/dayin thelife.html`

Forests

When you think of a forest, you most likely think of thousands of acres of trees in an area that includes streams, meadows, and wildlife. What many don't realize is that forests are one of the most critical ecosystems on the planet. Managing forests — whether they are old growth, second growth, industrial, park lands, or urban — is a crucial part of bringing the planet back into balance.

Forestry is a broad term used to refer to the management of natural forests, industrial forests, and the other natural resources found within forests. Many refer to this profession as a science, an art, and a practice. To succeed you must rely on your knowledge of biology, quantitative abilities, and technical skill. In addition, you must have managerial skills and know how to encourage people to act in ways that conserve forests. The goals of a forester are many:

- Growing and managing the forest
- Extracting the timber in a sustainable way and processing it as a raw material for use in a huge array of products

> ✔ Reforesting, restoring, and remediating forests that have been degraded, damaged, or destroyed
>
> ✔ Managing and protecting wildlife habitat, watershed area, and water resources found in the forested areas
>
> ✔ Providing recreation opportunities
>
> ✔ Maintaining air quality and water quality while naturally sequestering carbon from the atmosphere

Forests provide us with a number of products that are critical to our economy and our lifestyle. Everything from raw lumber for construction and furniture to fibers and pulp for paper and packaging. A number of fuel sources such as firewood, pellets, biomass, and charcoal are derived from forests.

Industry's current status

The U.S. Forest Service is actively working to understand the state of the nation's forests (www.fia.fs.fed.us) and the impact of possible climate change scenarios (www.fs.fed.us/research/climate). In addition, the U.S. Forest Service has received $936 million from the American Recovery and Reinvestment Act (ARRA) to invest in the 93 million acres of public lands it manages; to go toward fire management, building and maintaining facilities, establishing and repairing trails and roads, restoring watershed areas, and dealing with abandoned mines. The projects have created jobs in 32 states (see www.fs.fed.us/news/2009/releases/07/projects.shtml).

According to the American Forest & Paper Association, the U.S. forest products industry that produces wood, paper, packaging, and related products "accounts for approximately 6 percent of the total U.S. manufacturing GDP, placing it on par with the automotive and plastics industries."

Threats of global deforestation sparked the 1993 establishment of the Forest Stewardship Council (www.fsc.org), an international forest certification system to encourage sustainable forest management practice. Working with various certification bodies such as the Rainforest Alliance (www.rainforest-alliance.org), the FSC provides certifications for organizations that grow and harvest forests, companies that use or sell forest products even though they don't grow trees, forest management companies that want to ensure that their wood is legally and ethically harvested, and companies that manage and harvest products such as seeds or nuts from forests.

Although several other certification programs exist, such as the Sustainable Forestry Initiative in North America (www.sfiprogram.org), the American Tree Farm System (www.treefarmsystem.org) for privately owned forests, and the Programme for the Endorsement of Forest Certification Council (www.pefc.org), the FSC program is generally seen as the industry standard. To compare systems, see www.certifiedwoodsearch.org/ matrix/matrix.aspx.

In addition to forest management changes, the forest products industry (www.afandpa.org) has made a concerted effort to recycle paper and pulp to recover paper fibers that can be used to generate recycled paper. According to the American Forest and Paper Association, 57.4 percent of the paper consumed in the U.S. was recovered for recycling in 2008 (www.afandpa.org/Recycling.aspx). By 2012, the paper industry would like to hit a goal of 60 percent paper recovery. Every ton of paper that is recovered by the industry saves considerable landfill space, energy, water, and trees.

Rating

The forestry industry is mature with a growing interest in sustainable practices.

Future trends (and caveats)

As the climate changes, the U.S. Forest Service's role as caretaker of the forests is likely to become more important and more difficult. As ecosystems shift in response to rising temperatures, pests and invasive species potentially take hold in new regions, wildfires may rage out of control, and prolonged droughts may take their toll on forested areas. For a detailed statement of the U.S. Forest Service goals and objectives from now until 2012, take a look at this report: www.fs.fed.us/publications/strategic/fs-sp-fy07-12.pdf.

The American Forest and Paper Association has created a road map to help all stakeholders look to the future of the industry. Read the report (www.agenda2020.org/PDF/FPI_Roadmap%20Final_Aug2006.pdf) to discover new technology options, new products, and sustainable business models.

The forest products industry has voluntarily committed to reducing its greenhouse gas emissions by 2012 through the Climate VISION program (www.climatevision.gov/sectors), a voluntary public-private partnership initiative to improve energy efficiency and greenhouse gas intensity in energy-intensive industrial sectors. The industry is utilizing biomass from their production process to produce steam that is then used to generate electricity and dry paper products. The added efficiency reduces carbon emissions and energy costs for forest product plants.

Forest2Fuel (www.forest2market.com), a company that provides pricing information to the timber industry, is tracking trends in the biomass/biofuel arena. Although forestry clearing projects, forest products manufacturing plants, and construction projects produce a variety of woody feedstocks that can be used as fuel, it's currently unclear whether bioenergy will be a viable new income stream for this industry. The viability depends on how biomass is defined by pending legislation and whether wood-related sources of biomass are designated as a viable source of renewable energy for the Renewable Energy Standard.

Sample job functions

Forestry has a number of sub-disciplines that cover a broad range of professions and applications. For more details about these and other sub-disciplines, visit www.forestrycareers.org/sub_disciplines.html.

- **Forestry and natural resource sciences:** Biologist, forester, botanist, naturalist, environmental protection specialist

- **Management and conservation:** Forester, urban forester, research forester, arborist, forest consultant, forestry technician, conservation biologist, habitat conservation specialist, natural resource specialist, lumberjack, firefighters

- **Environmental science and technology:** Forestry GIS analyst, air and water quality specialists, environmental health specialist, water recycling, watershed program director, water quality specialist, environmental scientists and consultant, and laboratory analyst

- **Wood and paper science:** Wood technologist, packaging engineer, resin technologist, energy specialist, wood fiber acquisition and sales, pulp and paper specialist, resin extractor, rubber tapper

- **Genetics and biotechnology:** Forest geneticist, tree breeder, biochemist, molecular biologist, genetic engineering specialist

Industry associations

- Society of American Foresters: www.safnet.org
- List of national and regional forestry associations: www.forestresources.org/ALLIES/ind-assoc.html

Continue your exploration

- Dictionary of Forestry: http://dictionaryofforestry.org
- American Forest & Paper Association (AF&PA): www.afandpa.org

✔ Explore the sub-disciplines within forestry: www.forestrycareers. org/sub_disciplines.html

✔ Movie about Forestry that Works: www.managingwholes.com/forestry

Land

Land management consists of managing a wide variety of lands including forests, croplands, rangelands, national parks, public lands, and urban areas. In addition to providing stunning views and beautiful vacation destinations, land provides us with a variety of resources including wood products, water, and energy (see Chapter 9). In addition, the land and vegetation perform critical services for us by cleaning the air we breathe, filtering the water we drink, and capturing the carbon we emit into the atmosphere.

Depending on your interests, you may be drawn to one or more of the following activities within land management:

✔ **Land Use or Zoning:** Generally handled through local government, each piece of land, whether developed or undeveloped, is governed by land use regulations or zoning. (See Chapter 11 for more information on planning.)

✔ **Conservation:** The goal of conservation is to protect habitats from irreparable damage. In some cases a particular species is at the core of the conservation effort.

✔ **Restoration:** Bringing damaged lands and waters back to a renewed state in such a way that they function as they did originally.

✔ **Remediation:** This term is typically used to refer to restoring an area that has been polluted or contaminated by prior uses. The land may need to be remediated for human health reasons or because the land is slated to be redeveloped for a new purpose.

Industry's current status

According to the U.S. Forest Service, nearly all the 770 million acres of rangelands in the United States are west of the Mississippi River, with the wet grasslands of Florida as the exception. *Rangelands* are unimproved lands with a high proportion of native vegetation that may be marshy, shrubby, grassy, or arid desert. According to the Society of Range Management, rangelands comprise almost half of all the lands in the world. Caring for these lands is critical to the well-being of the planet.

The Omnibus Public Lands Management Act of 2009 converted million of acres of Federal lands and miles of rivers into wilderness. With the signing of this law, the 26 million acres of public lands within the National Landscape Conservation System are permanently protected under the Bureau of Land Management. For details read the press release: www.whitehouse.gov/the_press_office/ Statement-from-the-Presidents-signing-statements-on-HR-146- the-Omnibus-Public-Lands-Management-Act.

A growing portion of private lands are managed by land trust organizations. In 2005 when the Land Trust Alliance conducted its National Land Trust Census (www.landtrustalliance.org/about-us/land-trust- census), it found land trusts had doubled to 37 million acres since their last census.

Rating

Overall land management is a mature industry. Sustainability practices that have developed over the last few decades are experiencing a surge of interest.

Future trends (and caveats)

An increasing number of land owners and managers are managing their land holistically or sustainably, using a triple bottom line approach that balances financial results, environmental impact, and community impact. Through monitoring and sustainable land management practices, land owners and managers make changes to restore the land. According to Holistic Management International, 30 million acres of land worldwide use its system of holistic land management. Results include improved biodiversity on managed lands, increased profits, better water conservation, restoring land, and increasing the land's capacity to support wildlife and domestic herds. By improving the land's function, carbon is naturally sequestered in grasslands and soil. For more information about this method of land management, see www.holisticmanagement.org. Take a look at the images on the home page to see the dramatic difference between holistically managed land and traditionally managed land.

As the interest in domestic renewable energy sources grows, land use issues are likely to take center stage as utilities and other energy developers scope out where to site solar farms, wind farms, geothermal plants, and smart grid transmission lines.

Sample job functions

- ✔ **Studying the land:** Biologist, geologist, botanist

- ✔ **Evaluating land issues:** Land law examiner, land surveyor, engineer, land use planner, realty specialist, land investment analyst, soil consultant, environmental policy analyst, risk analyst, urban planner, regional planner, energy planning, energy policy analyst, environmental planner. See also Chapter 11 for more planning job titles.

- ✔ **Conservation and restoration:** Rangeland management specialists natural resources specialist, conservation biologist, environmental protection specialist, habitat conservation specialist, land rehabilitation specialist, mining reclamation specialist, soil and water conservation, landscape architect

- ✔ **Recreation uses:** Outdoor recreation planner

- ✔ **Protecting the land:** Firefighter, fire management officer, law enforcement, ranger

Industry associations

- ✔ Student Conservation Association: www.thesca.org
- ✔ Society for Range Management: www.rangelands.org

Continue your exploration

- ✔ Land Trust Alliance: www.landtrustalliance.org, including
- ✔ Find a land trust: www.ltanet.org/landtrustdirectory
- ✔ U.S. Department of Agriculture Economic Research Service's conservation policies: www.ers.usda.gov/briefing/ConservationPolicy

Waste

Unfortunately, one of the most abundant resources we have on the planet is waste. According to the EPA, in 2007 each person in the United States produced 4.6 pounds of waste per day. When you add it up, that waste takes a lot of energy and land to collect and manage. The sheer volume of waste we produce is becoming a problem.

Thankfully, recycling education efforts are beginning to pay off. Of that 4.6 pounds of waste each person produces each day, 33 percent is now reused or recycled according to the EPA. Only 54 percent of residential municipal solid waste went to landfill as of 2007, as opposed to 89 percent in 1980. For more details, see www.epa.gov/epawaste/nonhaz/municipal/pubs/ msw07-fs.pdf.

Managing waste streams requires a coordinated effort by a number of waste management teams. After your garbage and recycling are collected from your curb, they are taken to a processing center where the waste is sorted and transferred to the right location. Some of it may end up in landfill while some may be sorted, cleaned, and sold as scrap for reuse.

Although you may not think much about what happens to your trash after it is picked up from your street, someone continues to manage your trash in the landfill for years to come. Even after a landfill is closed, the property and the gases emitted from the trash must be managed indefinitely. Some waste management companies are converting the emitted methane gas into renewable energy. Others use a technology called waste-to-energy to incinerate the trash in carefully designed plants (see Chapter 9 for more).

Industry's current status

The EPA's most visible waste program is the Resource Conservation Challenge (RCC), which aims to encourage all Americans to pay attention to how they are handling waste. The key priorities include

- ✔ Recycling 35 percent of the municipal solid waste from businesses, industries, and residences. In the first phase, the targets are paper, garden waste, and packaging. Special programs are being put in place to help large waste producers recycle with ease.

- ✔ Recycling all electronics through special disposal programs with retailers and manufacturers. Electronic items contain toxins that have serious health consequences. By harvesting these chemicals and components, we can reuse them rather than extracting more from the Earth.

- ✔ Recycling industrial and construction waste can make a considerable impact due to the volume and nature of the waste produced by industrial plants and construction projects.

- ✔ Reducing the use of chemicals that are toxic and have been deemed particularly harmful to human health and the environment.

Although programs are a critical piece of the puzzle, without effective marketing and education, waste reduction programs do not produce results. The key to success is reaching out to people to show them how to take new actions and establish new habits around waste. One of the tools the EPA is using in its marketing campaign is a report with success stories for each of their main goals: www.epa.gov/epawaste/rcc/resources/rcc-rpt4.pdf.

Rating

Though the overall waste management industry is mature, necessity is the catalyst for new innovations and goals.

Future trends (and caveats)

In addition to ramping up various programs to encourage individuals and businesses to reduce, reuse, and recycle, the waste management industry is making other moves. A number of collection companies are replacing their truck fleets with vehicles that run on alternative fuels to reduce greenhouse gases emitted during the transfer of waste from one location to the next.

Municipalities are also implementing innovative solutions to reduce the waste that goes to landfill. In the summer of 2009, San Francisco passed a Universal Recycling and Composting Ordinance that requires everyone in the city to sort their waste into three categories: recyclables, compostables, and waste. Fines await those who don't participate. To handle the organic compostable material, the city's waste management service has created a processing center just for food scraps, green waste, and those pizza boxes you never know whether to recycle or not. According to SFRecycling (www.sfrecycling.com), 75 percent of the city's restaurants are participating in the commercial version of the composting program.

One innovative company, BigBelly Solar (www.bigbellysolar.com), is changing the way cities manage trash in public areas. Their trash cans are really trash collectors that use solar energy to compact the trash when it reaches the top of the can. When the can is full, BigBelly notifies the waste collectors to tell them it's full. When Philadelphia recently replaced 700 public trash cans with 500 of these newfangled garbage cans, they ended up reducing their collection runs for public areas by 75 percent. Imagine what that can do for a city's trash collection budget.

Industry is also getting into the waste reduction game by rethinking manufacturing processes to eliminate sources of waste, find ways to reuse waste in their own processes, or sell it to other companies that can use it. Interface, a worldwide carpet manufacturer, has spent the last 15 years finding ways to become more sustainable. According to its Web site, www.interfaceglobal.com/Sustainability/Progress-to-Zero.aspx, the company kept 100 million pounds of waste out of landfills and saved $372 million dollars that would have been spent on waste removal in the 12 years between 1995 and

2007. What's the secret? Interface actually solicits worn-out carpet to disassemble it and reuse the backing and fibers in new carpet. In addition, it recycles trimmings right back into the production cycle.

It's not just global companies that are finding innovative ways to transform trash into value. Shane McQuade, founder of Voltaic Systems, Inc., found a way to turn soda bottles into backpacks and messenger bags that have a solar panel to recharge cellphones. His latest feat is a briefcase with enough solar power to recharge a laptop. Stay tuned — this guy seems to be on to something: www.voltaicsystems.com.

For some, the ultimate approach to waste is something called zero waste. See the nearby sidebar, "Zero waste," for more information about this innovation.

Sample job functions

- ✔ **Recycling:** Recycling program specialist, waste minimization specialist, recycling supervisor, environmental specialist, environmental coordinator, municipal recycling coordinator, e-waste professional

- ✔ **Waste management facilities:** Public works services supervisor, operations supervisor, sanitation supervisor, hazardous waste engineer, hazardous waste coordinator, landfill operator, waste collector

- ✔ **Communication, education, and marketing:** Recycling education officer, communications manager, environmental educator, program services specialist

- ✔ **Industrial waste:** Resource manager, resource coordinator, industrial waste outside sales, industrial waste account executive, specialty waste senior national account manager, industrial waste inspector

Industry associations

- ✔ Air and Waste Management Association: www.awma.org
- ✔ Solid Waste Association of North America: www.swana.org
- ✔ International Solid Waste Association: www.iswa.org

Continue your exploration

- ✔ The Story of Stuff: www.thestoryofstuff.org
- ✔ U.S. Environmental Protection Agency: www.epa.gov/epawaste

Zero waste

Imagine a world without waste! Zero waste proponents believe we need to rethink our entire relationship with waste. They would like us to take inspiration from nature, where every output is an input to another process. With this perspective, every kind of waste become a potential resource to be used for another purpose.

With some proper prior planning, we can avoid using hazardous materials in products and production processes so we don't have to worry about the waste when the product is thrown into landfills. In addition, we can think ahead to determine waste streams from the production process and the end-of-life process for the product. With ingenuity, it's possible to convert these waste streams into an input for another product or the next generation of the same product.

To achieve this goal of zero waste, companies must use innovation to rethink every stage of the product life cycle to eliminate all inefficiencies. Those who work with waste must reframe their tasks to focus on reusing materials as much as possible. In the end, a zero waste philosophy reduces costs for extracting resources and disposing of waste, increases efficiencies, and increases profits.

Continue your exploration:

- Zero Waste Alliance: (www.zerowaste.org)
- Zero Waste International Alliance: (www.zwia.org)
- For information on implementing a zero waste initiative: www.zerowaste.org/approach.htm

Water

Water is one of the most essential natural resources on the planet. In some areas clean, high-quality drinking water is abundant and accessible. In other areas that suffer from drought conditions or inadequate water infrastructure, what little water there is may not be fit to drink. Although fresh water supplies are naturally regenerated through rainfall, the demand on fresh water supplies is often higher than the supply. It's likely that this burden will become even more extreme if climate changes continue to accelerate.

In addition, water usage has a direct impact on greenhouse gas emissions. According to the EPA, "an estimated 3 percent of national energy consumption, equivalent to approximately 56 billion kilowatt hours (kWh), is used for drinking water and waste water services. Assuming the average mix of energy sources in the country, this equates to adding approximately 45 million tons of greenhouse gas to the atmosphere."

Water resource management consists of the following components:

- ✔ **Treating water for end use:** Whether water is to used for drinking, industrial uses, or medical uses, or is waste water that is ready to be returned to the natural water cycle, it must be clear of contaminants and cleaned. Local water treatment facilities process water through a series of steps to provide high-quality water required by users.

- ✔ **Distributing water through irrigation:** In arid areas, water management includes moving water resources to the areas that need them for growing crops or other agricultural applications.

- ✔ **Managing flood waters:** In coastal areas or on land near rivers and lakes, local authorities must manage the overabundance of water to keep residents, business owners, and land safe.

- ✔ **Water conservation:** As water becomes more difficult to come by, finding ways to conserve it is the focus of water utilities throughout the country.

Industry's current status

Much of the U.S. water system was built in response to the population boom after World War II. As a result, the water mains, pipes, pumps, and water treatment plants are now showing their age. Although our water infrastructure isn't in dire straits at the moment, that situation is just a matter of time unless we create a strategic plan to update the system and finance the work. The EPA advocates the Sustainable Infrastructure Initiative to help local water utilities plan for repairs and enhancements over time. For more about this initiative, see www.epa.gov/waterinfrastructure/basicinformation.html.

To ensure that local and regional water utilities have the tools, knowledge, and support they need to implement changes to their infrastructure, the EPA joined with six water associations to create "Ten Attributes of Effectively Managed Water Sector Utilities." You can read all about this program at www.watereum.org. By laying out best practices for the nation's water utilities, local organizations can focus their efforts on working with industry on conservation measures, building their capacity to provide adequate supplies of drinking water, and finding energy efficient ways to process water (www.epa.gov/waterinfrastructure/bettermanagement.html).

Rating

Water resource management is a mature field, though expected changes in the climate are likely to spur a new level of innovation as water shortages are expected locally and worldwide.

Future trends (and caveats)

The Clean Water Act of 1972 gave the EPA regulatory methods to clean local waterways. The Water Quality Act in 1987 bolstered that toolkit. Then Supreme Court decisions weakened the water protection system significantly. The proposed Clean Water Restoration Act of 2009 `http://feingold.senate.gov/record.cfm?id=311001`,making its way through Congress at this writing, means to restore the strength of the original laws.

Existing and anticipated water shortages, both locally and globally, are inspiring water resource managers to look at innovative ways to meet the demand for water for various uses:

- The EPA is encouraging local governments to explore the natural watersheds in their regions to discover ways to repair or restore the natural flow of water. Although natural watershed areas may cross state or local district boundaries, it's essential to develop partnerships to work together to enhance this water delivery option. For more information visit `www.epa.gov/waterinfrastructure/watershedapproaches.html`.

- Water reclamation (also known as water recycling and water reuse) systems are being built to treat waste water such that it can then be used for irrigation, industrial uses, landscaping, flushing toilets, and a variety of other uses. Some municipalities are actually creating potable or drinkable water from their waste water. Although not palatable to many of us who are unaccustomed to this notion, water has been reclaimed in this manner by Israel, Jordan, and Australia for some time. Arizona, Texas, Virginia, and Florida commonly add treated water to their underground water reserves that are used for drinking water (`www.sandiego.gov/water/recycled/faq.shtml`). To find out more about this option, visit `www.watereuse.org`.

- Desalination or desalinization aims to produce fresh water from salt water. It's expensive and energy intensive, so researchers are on the hunt for technology that will enable salt to be removed from salt water. Plants currently exist in Tampa Bay, Florida, and the United Arab Emirates.

Water conservation by residents, and more important, industrial users, is a key component of any water management plan. When industrial manufacturers rethink their processes, install sensors, and eliminate waste streams, massive amounts of water are conserved for other use. As companies face this issue, they are likely to rely on water management experts to determine the best way to minimize water use in their plants. Is that where you come in?

Sample job functions

- ✔ **Designing and building water treatment systems:** Project manager, civil engineer manager, hydraulic engineer, hydrologist, supervising engineer, hydrogeologist

- ✔ **Managing and treating water resources:** Water resources director, water resources engineer, water resources analyst, water hygiene consultant, water hygiene engineer, water treatment consultant, water treatment engineer, water sales engineer, district manager, deputy water manager

- ✔ **Irrigation:** Irrigation engineer, irrigation specialist, irrigation technician, field irrigation manager

- ✔ **Forecasting water conditions and taking mitigating action:** Waste water network modeler, flood risk modeler, flood risk engineer, river modeler, coastal modeler

Industry associations

- ✔ American Institute of Hydrology: www.aihydrology.org
- ✔ American Water Resources Association: www.awra.org
- ✔ American Water Works Association: www.awwa.org
- ✔ International Water Association: www.iwahq.org

Continue your exploration

- ✔ Vital Water Graphics: An Overview of the State of the World's Fresh and Marine Waters: www.unep.org/dewa/vitalwater
- ✔ U.S. Department of Energy, Office of Water: www.epa.gov/water
- ✔ World Health Organization, Water Sanitation and Health: www.who.int/water_sanitation_health/resources/en/
- ✔ Water Conservation Portal and Search Engine: www.waterconserve.info

Chapter 9

Angling for Jobs in Alternative Energy

· ·

· ·

*O*ne of the foundations of the green economy is *renewable energy* — energy that is derived from resources that are readily available all over the world. In many cases the resources are natural, but in a few instances man-made waste is also being converted to power. The crucial feature of renewable energy is that by tapping into its power, you don't deplete the resource, nor do you inflict damage on the environment or the planet as a whole.

The transition from fossil fuel–based energy to renewable energy is motivated by the threat of global warming, climate change, and the long-term threat of dwindling oil supplies. Many in the United States are also advocating for energy independence to increase national security, take responsibility for fuel production domestically, and stabilize fuel production costs.

At this point no one can predict which renewable energy technologies will become standard and which will fade away or be relegated to specialty applications. The mix of renewable energy sources will vary geographically based on local resources, existing infrastructure, funding sources, regulations, incentives, and what needs to be powered (cars, homes, factories, and so on).

I identify eight main renewable energy sources:

  ✔ Onshore wind

  ✔ Offshore wind

  ✔ Solar photovoltaics

- Solar thermal electricity generation
- Municipal solid waste-to-energy
- Sugar-based ethanol
- Cellulosic and next generation biofuels
- Geothermal power

Shaping the Lower-Carbon Economy

Policies and treaties are likely to set the standards that motivate investors, industries, businesses, and citizens to make the transition from fossil fuels to lower-carbon alternatives. The following policies are in the works:

- **The Renewable Energy Standard**, also referred to as the Renewable Portfolio Standard, requires that a certain percentage of electricity come from renewable sources by a specific date. At the time of this writing, 37 states have standards or goals in place. You can see them for yourself at www.pewclimate.org/what_s_being_done/in_the_states/rps.cfm. Click on each state to read its Renewable Energy Standard.

- A **National Renewable Energy Standard** would create a built-in market for renewable energy companies nationwide. When, and if, this standard becomes law, the actual details of the plan will define the future for the renewable energy industries. Watch for the percentage of electricity to come from renewable energy sources and for which renewable sources are deemed acceptable. Any source of renewable energy that is not included in this standard will become less attractive to investors and utilities. You can bet that all the renewable energy industries described in this chapter are lobbying hard to be included. To read the case for a National Renewable Energy Standard, see www.renewable energyworld.com/rea/news/article/2009/09/getting-to-a-national-renewable-energy-standard.

- A **cap and trade system** is also likely to be implemented at some point in the United States to discourage companies from producing green-house gas emissions. In this system, entities that generate greenhouse gases above a set cap must purchase emissions credits from entities that produce less pollution. As this system is set up, the defined cap and the designated industries will shape the form of the green economy. For more details about this system, see Chapter 8.

Policies and financing put into place by the American Renewal and Reinvestment Act (February 2009) have given new life to emerging and growing renewables. Although the details vary by industry; grants, investment tax credits, production tax credits, and residential tax credits provided by the act encourage and enable investors, companies, local governments, businesses, and individuals to take more sustainable actions.

Converting Waste into Energy

Sad to say, one of the most abundant resources on the planet at this time in history is waste. Traditionally, waste has been buried in landfills. Landfills, because of microorganisms that see them as food sources, emit methane gas, a greenhouse gas that is 21 times more dangerous to the planet than carbon dioxide. For a detailed explanation, see www.epa.gov/methane/scientific.html. What if we could take all this waste and use it to generate energy?

The Environmental Protection Agency (EPA), Federal Power Act, and the Internal Revenue Service (IRS) consider waste-to-energy to be a renewable source of energy because the power is created from a sustainable, abundant resource that is available locally. Thanks to innovations in waste management, two overlapping technologies have arisen that relieve pressure on close-to-capacity landfills while producing energy at the same time:

- **Biomass power (or biopower):** Biopower creates electric power from organic material such as manure, crops, wood resources and processing residue, food and yard waste, and municipal bio waste. Biomass can be converted to electricity, biofuels, space heating/cooling, or process heat. (See www.nrbp.org/bioenergy/products for more on biomass power.)

  When you consider the entire life cycle of biomass power, you can see that using biomass power reduces greenhouse gases. Organic materials consume carbon as they grow. When the same organic material is processed as biomass, it releases carbon back into the atmosphere, but the amount of carbon emitted is less than it took in while growing. Furthermore, by converting these biomass materials into power, the waste is diverted from disposal methods such as landfills, open burns, forest accumulation and fires, and composting, which all produce large quantities of greenhouse gases. For a full description of this process, see the diagram at www.usabiomass.org/docs/Biopower_is_Carbon_Neutral_Fact_Sheet2.pdf. Research indicates that for every megawatt of biomass power produced, 1.6 tons of carbon dioxide is avoided (www.usabiomass.org/docs/pri_one_pager.pdf).

- **Waste-to-energy (WTE):** WTE facilities burn organic and manufactured waste in carefully designed boilers with modern pollution control equipment to scrub the emissions from the burn and maintain precise heat conditions to ensure that all waste matter is combusted completely. For each ton of municipal solid waste combusted, 500–600 kilowatt-hours (kWh) of electricity are produced. The electricity can be added to the grid, while the steam produced can heat buildings. Since the mid-1970s, the process has been perfected to handle acid gas, particulate matter, nitrogen oxides, mercury, and organic emissions safely. For more, see www.broward.org/solidwaste/wastetoenergy.htm.

Although the combustion process does emit carbon dioxide, the process removes far more greenhouse gas emissions than it creates. In fact, when one ton of trash is processed at a waste-to-energy plant, one less ton of carbon dioxide is emitted into the atmosphere. For a detailed explanation of this, see the detailed answer for the second question on www.wte.org/faq.

Industry's current status

The United States currently has more than 100 biomass power plants in 20 states (www.biomasspowerassociation.org/pages/facts.php). According to the Department of Energy (DOE), with the exception of hydro-power, biomass power produces more electricity than any other renewable energy resource in the United States. The biomass power industry is likely to be concentrated in rural areas of the West Coast, the Mississippi Valley from the upper Midwest to the mouth of the Mississippi River, the Southeast, and Maine. For maps illustrating the reach of this industry, see www.nrel.gov/gis/biomass.html. As of fall of 2009, the biomass industry is rallying their forces to convince Congress to extend existing tax credits due to expire at the end of 2009. If you're interested in entering this field, track updates on this topic here: www.biomassmagazine.com/article.jsp?article_id=3095.

Eighty-seven of the waste-to-energy plants built since the 1970s are still in operation in 27 states (http://swana.org/Education/TechnicalDivisions/WastetoEnergy/tabid/108/Default.aspx). These plants process only 8 percent of the waste produced in the U.S. each year, meaning that the industry has ample room to expand. For a list of organizations and local governments that operate waste-to-energy plants, see www.wte.org/about. More than 500 waste-to-energy plants have been built worldwide.

Rating

The biomass and waste-to-energy industries have the potential to grow. The technology has been perfected over the last three decades and is proven to work. The technology could be expanded throughout the United States and the world to produce energy and contend with waste generated locally.

Future trends (and caveats)

Sources for biomass power abound. The DOE estimates that 14 percent of our electricity could come from crops grown for energy production and from waste generated from agricultural crops. Currently 39 million tons of crop residues are wasted annually in the U.S. alone. Food waste from groceries, restaurants, and homes also produce tons of biomass.

Some coal plants are now adding up to 20 percent biomass in a process called *co-firing*. In addition to lowering the cost of operations, adding biomass reduces greenhouse emissions. A 2009 study in *Science* demonstrated that fueling cars with electricity from biomass was 80 percent more efficient than using the same biomass to produce biofuels. That means investment dollars may be diverted to biomass electricity production from liquid biofuels.

One of the most important next steps for this industry is to create demonstration plants to familiarize the public and politicians with the process and the benefits of biomass power. Building confidence in the technology is likely to lead to more interest in commercial applications. Another key determinant is how it is classified in the climate change policy discussions. If biomass is categorized as a carbon emitter, then all the carbon tax or trading rules will apply to the industry. The industry might contract as a result of additional taxes or fees. If it's designated as a source of renewable energy, then incentives to use this methodology will be put in place.

The waste-to-energy industry must overcome some history. Back in 1994 the Supreme Court ruled that urban areas must transport their waste long distances to newly created landfills. As a result, development of new WTE plants stopped. A more recent ruling by the courts has restored communities' ability to determine where their waste goes for processing. Concerns stem from the fact that early WTE plants didn't adequately address environmental issues. These issues have now been addressed, and some of the biggest companies are winning awards for their environmental work. The other concern environmentalists have is that people will stop recycling if they know their trash will be taken care of by the local WTE plan. Studies indicate, however, that the average recycling rate is higher than average in WTE communities.

 Both biopower and WTE plants are most cost-effective when located near the source of biomass. Agricultural and forestry-related businesses in rural areas of the country could add new income streams and put local residents to work as a result of thriving waste-to-energy and biopower plants.

Sample job functions

- ✔ Research and development efforts at universities, national laboratories, and industry require chemists, agricultural specialists, microbiologists, biochemists, and engineers.

- ✔ Engineers and construction workers are needed to design and build bio-energy plants, while electrical/electronic and mechanical technicians, engineers (mechanical, electrical, and chemical), mechanics, and equipment operators are needed to run and maintain them. Some want cross-training in engineering and biology, or chemistry and agriculture.

- ✔ As the industry develops, farmers and foresters will be needed to produce and harvest biomass, and waste-management employees will be needed to collect and move waste materials.

The basics of biofuel

Organic matter can also be processed into liquid fuels such as ethanol, biodiesel, and hydrogen that are capable of powering vehicles. Researchers are testing three generations of biofuels to find the most cost-effective, environmentally sustainable technologies to produce liquid fuels.

- **First generation:** Biofuels in this category are made from basic feedstocks of food quality, such as seeds and grains. The sugars, starches, vegetables, or animal fats in them are used to make vegetable oil, biodiesel, bioalcohols (commonly ethanol), and other gases.

- **Second generation:** Non-food crops, including waste biomass, agricultural waste, and biomass crops (switchgrass and miscanthus) grown for this purpose, create fuels such as biohydrogen, biomethanol, biohydrogen diesel, mixed alcohols, and wood diesel.

- **Third generation:** More recently, attention has turned to algae as a feedstock for biofuel. It has the potential to yield 30 to 40 times as much energy per acre than land crops. Even more remote is the idea of using fungi to generate biodiesel: www.wired.com/wiredscience/2008/11/rainforest-fung. *Potential* is the key word as companies work to unlock the best way to harvest this energy.

Advanced technology and experimentation now allow scientists to determine the net energy balance for various feedstock sources. To be viable, the amount of fuel created with a feedstock must be far greater than the energy required to grow, harvest, process, and transport the fuel.

According to a study by the U.S. Department of Agriculture (USDA), corn-based ethanol, once the darling of the industry, produces 67 percent more energy than is required to grow, harvest, refine, and transport the fuel. Researchers from the University of Nebraska-Lincoln grew switchgrass and found that biofuel from switchgrass produced 540 percent more energy than was required to produce it. (Fossil fuel gasoline is rated as a negative 19 percent, meaning it takes more energy to produce the fuel than you get out of it. For additional comparison ratings for various biofuels, visit http://help fuelthefuture.org/web/content/view/20/35).

To thrive, the biofuels industry must resolve several issues. First, biofuel feedstock must be grown in a way that doesn't negatively impact food crops, the soil, or the surrounding environment. One solution is to include waste sources as feedstock (see the earlier section "Converting Waste into Energy"). The Rocky Mountain Institute reports that biofuels can be created in a sustainable fashion as long as growing sites are chosen with care. Second, in addition to having a favorable net energy balance, biofuels must be produced by methods that ensure the best price and the lowest carbon emissions. The final hurdles for the industry are scaling (expanding) the favored production process to produce large quantities of fuel to meet demand at a cost-effective price and creating cost-effective distribution systems.

Currently 170 ethanol biorefinery plants exist in 26 states, with a high concentration in the Midwest (www.ethanolrfa.org/industry/locations). If you're interested in this industry, you may also want to track developments on Earth2Tech's Biofuel Deathwatch Map, www.earth2tech.com/maps, which tracks projects on hold due to funding issues and industry trends. In 2008 America's ethanol industry produced 9 billion gallons of ethanol and is expected to produce

10 billion gallons in 2009, 9 percent of the U.S. gasoline supply. Various blends of ethanol are in use. Biodiesel is also becoming more readily available.

The Renewable Fuel Standard program (www.epa.gov/OMS/renewablefuels/420f09023.htm), run by the EPA under the Energy Independence and Security Act of 2007, requires that a certain percentage of renewable fuel be blended with gasoline. In May 2009 the EPA announced new regulations for each year from 2010 to 2022 to extend the first Renewable Fuel Standards originally established in 2005. The proposed ruling specifies volume standards for cellulosic biofuel, biomass-based diesel, advanced biofuel, and total renewable fuel that must be used in transportation fuel each year. For the first time, greenhouse gas emissions thresholds have been set for each kind of biofuel. Requirements defined in this regulation will apply to domestic and foreign producers and importers and cover all transportation fuel, which includes gasoline and diesel fuel used in highway vehicles and engines, as well as locomotive and marine engines.

If these changes to the Renewable Fuel Standard are approved, the biofuels industry is likely to grow and develop. Using funds from the American Reinvestment and Recovery Act, the DOE is investing $786.5 million in advanced biofuels research and development and committing $480 million to demonstration-scale projects called *integrated biorefineries* that produce advanced biofuels, biobased products, power, and heat from the same plant. In addition, $176.5 million has been dedicated to several commercial-scale biorefinery projects that are under construction.

For more on biofuel, see the following Web sites:

- American Biofuel Council: www.americanbiofuelscouncil.com
- Bioenergy Power Association: www.usbiomass.org
- Biodiesel information by Next Diesel: http://nextdiesel.net/home.html
- International Biofuels Commission: http://helpfuelthefuture.org/web/content/section/6/33
- Industry outlook for ethanol: www.ethanolrfa.org/industry/outlook

Industry associations

- Bioenergy Power Association (ABA): www.usbiomass.org
- Energy Recovery Council (ERC): www.energyrecoverycouncil.org
- American Society of Mechanical Engineers (ASME), Solid Waste Processing Division (SWPD): http://divisions.asme.org/swpd

Continue your exploration

- ✔ Energy Recovery Council FAQ: `www.energyrecoverycouncil.org/faq`

- ✔ "Waste-to-Energy: A Renewable Energy Source from Municipal Solid Waste": `http://files.asme.org/Divisions/SWPD/17157.pdf`

- ✔ Powerpoint presentation about biomass by Biomass Power Association: `www.usabiomass.org/pages/facts_power_point.php`

- ✔ National Biofuels Action Plan: www1.eere.energy.gov/biomass/pdfs/nbap.pdf

Geothermal

Geothermal energy taps the heat from the core of the Earth to generate electricity and provide heating and cooling applications. Geothermal energy is a clean, reliable, renewable resource available throughout the world. Estimates suggest that the Earth's heat translates to 42 million megawatts of energy, which is said to be a virtually unlimited source of energy.

Geothermal energy is divided into three categories:

- ✔ **Geothermal electricity production:** Drilled wells bring hot water from geothermal reservoirs to the surface of the Earth where the heat is converted to electricity at a geothermal power plant.

- ✔ **Geothermal direct use:** Hot water from the Earth is used directly without converting it to electricity. Examples include heating/cooling individual buildings or districts, melting snow on roads, bridges, and sidewalks, heating greenhouses, drying crops, and using it in spas, agriculture, and aquaculture.

- ✔ **Geothermal heat pumps:** Continuous closed-loop pipes run underground and then back through the adjacent building. The constant temperature of the ground transfers to the water or substance in the pipes. On cold days the water is circulated throughout the building to provide warmth. On hot days, the process is reversed to take the heat from the room. The Environmental Protection Agency considers this technology to be the most efficient heating and cooling system available. (See page 18, `www.zebralliance.com/docs/geothermal_report_12-08.pdf`, or `www.newportgeo.com`.)

For a more detailed description of these systems and others, see Geothermal 101: Basics of Geothermal Energy Production and Use at `www.geo-energy.org/publications/reports/Geo101_Final_Feb_15.pdf`.

Industry's Current Status

According to the Geothermal Energy Association's May 2007 interim report (www.geo-energy.org/publications/reports/GEA%20World%20 Update%202007.pdf), 24 countries convert geothermal energy to electric power, and another 22 plan to start doing so by 2010. In 2007 the U.S. was the largest producer of geothermal energy in the world, generating 14,885 GWh (gigawatt-hours) of electricity. See Geothermal 101 for more details. Geothermal heat pump installations and direct use applications are also increasing.

Current technology is scalable. Larger plants can service larger communities, and smaller plants are adequate for smaller communities. The key hurdles to building geothermal power plants are construction capital and overcoming the financial risks of searching for the proper geological configurations. Operating costs are reasonable and do not fluctuate. The geothermal industry will develop where the Earth's geothermal resources are most abundant. Within the United States, the majority of geothermal activity is in 13 Western states, including Hawaii and Alaska. As of August 2008, these states had 103 geothermal energy plants in development for almost 4 GW (gigawatts).

Rating

The geothermal industry is maturing. Plants are in place, and the technology is perfected. Challenges to expansion relate to identifying new geothermal sites and ensuring that the necessary equipment is available when needed.

Future trends (and caveats)

The American Recovery and Reinvestment Act of 2009 has provided a number of valuable incentives to the geothermal energy industry. Production tax credits, investment tax credits, and grants are available for projects that will be in service by December 2013. Homeowners will receive a tax credit of up to $2,000 for qualified geothermal heat pumps. A similar tax credit incentive has contributed significantly to the growth of the residential solar industry.

Technological advances are expected to reduce the costs and risks of using geothermal energy. Some of the technologies to watch can be found at www. geo-energy.org/aboutGE/basics.asp.

Issues that must continue to be addressed by the industry include maintaining the quality of drinking water near geothermal plants, finding ways to sequester the carbon released by geothermal processing, and minimizing earthquakes that may occur while creating new geothermal plants.

Sample job functions

- ✔ Locating, assessing, and accessing the reservoirs is the job of geologists, geochemists, geophysicists, hydrologists, reservoir engineers, mud loggers, hydraulic engineers, and drillers.

- ✔ Direct-use geothermal technologies create jobs for heating engineers and employees within the green building industry and agricultural industries.

- ✔ Electricity production necessitates building power plants, requiring electrical and mechanical engineers, construction workers, electrical technicians, electricians, electrical machinists, welders, riggers, and mechanics.

- ✔ Manufacturing and installing geothermal heat pumps create employment for mechanical engineers, geologists, drilling crews, heating contractors, ventilation contractors, and air conditioning contractors.

- ✔ The research and development sector of the geothermal industry must have highly qualified mechanical engineers, electronic engineers, geologists, chemists, and materials scientists.

Industry associations

- ✔ Geothermal Energy Association: www.geo-energy.org
- ✔ International Ground Source Heat Pump Association: www.igshpa.okstate.edu

Continue your exploration

- ✔ Overview of the future of the geothermal industry: www1.eere.energy.gov/geothermal/future_geothermal.html

- ✔ NREL's overview of geothermal technologies: www.nrel.gov/geothermal

- ✔ Geothermal 101: Basics of Geothermal Energy Production and Use: www.geo-energy.org/publications/reports/Geo101_Final_Feb_15.pdf

- ✔ Virtual geothermal plant: www.geothermal.org/virtualgeo.html

- ✔ DOE Report on Geothermal Heat Pumps: www.zebralliance.com/docs/geothermal_report_12-08.pdf

Hydrogen: An industry to watch

Hydrogen (H$_2$) is the most abundant element in the universe. It is a light, odorless, colorless gas that stores and delivers energy in an easy-to-access form. When used, hydrogen power produces two by-products: heat and water. Many refer to hydrogen as a *universal fuel* because it can be produced in a number of ways, depending on the resources locally available. Issues surrounding the hydrogen industry include the following:

✔ To determine whether hydrogen is renewable, look at the production process used to create the hydrogen. If a renewable energy source such as solar energy, wind, or bio-fuels, is used, then the hydrogen is indeed considered green, or renewable. If coal or natural gas are used to produce hydrogen, the end result is decidedly not green in nature.

✔ Although it takes more energy to produce and distribute hydrogen than it does for gasoline fuel, hydrogen combustion engines (HCEs) and fuel cells are far more efficient than the traditional combustion engines, which means they need to use less fuel to travel the same distance.

✔ Applications for fuel cell technology are growing in the area of stationary power sources, specialty vehicles such as forklifts, and portable power for emergency backup.

✔ As hydrogen evolves, forecasts indicate a move toward electricity generation for buildings on the grid and in remote locations, portable consumer electronics devices, military applications, and vehicles, from two- and three-wheelers to delivery trucks and buses.

Hydrogen proponents' vision of a hydrogen-based economy includes using fuel cells as an efficient, versatile way to power a variety of applications. If we switched to hydrogen technology, internal combustion engines, turbines, and batteries would go the way of the horse and buggy. For the move to a hydrogen-based economy to happen, several key issues must be addressed:

✔ The methods for producing hydrogen from green, renewable, domestic sources must be identified and perfected.

✔ Costs to the user must be ascertained. The DOE is targeting a cost of $2–$3 per gallon of gasoline equivalent; current technology produces hydrogen at a cost of $3–$6 per gallon of gasoline equivalent.

✔ Distribution of hydrogen and the associated infrastructure must be resolved. Current estimates indicate that $9 billion to $15 billion dollars would be required to build hydrogen stations to support 1 million fuel cell electric cars in the top 100 metro areas. If built out according to this plan, 70 percent of the U.S. would live within two miles of the nearest hydrogen station.

For more on hydrogen, check out the following Web sites:

✔ National Hydrogen Association: `www.hydrogenassociation.org`

✔ Increase your H$_2$ IQ: `www1.eere.energy.gov/hydrogenand fuelcells/education/h2iq.html`

✔ Hydrogen projects by DOE Hydrogen Program: `www.hydrogen.energy.gov/offices.html`

✔ Maps of current hydrogen infrastructure and hydrogen production sites (`www.h2 andyou.org/pdf/nightLights.pdf`) and maps of consumer demand, proposed refueling stations, and potential hydrogen from renewable energy sources (`www.nrel.gov/gis/hydrogen.html`)

Solar

Sunlight is the source of most renewable energy power. By incorporating solar into our energy mix, we have access to a very reliable, abundant, accessible source of energy that can be produced domestically with little or no impact on the environment. The solar industry is generally divided into residential, commercial, and large utility-scale projects. Although the basic solar principles are the same in each of these applications, the equipment that is deemed most efficient and cost-effective varies by application.

- **Solar electricity:** Sunlight is converted directly into electricity with the use of photovoltaic (PV) technology. Rooftop solar arrays are built according to the size of the project. *Thin-film solar*, a competing technology, is often referred to as CIGS, for the chemicals — copper, indium, gallium and (di)selenide — used to absorb light. Some companies are already offering roof tiles that have embedded PV qualities. Solar electricity is a viable energy source for a wide range of situations, from small consumer items, to remote buildings and equipment, to solar farms that cover thousands of acres. Electricity from solar projects can charge batteries and contribute to the grid.

- **Solar heating:** Solar thermal systems harness the power of the sun to heat liquids that then transfer the heat to a building, swimming pool, or household water needs. These systems are either *passive*, where the system is designed to move the liquid through a loop, or *active*, where a pump is installed to force the water somewhere else. Some systems are *direct*, in that the water itself is moved through the solar thermal equipment, whereas other systems are *indirect* and have another substance run through the loop.

- **Concentrating solar power (CSP):** Typically used in utility-scale projects, CSP uses a large array of mirrors to focus sunlight onto receivers. As the receivers collect the solar energy, they convert it to heat. Several designs are in use, including a mirrored dish, a power tower with mirrors encircling the tower, and linear trough systems.

Industry's current status

The Emergency Economic Stabilization Act of 2008 (EESA), often referred to as the bailout package, included several key wins for the solar industry. Enhanced tax credits for investors and homeowners provide a much-needed long-term framework for the industry. This stability is likely to help the industry grow. For more details on the status of the overall solar industry and by technology and by state, see www.seia.org/galleries/pdf/2008_Year_in_Review-small.pdf.

States and municipalities with incentive programs above and beyond the federal rebates are seeing tremendous growth in photovoltaic installations. As I write this, New Jersey had just moved ahead of California in PV installations. Solar installers in Pennsylvania, New York, Colorado, and Delaware are also benefiting from generous rebates. Florida and southern Texas are seeing a jump in thermal solar. States are likely to change positions in the rankings as new rebates are approved in different areas.

Global competition is heating up in the solar industry, from manufacturing to installation in each technology area. Key players are Europe, the U.S., Japan, and China. The market climate in each of these countries and regions is impacting how this industry is developing.

 The highest potential for domestic solar power is in the Southwest region of the United States (see `www.nrel.gov/gis/solar.html`). Scroll down on that pages for detailed maps of various solar technologies within the U.S. For a map of solar potential globally, visit `www.solar4power.com/map1-global-solar-power.html`.

Rating

The solar industry is growing and developing. Technology exists to create solar power at the residential and utility level, and research and development continues to push toward more efficient technology. As the industry matures, key technologies will become standard, and others are likely to drop away.

Future trends (and caveats)

As with other renewable energy industries, the American Recovery and Reinvestment Act is providing a financial infusion into the solar industry through investments in research and development, demonstration projects, and commercial projects. Grants at the commercial level and tax credits for residential solar installations motivate activity.

To break through to the next level of production, the solar industry must find ways to deliver solar electricity into the electric grid through high-voltage transmission lines. The National Renewable Energy Laboratory (NREL) at `www.nrel.gov/pv` is dedicating part of its research agenda to defining and resolving the regulatory, technical, and economic barriers to this integration. For more about this topic, see Chapter 10.

The NREL is also searching for ways to improve the efficiency of thin-film solar and concentrator technology and integrate solar technology into building materials from shingles to paint. Nanosolar's thin-film technology is also garnering interest as new developments allow the company to print solar cells on very thin foil (www.nanosolar.com/technology). As the thin-film industry takes off, expect to see new solar energy collection systems.

As the solar industry looks to build more utility-scale solar farms and CSP installations, land access and land use issues must be resolved. Public lands in the Southwest, managed by the Bureau of Land Management (BLM), continue to be prime territory for large-scale solar projects. In 2008, the BLM launched a two-year study that's likely to speed up application processing in the future.

Sample job functions

- ✔ Solar research and system design depend on scientists and engineers.
- ✔ Manufacturing of solar systems and the components that go into making solar products, such as glass and steel manufacturing, require technicians, operators, machinists, electricians, production manager, scheduler, materials manager, supervisors, and plant managers.
- ✔ Solar systems must be marketed and sold.
- ✔ Installation of residential applications, commercial systems, and utility-scale rely on contractors, electricians, plumbers, and carpenters.
- ✔ Operation, inspection, maintenance, repair, and troubleshooting solar systems requires maintenance supervisors and maintenance personnel.

Industry associations

- ✔ The Solar Energy Industry Association: www.seia.org
- ✔ American Solar Energy Society: www.ases.org
- ✔ Solar Electric Power Association: www.solarelectricpower.org
- ✔ Global Solar Thermal Energy Council: www.solarthermalworld.org

Continue your exploration

- ✔ How solar works: www.southface.org/solar/solar-roadmap/solar_how-to/solar-how_solar_works.htm
- ✔ Solar Energy Technologies Program (SETP or Solar Program), with detailed descriptions about applications, technologies, and research: www1.eere.energy.gov/solar
- ✔ "A Solar Grand Plan" in *Scientific American*: www.scientific american.com/article.cfm?id=a-solar-grand-plan
- ✔ Solar research by the NREL: www.nrel.gov/solar

Low-impact hydropower

Historically, hydroelectric power plants have come in the form of large-scale dams. Although the energy they produce is deemed clean, renewable energy, the impact of the dams during construction and operation has not always been environmentally sound. Nevertheless, hydropower plants contribute one-fifth of the world's energy, and hydropower is the major source of power for 55 countries.

As the impact of climate change started becoming apparent, the hydropower industry took on the challenge to find more sustainable ways to provide power. The following list includes several key initiatives that address the sustainability of hydropower:

✔ The Sustainable Hydropower Web site provides an in-depth look at the advantages and disadvantages of hydropower from an economic, social, and environmental point of view. Visit www.sustainable hydropower.org and click on the segments of the globe to dig into issues and solutions. For a chart of the strengths and weaknesses of the technology, click on the About Sustainability in the Hydropower Industry link at the top of the home page.

✔ The non-profit Low Impact Hydropower Institute (LIHI) is working to reduce the impact of hydropower plants by certifying projects that have reduced their environmental impact. The certification allows consumers to support hydropower dams that become more environmentally sound. For more, see www.lowimpacthydro.org/content/about.aspx. While you're on the site, check out the project map and list of certified projects and projects that are moving through the application process.

✔ Small-scale or *micro hydro* technologies are also gaining popularity because they have little to no impact on the surrounding environment. These systems capture the power of river flow without altering or interfering with the river — just as mills used to do. Typically these systems produce up to 300 kilowatts. Micro hydro projects are in place around the world, often in areas that couldn't afford a larger facility. For more about this sector, see www.alternative-energy-news.info/micro-hydro-power-pros-and-cons/.

To continue your investigation of hydropower, check out these Web sites:

✔ The International Hydropower Association: www.hydropower.org

✔ National Hydropower Association: www.hydro.org

✔ Overview of the hydropower industry: www1.eere.energy.gov/windandhydro/hydro_how.html

Tidal and Marine

The oceans, which cover 70 percent of the earth's surface, are constantly in motion due to lunar phases, gravity, tides, wind, and solar heating of the water's surface. That movement provides a promising source of renewable, non-polluting electricity. Energy can be pulled from oceans in the following ways. Each source has benefits that are unique to the corresponding technology:

✔ **Tidal energy:** Energy can be captured and converted to electricity as tidal waters move into and out of a bay. Although electrical power generated from tidal action is cyclical, with two high and two low tides each day and no generation at the six-hour mark in between, the peaks in production are predictable and reliable. This sort of energy is best suited to displace electricity that would have been generated by fossil fuels.

✔ **Wave power:** As waves move, the change in their height and speed creates energy. The Ocean Energy Council calculates that "an average 4-foot, 10-second wave striking a coast puts out more than 35,000 horsepower per mile of coast." (One horsepower is equal to a little over 700 watts — meaning one wave has the energy of 24 megawatts (MW). Using one of a variety of devices (buoys, floats, oscillating water column devices, or a tapered channel), the wave's movement can be added to the electric grid.

✔ **Ocean current energy:** This source of energy takes advantage of strong currents that occur naturally between islands, near headlands, and at the entrances of bays and harbors. Underwater turbines capture the energy created by currents that have a velocity of 5 or more knots.

✔ **Ocean thermocline energy (OTEC):** This method relies on temperature differences between the warm water on the surface of the ocean and the cold water at deeper depths. By building thermal energy conversion plants in areas with a large temperature differential, surface water can be used to create steam which is passed through a turbine generator to make electricity. Although costly to build, such a plant can continually produce clean, renewable electricity. And after the warm or cold water has been pumped into the system, it can be used for other purposes, including air conditioning, desalination, and aquaculture.

See www.oceanenergycouncil.com/index.php/Tidal-Energy/What-is-Ocean-Energy.html for more on each of these power sources.

Industry's current status

The good news about tidal power is that the technology required to capture power from the ocean is well developed and is very similar to technology used by hydroelectric plants for the last 120 years. The more challenging part of the story is the construction itself. Oceanic projects require a large investment of time and money, with construction lasting as long as ten years. Nevertheless, companies, utilities, and governments are actively working on projects around the world. The location of the early adopters depends on the geological phenomenon needed to leverage each type of technology:

✔ **Tidal energy:** Operating a tidal energy operation requires a difference of at least 7 meters between the low and the high tide. Several tidal power plants exist now on the northern coast of France, in the Bay of Fundy in Nova Scotia, near Murmansk in Russia, and several locations in China. Research studies point to several other promising locations, including Alaska, British Columbia, Washington, Maine, the Severn River in England, and the White Sea of Russia. If we could harness tidal power around the world, we could generate 64,000 MW of power.

✔ **Wave power:** Wave power plants are most likely to be sited on western coastlines that experience fast series of pounding waves. In keeping with this fact, WaveGen (www.wavegen.co.uk) built the first commercial-scale wave power plant in the Isle of Islay, Scotland. Other projects are underway around the globe in countries such as Portugal, Norway, the U.S., China, Japan, Australia, and India. The U.S. alone could produce 23 GW from wave power.

✔ **Ocean current energy:** To capture energy from ocean currents, the current must be moving at 5 knots or more. Various areas around the world including the UK, Italy, Japan, the Philippines, the Florida Current, and the Gulf Stream are well suited for this industry. In 2000, Blue Energy, Inc., estimated the power from this energy source to exceed 450 GW.

✔ **Ocean thermocline energy (OTEC):** This technology is typically most effective near the equator where the warm shallow waters around an island drop off dramatically to deep waters with cold temperatures. Although studied by scientists since the late 1800s, only a few plants have been constructed — off Hawaii, India, and Guam.

Experts say that the ocean energy industry is where wind power was in the early 1980s, when many technical designs were in play and no clear indication of the ultimate direction of the industry was apparent. The ocean energy industry has a couple advantages over the early years of the wind industry, however. The cost per unit of energy is already competitive with wind, lower than solar, and expected to drop farther. In addition, the development of industry standards is progressing more quickly than in wind, shortening the time between product prototype and commercialization.

Rating

Although some ocean power technologies are more mature than others, the industry as a whole is still in early stages of development.

Future trends (and caveats)

Although the industry is not yet ready for large-scale development, there are some positive signs that the industry is progressing. The capital costs per net kilowatt compete with wind projects and are lower than solar power projects.

Growth potential is also projected to be quite promising. In a report entitled *Forecasting the Future of Ocean Power*, Daniel Englander and Travis Bradford forecast the ocean power industry can move from the current 10 MW installed capacity to over 1 GW over a span of six years. They estimate the annual market for this industry to be $500 million and that more than $2 billion will be invested to manufacture and install these ocean power plants. Several large corporations, including G.E., Chevron, and Shell, are investing in ocean power companies. For a summary of this report, see `www.gtmresearch.com/report/forecasting-the-future-of-ocean-power`.

To thrive, the ocean power industry needs the same kinds of support that the solar and wind industries have been receiving.

- ✔ Financing is of key importance. As an early-stage industry with promise, funds are needed for technological research, testing devices in ocean settings, and building demonstration projects to increase awareness of the industry and encourage commercial projects.

- ✔ The industry could also use some assistance to smooth out the environmental impact studies, planning requirements, and the permit process. The bureaucratic nature of the process is causing undue delays and putting the U.S. behind many other countries.

- ✔ As carbon regulations take form, it's critical that ocean power be included as a viable source of clean energy. Adding it to clean energy incentive programs such as the Renewable Energy Portfolio would open up options for utilities that must provide a certain percentage of renewable energy to their customers.

Companies working in this industry must conduct studies and make adjustments as needed to minimize the impact on wildlife. Although questions and concerns about the environmental impact of capturing the power of the sea exist, several early studies indicate that the impact is minimal. Another challenge for this industry is determining the best way to build machinery to withstand hostile undersea conditions. The industry will need to rely on software simulations and precise engineering to discover the most effective building methodologies. In the early stages, companies may need to develop their own equipment or modify equipment used in offshore drilling.

Sample job functions

✔ Mechanical engineers, control and instrumentation engineers, sustainable energy engineers, structural engineers, and geotechnical engineers build and maintain the power generation systems.

✔ Oceanographer engineers, rivers and coastal engineers, marine ecologists, and hydraulic modelers are needed to identify the best locations for power technologies and to work with engineers on operations and maintenance issues.

✔ Electrical designers, electric design managers, and software engineers manage the electricity generated by the power generation systems.

✔ As new systems go online, workers must install, service, and maintain equipment. Diving and working underwater is likely a desired skill.

Industry associations

✔ Ocean Renewable Energy Coalition: www.oceanrenewable.com

✔ Ocean Energy Council: www.oceanenergycouncil.com

✔ Ocean, Tidal and New Technologies Council of National Hydropower Association: www.hydro.org

Continue your exploration

✔ What is Renewable Energy? tutorial by American Council on Renewable Energy: www.acore.org/what_is_renewable_energy/ocean

✔ What is Ocean Energy? by the Ocean Energy Council: www.ocean energycouncil.com/index.php/Tidal-Energy/What-is-Ocean-Energy.html

Wind

As the sun heats different parts of the earth at different rates, hot air rises and cooler air is drawn in to replace the warmer rising air. The result is wind — which can be converted into electricity. Wind is inexhaustible, affordable, and is fairly predictable in certain regions of the world. Wind energy has been harnessed for centuries (have a look at old Dutch paintings).

The most common modern turbines have a propeller design and can be up to 300 feet tall with turbine blades that are 65 to 130 feet long. The amount of energy collected from wind depends on the size of the wind turbine and the speed of the wind moving the rotor. As the wind moves the turbine blades, they turn a gearbox and electrical generator to produce electricity.

Industry's current status

Although the economic crisis of 2008–2009 slowed the growth of the wind industry, the American Recovery and Reinvestment Act included a number of financial incentives for future wind power installations. Experts predict that wind power installations will exceed 2008 growth within a few years.

As of April 2009, the United States became the world leader in wind with 28.6 GW of installed capacity. These installed wind farms were projected to generate over 60 billion kWh of electricity in 2009, which would power over 5.5 million homes. Industry experts forecast that wind power is capable of providing 20 percent of the energy of the United States by 2030. For more information, see http://www.awea.org/newsroom/releases/year_end_wrap_up_22dec08.html. For a look at how the wind industry has evolved in the U.S. over the last decade, see www.windpoweringamerica.gov/wind_installed_capacity.asp.

Europe and China are the other wind powers. In 2008, China's wind power capacity doubled for the fourth year in a row. Chinese manufacturing production is expanding as well.

Rating

The wind industry is growing. Safety guidelines and manufacturing guidelines for utility-scale and small-scale wind turbines are likely as the wind industry matures.

Future trends (and caveats)

Wind turbines are immense machines full of finely machined parts. The industry depends on the availability of several key ingredients: steel, large-scale manufacturing equipment, heavy-duty transportation, and experienced workers. In addition, the success of the wind industry, and many other renewable energy sources, depends on the creation of a new electric grid that provides for the transmission of electricity from renewable sources in all parts of the country.

Small-scale wind power systems are those that generate up to 100 kW of electricity. Residential units are also gaining popularity and produce up to 1 kW. With a federal-level investment tax credit of 30 percent of installed costs available through December 2016, consumers are expected to purchase more small wind turbines for their homes, businesses, and farms. Community wind farms are likely to gain appeal.

The next frontier for wind may be offshore. One glance at the wind resource map (www.windpoweringamerica.gov/wind_maps.asp) that includes coastal wind resources demonstrates why. Although the costs of offshore wind are higher upfront, windier conditions at sea produce more energy than on land. Offshore wind farms are also likely to be near urban centers. Generating wind where it is used reduces the cost of transmission. Although not feasible yet, it may be possible to set up floating wind farms in the future.

Sample job functions

- ✔ Mechanical, electrical, and aeronautical engineers with advanced degrees, and experienced technicians work together to conduct research and development to improve wind turbines and their capacity.

- ✔ Meteorologists help engineers identify the best sites for wind farms.

- ✔ Project development managers, transmission design engineers, and utility wind-program managers work on turning a potential wind site into a fully functional wind farm. In addition to technical knowledge, the people in these roles must be able to work diplomatically with the local utility, elected officials in the region, and community members.

- ✔ Manufacturing plants with skilled machinists and welders create the components of the wind turbine.

- ✔ Construction managers and workers build and install the wind turbines.

- ✔ Large-load transportation specialists transport extremely large turbine blades to the wind farm site.

- ✔ Mechanical and electrical technicians, called windsmiths or wind technicians, keep the wind turbines working effectively.

- ✔ Wind turbine sales managers and specialists sell the wind turbines.

Industry association

America Wind Energy Association: www.awea.org

Continue your exploration

- ✔ Wind Web Tutorial: www.awea.org/faq/
- ✔ Ten Steps to Building a Wind Farm: www.awea.org/pubs/
  factsheets/Ten_Steps.pdf
- ✔ United States Wind Projects: www.awea.org/projects/

Chapter 10

Careers in Rebuilding the Infrastructure

. . . .

In This Chapter

▶ Gaining a clear understanding of what cleantech is

▶ Uncovering ways the technical world is becoming energy efficient

▶ Nailing down all the aspects of green building

▶ Understanding how to green the manufacturing sector

▶ Wrapping your mind around the smart grid

▶ Finding the best way to move products, materials, and people from here to there

. . . .

*O*ur world consists of an array of interrelated systems, sectors, and processes that consume a lot of energy, create a tremendous amount of waste, and incorporate materials that are actually hazardous to our health when they aren't handled properly. To make a dent in our impact on the planet, these industry sectors must become more sustainable. The sooner the better.

The sections in this chapter refer to different sectors of our economy. As a result, the profiles in this chapter include a collection of interrelated industries that must collaborate to green their processes. Although some sectors are just beginning their green adventure, others are making great strides. The trends highlighted in this chapter provide a sampling of what's happening in the overall sector. As you drill down into each industry, you will discover even more trends that deserve your attention.

Cleantech

According to the Cleantech Group, the originators of the term *cleantech*, "determining what is or isn't cleantech isn't always easy." When key industry experts don't agree on a single definition and they continue to tweak the description as the scope of the sectors evolves, you know that you are on the frontlines of innovation. A few definitions of cleantech follow.

Clean Edge (www.cleanedge.com), a cleantech research firm: "A diverse range of products, services, and processes that harness renewable materials and energy sources, dramatically reduce the use of natural resources, and cut or eliminate emissions and wastes."

Pernick and Wilder, authors of *The Clean Tech Revolution: The Next Big Growth and Investment Opportunity:* "Any product, service, or process that delivers value using limited or zero non-renewable resources and/or creates significantly less waste than conventional offerings."

The Cleantech Group, a network of entrepreneurs and investors, http://cleantech.com/about/cleantechdefinition.cfm: "... cleantech represents a diverse range of products, services, and processes, all intended to: provide superior performance at lower costs, while greatly reducing or eliminating negative ecological impact, at the same time as improving the productive and responsible use of natural resources."

Green Building

According to the U.S. Green Building Council, residential homes and commercial buildings consume 72 percent of the country's electricity, 39 percent of all energy sources, 40 percent of the raw materials, and 14 percent of the potable water. Buildings emit 38 percent of the country's carbon dioxide and produce 30 percent of the country's waste.

To counteract these effects, the building industry is becoming more and more dedicated to building green, sustainable structures. Changes are being implemented throughout the process, from rethinking how building materials and supplies are manufactured to how buildings are constructed, decorated, and maintained. The benefits of green building are many. The environment is better off as natural resources are used more effectively, and the surrounding areas are improved by better air and water quality and less waste. The building owners and renters save money because operating these building is less costly. The people who live and work in the buildings are generally healthier, more productive, and more comfortable.

The greening of the building industry is occurring in the following areas:

- **Architecture:** Those who design buildings try to find innovative solutions that result in little impact on the environment. Green roofs handle water runoff, insulate the building, and enhance the biodiversity of the local environment. More buildings are designed to generate their own power through a variety of methods. Waste water that used to flow into the sewer system is divided into *true waste* and *gray water*. Gray water can be used to flush toilets and water the garden. Rain water that used to travel to the gutter is now stored for other uses.

- **Building supplies and materials:** All the materials, such as roofing, windows, doors, foundations, insulations, paints and plumbing, used in building new construction and remodeling projects must be built from sustainable materials with green manufacturing processes.

- **New construction and remodeling:** Contractors seek new knowledge, skills, and experience to implement the architect's plans while finding innovative ways to manage the building industry's waste stream.

- **Energy-efficiency audits and retrofitting:** A new emphasis in the building trade is evolving to assess the environmental impact of existing buildings and to retrofit them to be more energy efficient.

- **Interior design:** Choosing the materials used to create the interior ambience of a building is just as important as the structure itself.

- **Furnishings:** Interior decorations must also be built sustainably, including furniture, window coverings, flooring, and lighting.

- **Landscaping:** With care and forethought, landscaping can decrease the energy used to heat, cool, and light a building. Water usage, waste management, and buying locally benefit green landscapers.

Industry's current status

The Architecture 2030 Challenge was founded by the architect Edward Mazria in 2002 to transform the building industry from being a contributor to greenhouse gas emissions to being part of the solution (`www.architecture2030.org/2030_challenge`). Buildings require a huge amount of power to build and operate. When that power is provided through coal-burning plants, the result is massive amounts of greenhouse gases that contribute to global warming. Reducing the power needed to build and operate buildings reduces greenhouse gas emissions. The Architecture 2030 Challenge asks all architects and building professionals to design, build, and retrofit buildings to emit 50 percent fewer greenhouse gas emissions than typical buildings of the same variety until, over time, that percentage increases and buildings are carbon neutral in 2030.

The Leadership in Energy and Environmental Design (LEED) certification system developed by the U.S. Green Building Council in 1998 provides all building professionals with a framework to create buildings that save energy, conserve water, improve indoor air quality, and reduce greenhouse gas emissions. Professionals can earn a certification in building construction, homes, interior design, operations, neighborhood development, and more. If you're interested in sitting for your certification, visit the Green Building Certification Institute: www.gbci.org.

The U.S. Green Building Council worked with the American Society of Interior Designers to create the REGREEN guidelines for residential remodeling projects (www.regreenprogram.org). This program provides information about building strategies and products.

Energy efficiency pros use a whole-house systems approach to assess energy efficiency of homes based on air leaks, insulation quality, cooling and heating systems, and lighting and appliances. Auditors use the data in steps to make a home more efficient. For more: www.energystar.gov/index.cfm?c=home_improvement.hm_improvement_hpwes.

Rating

The industry is mature with room for continued growth and expansion.

Future trends (and caveats)

Key players clearly spell out plans and goals on their Web sites. If you want to explore where this industry is heading, see these documents:

- ✔ AIA 2030 Commitment: www.aia.org/about/initiatives/AIAB079458
- ✔ U.S. Green Building Counsel Strategic Plan through 2013: www.usgbc.org/DisplayPage.aspx?CMSPageID=1877&
- ✔ American Institute of Architects: www.aia.org/about/initiatives/AIAB079544

The U.S. Department of Energy's (DOE) Energy Efficiency and Renewable Energy department has put forth the Net-Zero Energy Commercial Building Initiative to encourage development of commercial buildings that "generate as much energy as they consume through efficiency technologies and on-site power generation": www1.eere.energy.gov/buildings/commercial_initiative.

Watch for intriguing new building materials with unusual qualities. Although these ideas are still in an R&D phase, many look promising: a polymer coating that repels oil and can be cleaned with water, dark roofing materials that don't generate heat, highly insulated windows and glass, soundproof windows, and drywall requiring 80 percent less energy to produce.

Sample job functions

- ✔ **Architecture:** Architect, project architect, laboratory planner, architectural services manager, senior project manager, senior design leader, architectural draftsperson, design architect, director of design, senior design architect/project manager, lead architect, project designer, resource architect, university architect, healthcare planner, staff architect, transit architect

- ✔ **Building:** LEED project manager, home performance retrofitter, senior home performance specialist, director of retrofitting operations, project manager, contractor, construction manager

- ✔ **Energy efficiency:** Residential energy auditor, energy efficiency project manager, home energy consultants

- ✔ **Designer:** Interior designer, senior interior design, furniture designer, assistant project manager, interior designer for hospitality projects, store designer, healthcare facilities design/planning consultant, design representative, junior designer, interior design manufacturer's representative, design/production assistant, interiors architecture project manager, interior design assistant, design consultant

- ✔ **Landscaping:** Landscape architect, senior landscape architect, landscape designer, grounds manager, facilities superintendent, landscaper, gardener, caretaker, landscaping supervisor, landscaping estimator, irrigation technician, coordinator of landscape and urban design

Industry associations

- ✔ American Institute of Architects, Committee of the Environment: www. aia.org/practicing/groups/kc/AIAS074686

- ✔ American Society of Landscape Architects: www.asla.org

- ✔ American Society of Interior Designers: www.asid.org

Continue your exploration

- ✔ U.S. Green Building Council: www.usgbc.org

✔ Sustainable Buildings Industry Council: www.sbicouncil.org

✔ Building Green: www.buildinggreen.com

✔ Greener Buildings: www.greenerbuildings.com

✔ National Association of Home Builders' National Green Building Program: www.nahbgreen.org

Green computing, green IT

Computers are energy hogs. And it takes nearly the same energy to power data centers and computers as it does to keep the systems cool. In 2007 the EPA noted that by 2011 data centers were likely to use twice as much power as they did in 2006. That energy amounts to 1.5 percent of total U.S. power usage, or $4.5 billion! The good news is that it's possible to cut power needs and cut costs dramatically, at the same time. The bad news is that only 25 percent of data center operators have a plan to reduce energy usage. Many organizations expect to build more facilities that will eat up even more energy. As energy costs go up and power capacity becomes limited, companies are likely to shift their thinking, if not for the environment, then for their own survival.

Green computing, also called *green IT*, is making strides in the following areas:

✔ **Energy efficiency and power utilization:** From data centers and virtualization to PCs, printers, and networks, equipment is being developed to use less power more efficiently.

✔ **Materials and product design:** Computer equipment itself is being redesigned with a closer eye toward energy-efficient operations and the materials being used in production.

✔ **Supply chain:** Innovative companies go back to the source to verify that all materials meet their environmental standards and are extracted and processed with integrity.

✔ **Procurement:** Companies that purchase large quantities of computer equipment have a huge opportunity to become more sustainable. The EPA's Energy Star program (www.energystar.gov) ensures that computer equipment meets government standards for energy efficiency. In 2009 these standards were extended to include servers, networks, routers, and other hardware. The Green Electronics Council recently extended its U.S.-based Electronic Product Environmental Assessment Tool (EPEAT) to computer equipment in 40 countries. Now buyers can factor environmental impact into their decisions.

✔ **Disposal:** Each piece of computer equipment contains hazardous chemicals and materials that cannot be tossed in a landfill. Standards are emerging to ensure proper disposal. Some companies dismantle equipment and reuse materials. The cost of the disposal process must be factored into the equation when purchasing electronic equipment.

Green IT 2.0 is right around the corner. The quest for higher energy efficiency, lower carbon emissions, and lower costs will become an integrated part of the IT mission (see www.greenercomputing.com/blog/2009/09/08/get-ready-green-it-20). For other trends likely to impact IT, read the "Smart Grid" section in this chapter. For more information about green computing, visit Greener Computing: www.greenercomputing.com.

Manufacturing

The manufacturing sector converts raw materials into finished goods, which may then be used in downstream products ultimately sold to the consumer. According to the U.S. Department of Commerce, "Sustainable manufacturing is defined as the creation of manufactured products that use processes that are non-polluting, conserve energy and natural resources, and are economically sound and safe for employees, communities, and consumers." The goods may have green uses, such as solar panels or green building supplies, or they may be traditional goods produced sustainably, such as toothpaste and carpet tiles.

Green manufacturing follows a *cradle to cradle* model, where materials from outdated models becomes an input to the production process. Manufacturers must review all the following components of the process:

- ✔ Extracting and processing raw materials for the manufacturing process
- ✔ Manufacturing and producing the products
- ✔ Moving materials and finished products to their intended locations
- ✔ Using the products
- ✔ Maintaining and repairing the products
- ✔ Reusing and recycling when parts become broken or obsolete

Obviously, this transformation doesn't happen overnight. Materials, products, manufacturing systems, factories, and distribution must all be redesigned. Some products may be redesigned to allow the final product to biodegrade more easily. Other products may be disassembled and the parts reused in manufacturing. Sustainable design applies a triple bottom line philosophy (profit, social responsibility, and environmental impact).

Industry's current status

Sustainable manufacturing is currently the key issue for the manufacturing sector. According to an Eye for Transport report, 95 percent of executives surveyed indicated that the trend toward green manufacturing will continue. Furthermore, 71 percent noted that costs to green their process were decreasing, and 43 percent were experiencing higher product quality and manufacturing efficiencies by moving to a green manufacturing process. But a survey conducted by the Society of Manufacturing Engineers found that only 16 percent of 1,046 manufacturing professionals understood what *environmental footprint* meant. Clearly, there's a ways to go before the entire manufacturing sector is completely onboard with this growing trend.

The U.S. isn't the only one either. China is taking the lead in sectors such as the electric car and solar, fueled by the country's enormous energy needs.

Rating

Although the manufacturing sector is mature (and some might say fading into the sunset), green, sustainable manufacturing is emerging.

Future trends (and caveats)

When manufacturers must account for the carbon footprint of the entire manufacturing process, the sector will need to shift its practices dramatically to remain financially viable. Companies that make efforts to green their manufacturing process voluntarily will be ahead of the curve. A major educational initiative must be implemented so that workers at all level understand what's at stake and what they can do to be more sustainable in their own actions to conserve energy and eliminate waste for the company.

One trend to keep an eye on is the role nanotechnology (very tiny manufacturing) will play. Creating non-toxic materials without hazardous substances is commendable. Who doesn't want to see fewer chemicals used in the manufacturing process? The trouble is, no one is quite sure yet what, if any, are the side effects of nanotechnology. Several organizations are studying the issue, including the Environmental Protection Agency and the University of Alabama's Center for Green Manufacturing.

Sample job functions

- ✔ **Management:** Vice president of manufacturing, division manager, general manager, plant manager, assistant plant manager

- ✔ **Design:** Researcher, industrial designer, engineering, manufacturing engineer

- ✔ **Project and production:** Project manager, project engineer, product manager, product development engineering manager, production manager, production supervisor, manufacturing technician, production technician, machine operator, production worker, production planner/scheduler, expediter, safety manager, safety coordinator, manufacturing production engineer, production engineering manager, quality control manager, quality assurance manager

- ✔ **Distribution:** Distribution manager, shipping and receiving manager, shipping and receiving supervisor, shipping and receiving clerk, green logistics specialist, packaging engineer

- ✔ **Materials:** Materials manager, materials handler, materials planner, purchasing manager, purchasing agent, buyer

> ✔ **Facilities:** Facilities manager, maintenance superintendent, maintenance supervisor, maintenance technician, machinist

Industry associations

> ✔ International Society for Industrial Ecology: www.is4ie.org
>
> ✔ Society of Manufacturing Engineers (SME): www.sme.org
>
> ✔ National Council for Advanced Manufacturing: www.nacfam.org

Continue your exploration

> ✔ *Managing Automation*: www.managingautomation.com/maonline/channel/GreenManufacturing
>
> ✔ Green Manufacturing blog: http://green-manufacturing.blogspot.com

Printing and publishing

Books, magazines, newspapers, marketing pieces, and packaging have a significant impact on landfills and our natural resources. The world would stop functioning without paper, and the printing and publishing industries are well aware of the issues at hand. Choices are being made at each step of the publishing process to reduce the industry's impact on the environment:

✔ **Design of project:** Some graphic, product, and packaging designers are making choices at the earliest stages of their projects to minimize environmental impact. Products and packaging are being designed to reduce production, waste, resources, toxics, and transportation: http://sustainability.aiga.org/sus_questions. Even fonts make a difference: Ecofont uses 20 percent less ink than conventional fonts: www.greentaxi.com/green-font/.

✔ **Supply chain:** Paper source is a critical part of greening the industry. Is the supply from sustainable forests, how is the land impacted, how is the health of the people in surrounding areas affected, how is the local economy influenced? Take a look at: www.greenpressinitiative.org/documents/socialimpacts factsheet.pdf. A variety of sustainable paper products are available: http://sustainability.aiga.org/sus_paper. See Chapter 8 for additional insights on paper sources.

✔ **Production:** The printing process must be changed as well. Using low-volatile organic compounds and eliminating bleach from the process can lower the environmental impact of the production process: www.greenpressinitiative.org/solutions/productionimpacts.htm.

(continued)

(continued)

✔ **Distribution:** Moving printed products to their final destination is part of the carbon footprint. See the section "Supply/ Distribution Logistics" for more on this.

The use of recycled paper has increased over the last few years (you're holding one example in your hands right now) — in fact, North American recycled paper manufacturers struggle to meet the demand. The Environmental Paper Network is strengthening paper recovery standards to ensure that paper sent to recycling is of high enough quality to allow the paper fibers to be used in manufacturing recycled paper. See www.environmentalpaper. org/repaperproject for more.

The Book Industry Environmental Council (BIEC) (www.bookcouncil.org) is addressing the environmental impact of the book publishing industry. In addition to creating a target for reducing greenhouse gas emissions, the group will also track the industry's environmental impact and certify book publishers that are reducing their impact on the environment. For more information about green printing and publishing, visit:

✔ Green Press Initiative: www.green pressinitiative.org

✔ Design Can Change: www.designcan change.org/#home

✔ AIGA Center for Sustainable Design: http://sustainability.aiga. org/sus_resources

Smart Grid

Electricity is such an integral part of our lives that we don't think about it much — until there's an outage. Then we realize just how much we depend on it. Although an outage is inconvenient to residents, it can be catastrophic for commercial and industrial entities who, according to the Electrical Power Research Institute (EPRI), lose $50 billion per year due to electric outages.

Given that our electric system was designed to generate, transmit, and distribute power from fossil fuels, we must make some significant changes to it to incorporate the renewable energy sources that will power our future. Thanks to decades of technological advancements, we're in a position to transform every part of the delivery system, while adding technology to help users manage power consumption. According to the U.S. Department of Energy (DOE), the resulting infrastructure is predicted "to provide improved reliability, security, efficiency, and ultimately lower cost to the user."

The term *smart grid* refers to an entire sector of our economy that will touch all of us in multiple ways. Before diving into the details, here's an overview of the components of the electricity supply chain:

✔ **Power generation:** At the front end are a variety of methods for generating power. See Chapter 9 for detailed descriptions of these topics.

- **Power transmission:** This portion of the supply chain moves high voltage electricity from one region to another.

- **Power distribution:** Distributing electricity from the substations to commercial, industrial, and residential users is the focus here.

- **Energy storage:** It's important to have the capability to store energy and use it when you need it. Utilities have always used a variety of storage systems such as compressed air, fly wheels, and banks of batteries for this reason. Residential and commercial users are beginning to see the need to store energy as well. The energy storage industry is developing various technologies to provide a wide range of storage equipment.

- **User consumption management:** To use energy efficiently, residential, commercial, and industrial customers must be able to manage their own consumption. Software systems help manage energy usage in real time.

Several entities play critical roles in delivering electricity to power our world.

- **Utilities:** Each region receives its power from the local utility. You likely write yours a check each month for electricity and gas.

- **Manufacturers:** Companies manufacture an array of equipment and software products for every phase of the electricity supply chain.

- **Making markets:** Financial experts are creating new markets and models to sell energy because the old markets don't work with the variety of energy sources that are being added to the electricity grid.

- **Services:** A variety of service providers will evolve as the smart grid transformation takes hold. It's likely that consultants, systems integration specialists, and other professionals will play key roles.

Industry's current status

Industry experts have known for some time that the electrical infrastructure in the U.S. was due for a major overhaul. The sheer costs, number of players, and inherent complexity of an end-to-end revision make this difficult.

The Energy Independence and Security Act of 2007 referenced the smart grid. This bill and the $4.5 billion in funding from the American Recovery and Reinvestment Act have motivated key players to help rethink the electric grid. Major IT companies, including Google, Microsoft, and Cisco, are creating products and services to address smart grid issues.

Several collaborative organizations have been formed to grapple with the myriad of issues associated with updating and reconfiguring our electric grid. Here are two you want to pay attention to:

- ✔ Federal Smart Grid Task Force convened to coordinate smart grid actions by various departments of the federal government.

- ✔ GridWise Alliance is a forum for smart grid stakeholders, from innovative companies contributing new technology to those creating policy, from local utilities to the federal government.

When the American Recovery and Reinvestment Act funds were originally announced, the DOE capped the amount of funds that could go to various smart grid projects at a level that was too low for companies to begin the project. Then the grant caps were raised to $200 million for smart grid projects and up to $100 million for demonstration projects such as regional grid projects, utility-scale storage, and grid monitoring.

Stimulus money to the tune of $10 million has also gone to the National Institute of Standards and Technology (www.nist.gov/smartgrid) to fund development of interoperability and cybersecurity standards. Vint Cerf, father of the Internet, sees the smart grid as the equivalent of an energy Internet. He believes, as do many, that the smart grid must be built with sophisticated standards that allow for transparency and security at all levels: http://earth2tech.com/2009/08/24/smart-grid-standards-road-map-coming-soon-vint-cerf-weighs-in/. This road map of standards is critical to the transition to the smart grid. Latest standards were released in September 2009. These standards, that frankly look Greek to me, and perhaps to you, allow various parts of the smart grid to communicate without any glitches and urge competing vendors to create interoperable hardware and software.

Key findings from the DOE report indicate several critical advances are gaining ground with great potential for growth, including smart meters (electric meters that allow for two-way transfer of pricing information, usage data, and electricity), distribution substation automation (remote monitoring and management), appliances that can automatically communicate with the grid to indicate energy needs and obtain energy pricing information, and distributed energy generation that is then stored for later use.

Rating

This is an emerging industry that has the potential to change our relationship with electricity from the ground up.

Future trends (and caveats)

The smart grid's potential to change our world could be larger than the impact of both the Internet and the telecommunications revolutions. According to the DOE, for the smart grid to reach its full potential, a social/cultural shift will be required. As real-time measurement of energy usage and automation are embedded in our world, we will develop a new relationship with electricity. If you think programming your VCR was hard, imagine having to set up all your appliances to communicate with the grid? Luckily, home energy management systems will give us one access point to manage all the things that go beep.

The telecommunication industry sees an opening here as well. For various parts of the smart grid to communicate with one another, an embedded communications system must be in place. Companies that power our cellphone communications are searching for ways to service the smart grid.

Complex analytical modeling software is needed to assist utilities and energy traders in projecting shifts in supply and demand of electricity. For example, networking operating centers will need to adjust electricity sources more frequently and manage energy coming from multiple sources, including intermittent renewable energy sources like wind and solar and decentralized energy from residential generation. New challenges require new technology.

Look for more energy storage options, and moving the storage site to more decentralized locations such as substations, residences, and remote sites. Cars may also become a vehicle of choice for energy storage.

Regulations that have the possibility of shaping both the pace and direction of smart grid technologies focused on distributed generation and storage include

- **Feed-in tariffs:** With this regulation, utilities must buy back excess energy generated by distributed generation sources. Utilities will have to accommodate a bidirectional flow of electricity.

- **Renewable portfolio standard:** Currently, the percentage of electricity required to come from renewable sources varies by state. Creating a national renewable portfolio standard would stimulate renewable energy industries throughout the country.

Workforce forecasts for the utility industry project that a large percentage of their experienced employees will retire in the next few years. This translates to ample job opportunities if you prepare and train for this kind of work.

Sample job functions

- ✔ **Systems:** Smart grid standards leader, smart grid chief technology officer, smart grid partner director, smart grid solutions architect, smart grid director, smart grid electrical engineer, smart grid engineer, transmission systems engineer, project manager, smart grid solutions architect/engagement manager, transmission systems engineer, test engineer, renewable systems engineer, systems project manager, distribution systems engineer, smart grid systems project manager, critical infrastructure consultant

- ✔ **Standards:** Smart grid standards leader, smart grid systems interoperability validation manager, grid security director

- ✔ **Software:** Smart grid software engineer, smart grid manager infrastructure development, software infrastructure subsystem leader, lead software engineer, software infrastructure quality assurance leader, software infrastructure test engineer, senior software systems engineer, advanced metering engineer

- ✔ **Marketing and sales:** Smart grid marketing, smart grid sales, director business development, strategic commercial manager

Industry associations

- ✔ GridWise Alliance: www.gridwise.org

- ✔ National Association of Electrical and Medical Imaging Equipment Manufacturers: www.nema.org/gov/energy/smartgrid

Continue your exploration

- ✔ U.S. DOE: www.oe.energy.gov/smartgrid.htm

- ✔ National Electrical Manufacturers Association: www.nema.org/gov/energy/smartgrid/upload/smartGrid_BuildingOnTheGrid_4web.pdf

Supply/Distribution Logistics

Look around you. See anything that's been manufactured or processed? If so, you are the recipient of the work of supply chain logistics specialists. Someone had to direct all the raw materials to the processing location, move partially finished inventory around the plant, distribute the product to the point of sale and then point of use. That's a lot of moving and shuffling.

Logistics specialists work with a broad range of channel partners. To work in this field you may be an in-house employee for the manufacturer, supplier, transportation intermediary, or third-party logistics company. Or you might work for a consultancy. You may interact with people around the world or across town to procure supplies and distribute final products.

In the past, logistics specialists focused on decreasing costs while bringing supplies and products to their location with just-in-time delivery. Now, many create sustainable supply chain management that achieves the same results, while minimizing the environmental impact of the process and being profitable. With so many moving parts in this process, there are numerous ways to minimize waste, cut energy use, decrease transportation costs, manage warehouses more effectively, and cut greenhouse gas emissions.

Industry's current status

Although the term *supply chain* is still used to describe this field, the better way to conceptualize it is to think of a vast network of suppliers spread throughout the world. To manage this multi-faceted system with numerous players efficiently, sophisticated software that allows all the players to understand the supply and demand needs and status is critical. E2Open is a key player in this arena: www.e2open.com.

Three reports describe how the supply chain industry is responding to the push toward sustainable management.

- ✔ The Carbon Efficient Supply Chain Report describes the current state of the industry and highlights future trends in the areas of measuring greenhouse gas emissions, making strategic decisions to lower emissions, and reporting results to consumers and partners. Unfortunately, you must purchase the report to read it (http://cscmp.org/resources/ioma.asp).

- ✔ Acceleration of ECO-Operation: A Milestone Study on Achieving Supply Chain Success and Sustainability (www.eco-opscenter.com/report.php) offers a comprehensive study of how companies are meeting sustainability goals. The downloadable report provides interesting statistics that indicate the sustainability message is getting out there, but the follow-through isn't quite meeting the mark.

A trend that is gaining more attention as the focus turns to environmental impact is *reverse logistics*, which refers to all post-sale logistics, from the support call center and field service to refurbishing, recycling, and reusing materials in a product at the end of its life cycle. According to the Reverse Logistics Association, this concept is also referred to as *aftermarket logistics*, *retrogistics*, and *aftermarket supply chain*.

Rating

This is an established industry that has begun the greening process.

Future trends (and caveats)

Several key elements must be in place to assist companies, and specifically supply chain managers, in putting sustainability goals into action:

- ✔ Cooperation among the myriad of supply chain managers, vendors, and intermediaries must be a central feature of a truly sustainable supply chain operation. By sharing demand and supply data more openly and collaborating to create best practices, the industry moves closer to becoming more efficient and more sustainable.

- ✔ Accurate, verifiable, transparent data about the environmental impact of all parts of the supply chain regarding one's own company's actions as well as those of vendors, suppliers, and customers are essential in this industry. If supply chain managers can't obtain data to determine which product or transportation method is more environmentally sound, they can't make decisions with any reliability.

A couple of verification systems are in the works. Walmart is gathering life cycle sustainability information from all its suppliers on every product it sells. Its goal in working with the Sustainability Consortium on this project includes encouraging buyers and suppliers to be more innovative and accountable about their products' sustainability, to help Walmart select the most environmentally preferred products and to enable it to track its own performance in regard to its supply chain. For more on this project, read www.greenbiz.com/blog/2009/07/14/inside-wal-marts-sustainability-index and review the consortium's Web site: www.sustainabilityconsortium.org.

A number of debates are in progress as to the most effective way to reduce the costs and emissions of transporting goods. Here are a couple ideas :

- ✔ **Reworking packaging:** Although reducing bulky packaging is important, it's not the only issue at play here. Supply chain managers are discovering the benefits of creating packages with dimensions that allow more products to fit onto a pallet or on a truck. More products per run means more cost-effective transit, fewer deliveries, less room required to store the supply, and less time to load. Redesigning the traditional milk carton resulted in savings all the way around: www.scdigest.com/assets/newsViews/08-07-16-1.php?cid=1801.

✔ **Pallet transitioning:** Transitioning from wooden pallets to plastic pallets could remove the insect pests criss-crossing the country in wood, and may eliminate the need for wooden pallets — which account for 40 percent of the hardwood harvest in the U.S. (and many pallets are being used exactly once!). Wood pallet waste amounts to 20 percent of the waste wood in landfill. Plastic pallets last 15 years, can be ground up and reused at the end of their life cycle, and are lighter than wood, but manufacturing them creates emissions. The jury is still out on which is better: `www.scdigest.com/assets/On_Target/09-09-10-1.php?cid=2728`.

One thing is clear, logistics specialists and packaging engineers can have quite an impact on the emissions and costs associated with supply chain activities. By working this problem from both perspectives, innovations are likely to continue well into the future.

Sample job functions

✔ **Sales:** Demand analyst, procurement pricing analyst, advanced sourcing director, commodity analyst, logistics sales, contracts and compliance manager

✔ **Supply chain:** Network planner, supply chain and logistics consultant, supply chain process lead, supply chain consultant, supply chain manager, vice-president of supply chain management, logistics manager, logistics engineers, logistics analysts

✔ **Operations:** Staff engineer for warehouse and logistics, operations development leader, operations professional, sales and operations planning analyst, operations manager, operations support manager, distribution center facilities manager

✔ **Global and export:** Export compliance specialist, trade compliance auditor, customs compliance manager, international trade compliance specialist, manager of export compliance, global logistics, global commodity manager

✔ **Transportation:** Freight broker, global transportation manager, distribution specialist, route engineer. (See next industry profile for more transportation titles.)

Industry associations

✔ Council of Supply Chain Management Professionals: `www.cscmp.org`

✔ Material Handling Industry of America (MHIA): `www.MHIA.org`

✔ Reverse Logistics Association: `www.rltinc.com`

Continue your exploration

- ✔ Supply Chain Digest: www.scdigest.com
- ✔ Global Supply Chain Management Solutions: www.thirdparty logistics.blogspot.com
- ✔ Supply Chain Brain: www.supplychainbrain.com

Transportation

The transportation sector has a huge impact on our lives and on the nation's carbon footprint. According to the U.S. Department of Transportation (DOT), transportation accounted for 28 percent of the nation's greenhouse gas emissions in 2006. The vast majority of the emissions are due to the carbon-based fuels used to power various forms of transportation. For more, see www.climate.dot.gov/about/transportations-role/overview.html.

The modes of transporting freight and human passengers are varied:

- ✔ Freight, packages, materials, and fuels are transported via a network of airplanes, heavy trucks, ships, trains, and pipelines.
- ✔ Specialty vehicles are used for specific purposes, such as farm equipment to work the land and tend to animals, and construction vehicles to build structures and the overall infrastructure.
- ✔ Public transportation systems such as subways, buses, trolleys, trains, and light rail are used in populated areas to move large numbers of people around as efficiently as possible.
- ✔ Individuals and families get around by way of automobiles and light trucks, recreational vehicles both on road and off road, and bicycles.

For each element of the transportation system, people are needed to design, manufacture, operate, and service vehicles. But it doesn't stop there, the systems upon which these vehicles run, such as highways, rail systems, subways, ports, and pipelines must also be designed, constructed, operated, and maintained.

Industry's current status

Several governmental departments are actively working to reduce the greenhouse gases emitted from vehicles of all kinds:

✔ The EPA's Office of Transportation and Air Quality (OTAQ) regulates air pollution from vehicles, engines, and fuels. See `www.epa.gov/OMS` for more information about this program.

✔ The EPA's SmartWay Transport Partnership is a collaboration with the freight industry to create incentives to encourage freight companies to clean up their act by increasing energy efficiency and reducing greenhouse gas emissions. For a full description, go to `www.epa.gov/smartway/transport`. Through the American Recovery and Reinvestment Act of 2009, the EPA provided grants and funding on several clean diesel programs at the national and state levels. For the details, see `www.epa.gov/otaq/diesel/projects.htm`.

✔ The DOE dedicated $300 million of the stimulus funds to 25 different Clean Cities projects intended to speed up the country's transition to alternative fuel vehicles: `www1.eere.energy.gov/cleancities/projects.html`.

✔ The DOE also invested $2.4 billion into developing electric vehicle technology, including battery technology, battery recycling systems, electric drive systems, test vehicles, and charging stations.

For additional government projects related to transportation, refer to this list of links: `www.epa.gov/otaq/climate/relatedlinks.htm`.

Freight companies are also moving beyond business-as-usual by updating their equipment in ways that improve fuel efficiency, reducing the length of time trucks idle, and rethinking distribution routes with the help of geographic information system GIS software than allows companies to create queries to evaluate different routes.

A new segment of the transportation sector is emerging to provide alternative vehicles for personal travel. These vehicles range from scooters and Segways to motorized bicycles and low-speed vehicles like electric golf carts.

Rating

Transportation is a mature industry that is having to rethink and redesign to become sustainable/green.

Future trends (and caveats)

The move toward alternative fuel automobiles is not stymied for lack of trying. Vehicles can be built to run on a number of fuel sources, including hydrogen, propane, natural gas, compressed natural gas (CNG), liquefied petroleum gas

(LPG, also called autogas) biodiesel, ethanol, and others. In addition, vehicles can be powered by fuel cells, such as battery-powered electric vehicles (BEVs), hybrid electrics, plug-in hybrids — even hybrid trucks: www.electricdrive.org/index.php?ht=display/ReleaseDetails/i/13954. For all this innovation, there are no set standards yet. It's possible that several technologies will evolve for different purposes.

In May 2009 the EPA proposed a plan to increase the use of renewable energy as required by the Energy Independence and Security Act of 2007. The plan calls for developing four kinds of renewable fuels, including cellulosic biofuels, biomass-based diesel, advanced bio fuels, and total renewable fuel. These fuels would be phased in through 2022 with different production goals for each fuel type.

An important piece of creating viable alternative vehicles is solving the battery challenge. Lithium-ion batteries have been used to power electric cars, but they're very costly. The quest for viable solutions is likely to birth a brand-new market segment over the next couple of decades, but there's no way to know now which technologies will win the race.

Air travel is also likely to become more environmentally sound as new fuels are developed. Several initiatives and incentives are planned to support this effort, including the Commercial Aviation Alternative Fuels Initiative (CAAFI — www.caafi.org) and government incentives (http://trade.gov/mas/manufacturing/OAAI/aero_links_altfuels.asp).

Ports are another likely place for clean innovations. Traditionally, ports are very dirty places that use a tremendous amount of energy. A few test projects suggest that innovation can turn these numbers around. Putting a cap over a ship's smokestack can control emissions for the short term until a more permanent solution can be invented and installed. A crane by Vycon Energy works like the brakes on a Prius, whereby the crane's actions allows it to store the energy and use it again. For details on these ideas and others read www.greentechmedia.com/articles/read/the-next-green-wave-ports.

Sample job functions

- ✔ **Vehicle design and engineering:** automotive engineer, mechanical engineer, aerospace engineer, aircraft engineer, industrial engineer, aircraft surveillance systems engineer
- ✔ **Battery development:** Battery technology manager, product manager electrical energy storage systems, director of electrical and electronics engineering, lithium battery development engineer, senior mechanical engineer advanced battery technology, charger/battery systems engineer

  ✔ **Transportation engineering:** Safety engineer, project geotechnical engineer, transportation engineer, civil engineer, construction engineer

  ✔ **Logistics and operations:** Freight agent, freight broker agent, freight planner, senior freight planner, planning analyst, transit planning analyst, transit office manager, air traffic controllers, transportation specialist, aviation safety inspector, information technology specialist, rail inspector, motor carrier safety specialist, highway safety specialist

For more job functions, see the section in this chapter on Supply/Distribution Logistics and the Planning profile in Chapter 11.

Industry associations

  ✔ Electric Drive Transportation Association: www.electricdrive.org

  ✔ National Transportation Operations Coalition: www.ntoctalks.com

Continue your exploration

  ✔ Transportation Research Board: www.trb.org

  ✔ EPA's Office of Transportation and Air Quality (OTAQ): www.epa.gov/OMS

  ✔ U.S. DOE's Clean Cities: www1.eere.energy.gov/cleancities

  ✔ Green Air Online, Independent Reporting on aviation and the environment: greenaironline.com

  ✔ DOT's Transportation and Climate Change Clearinghouse: www.climate.dot.gov

  ✔ Energy Information Administration: www.eia.doe.gov

  ✔ Transportation for America: www.t4america.org

Chapter 11

Working to Shape the Green Economy

*E*ven if you don't know how to manufacture or install a solar array, design a green building, or manage natural resources, you can still play a role in the green economy. In fact, the role you play may be critical in defining its future form.

Whether you are drawn to working in the financial industry, the legal field, planning profession, or enforcement, you have the potential to strengthen the green economy. By contributing your knowledge, passion, and commitment, you can help companies, communities, governmental agencies, and financial institutions take steps to act more sustainably.

Law

Over the last few decades the United States has enacted a number of key pieces of legislation to protect the environment from negative human and industrial impacts. As this body of law has developed, it's become layered and nuanced. Those in this field combine their knowledge of the law and scientific concepts of conservation, sustainability, and ecology to enforce and enhance these laws.

Attorneys practicing in this specialty may work in environmental agencies, interest groups, private and public corporations, nonprofit organizations, law firms, and governmental agencies at the local, state, federal, and international levels. What they do during their work day is not substantially different from what other attorneys do.

Depending on their setting they may

- ✔ Develop, analyze, and draft laws, regulations, briefs, contracts, and legal pleadings
- ✔ Settle disputes through negotiation, mediations, and litigation
- ✔ Conduct research into case law, interview, and take depositions
- ✔ Prepare licenses, permits, applications, and patents
- ✔ Monitor compliance with regulations

A section of the American Bar Association is devoted to lawyers who practice in this area. They divide the specialization into three main topics:

- ✔ **Environmental law** addresses a wide range of environmental topics, from air quality and waste management to climate change and endangered species.
- ✔ **Energy law** grapples with an array of energy sources, from traditional oil and gas and hydropower to renewable energy, carbon, and restructuring the electric grid.
- ✔ **Natural resources law** focuses on issues associated with the Earth's resources, such as water, forests, marine areas, and public lands.

Because the energy and natural resources areas overlap, they are often combined in discussions of the field. For a more detailed outline of these disciplines, visit www.abanet.org/environ/committees.

Industry's current status

A number of the laws that have governed the environment — including the Endangered Species Act, Clean Air Act, Clean Water Act, and Superfund — were enacted in the 1970s and 1980s. Now, with the ObamaAdministration in place, more legislation that impacts the environment and the energy industry is likely to be enacted at the federal, state, and local levels.

As businesses, developers, local agencies, venture capitalists, and other entities face these new laws, they are going to need guidance to understand what's expected of them and to work through any legal issues that arise. Legal experts expect growth in the field throughout the country, in private practice, nonprofit agencies, businesses, and government agencies.

Rating

All three areas of law that touch on environmental/energy issues are growing. This trend is not likely to slow down any time soon.

Future trends (and caveats)

The growing interest in new energy sources is expanding the field of **energy law**. Originally this specialization worked on issues within the oil and gas industry, but now new opportunities are opening up as the energy industry explodes. The issues that someone in this specialty might address include new energy generation, transmission, and storage technologies and new logistics regarding where and how energy is generated, delivered, and sold.

Developments in the green economy will lead to new specialties in the legal field.

- ✔ **Carbon trading** is a topic that sits on the horizon as we await new legislation to define how this system will work. As more details are known, attorneys will undoubtedly discover that their services are in demand.

- ✔ **Modernizing the electric grid and transmission system** is bound to raise issues about property rights, partnerships, security, and other issues we have yet to define.

- ✔ **Cleantech law** is another specialty that is poised to grow. At one level, this specialty focuses on traditional legal activities associated with patent law, intellectual property, and licensing. The cutting edge aspect of this specialty is the challenge of guiding cleantech inventions from concept to commercial venture. Given that the cleantech segment is emerging in a number of different directions, everything about this legal specialization is likely to be evolving for some time. (For more details about cleantech, see Chapter 10.)

Sample job functions

- ✔ **Attorney:** Litigation attorney, county counsel, in-house attorney, corporate attorney, environmental attorney, managing counsel, energy regulatory counsel, senior counsel, energy/infrastructure attorney

- ✔ **Subject matter expert:** Land use law analyst, water rights specialist, environmental protection specialist, legislative analyst, environmental legal consultant, litigation associate, environmental and energy associate

- ✔ **Support:** Paralegal, litigation paralegal, legal secretary, litigation support, administrator, litigation secretary

Industry associations

✔ American Bar Association: www.abanet.org/environ/committees

✔ Energy Bar Association: www.eba-net.org

✔ National Association of Environmental Law Societies: www.naels.org

---

Environmental justice

Although many special interest groups focus on particular segments of the environment, we must also remember that human lives are negatively impacted by practices that harm the environment. In the 1980s those involved in social justice and civil rights joined with environmentalists to raise awareness about the fact that disadvantaged communities are often exposed to more than their fair share of toxins, hazardous waste, and pollution — and suffer with a higher incidence of health problems as a result.

If you've seen *Erin Brockovich,* you've seen a dramatization of a real-life instance of environmental justice. In that movie, the lead character investigates a cluster of health problems in a rural California community. Through her research she discovers that the residents were being exposed to a toxic chemical that had leaked into the groundwater from a nearby electric plant. As the result of her research, a lawsuit is filed, and the company ends up paying a very large sum of money to the residents of the area.

According to the U.S. Environmental Protection Agency (EPA), "Environmental justice is the fair treatment and meaningful involvement of all people regardless of race, color, national origin, or income with respect to the development, implementation, and enforcement of environmental laws, regulations, and policies."

In 1994 President Clinton signed an executive order to form an interagency working group to ensure that environmental justice was incorporated into all environmental programs throughout the country. The working group is led by the EPA and includes 11 government departments and White House offices. For a visual representation of this collaboration take a look at http://cfpub.epa.gov/compliance/newsroom.

A wide variety of environmental justice organizations exist at the international, national, state, regional, and city levels. These organizations may be governmental agencies, nonprofits, or academic departments.

For more on environmental justice, check out the following Web sites:

✔ EPA: www.epa.gov/oecaerth/basics/ejbackground.html

✔ List of environmental justice organizations: http://courses.ma.org/sciences/Gottlieb/EJ/arrrrr/organizations.html

✔ Multicultural Environmental Leadership Development Initiative: http://meldi.snre.umich.edu/directories_databases_and_resources_guides

Continue your exploration

- ✔ EnviroEducation: `www.enviroeducation.com/majors-programs/env-law.html`

- ✔ Environmental Lawyers: `www.environmentallawyers.com`

- ✔ Global Climate Change and U.S. Law: `www.abanet.org/abapubs/globalclimate`

- ✔ HG.org legal directories: `www.hg.org/energy.html`

Planning

After World War II, most urban areas shifted from a tight neighborhood plan to suburban sprawl. Land availability, population growth, and abundant natural resources allowed for unchecked development in many regions. As a result of this planning philosophy, planners have been focused on issues associated with growth such as housing needs, traffic patterns, and parking issues. At the same time, some rural areas and inner city neighborhoods have been shrinking. The economic base these communities depended on may have disappeared or moved away. Planners for these areas focus on revitalization strategies.

No matter what the planning challenge, planners in rural areas, small towns, cities, counties, regions, and federal lands have the complex task of figuring out how to use the land and resources effectively for a number of interrelated purposes:

- ✔ Establishing an economic base for the community

- ✔ Incorporating the needs of the surrounding environment and wildlife

- ✔ Managing natural resources in the region and establishing local utilities

- ✔ Establishing reliable energy sources locally

- ✔ Transporting people, raw materials, finished goods, and waste

- ✔ Housing residents, businesses, and institutions

- ✔ Integrating technology needs into the plan

- ✔ Engaging residents in recreational activities

- ✔ Ensuring that all members of the community thrive

- ✔ Preserving the ambience and enhance the quality of life of the region

Industry's current status

More cities and towns are realizing that constant growth has its limits. With nearly 1,000 mayors signing on to the U.S. Mayors' Climate Protection Agreement (see map at http://usmayors.org/climateprotection/ClimateChange.asp), cities are now focused on how to reduce greenhouse gases in their regions to comply with the Kyoto Protocol.

Planning a sustainable community from scratch is one thing. It takes a lot of coordination, forethought, and investment. Transforming a traditional community into one that is sustainable carries with it even more challenges as various systems of the community must be reworked to be sustainable.

Several planning and design philosophies — Smart Growth, New Urbanism, and transit-oriented development (TOD) — have gained popularity in the U.S. over the last three decades. Although born from different traditions, each of these philosophies gives planners new tools and strategies to move away from the idea of suburban sprawl that requires a significant amount of automobile travel. Now planners are looking toward empty or underused sites within city limits to create compact mixed-use developments that encourage walking and bicycling. According to New Urban News, 500 communities have been built within the New Urbanism philosophy (www.newurbannews.com/aboutnewurbanism.html).

In June 2009 the EPA, the U.S. Department of Housing and Urban Development (HUD), and the U.S. Department of Transportation (DOT) created an Interagency Partnership for Sustainable Communities (www.epa.gov/smartgrowth) to help local communities grown in a sustainable way. The stated goal of this partnership is to "coordinate federal housing, transportation, and other infrastructure investments to protect the environment, promote equitable development, and help to address the challenges of climate change."

The New Urban News reports how money from the American Recovery and Reinvestment Act impacts sustainable transportation options in urban areas (www.newurbannews.com/14.2/mar09fedstimulus.html).

Rating

The industry is mature, with a developing focus on sustainable design.

Future trends (and caveats)

The push toward Smart Growth and New Urbanism that brings neighborhoods together in ways that reduce greenhouse gas emissions will continue.

Another component of Smart Growth is ensuring that communities have sufficient water resources to be sustainable. Designing cities to align with the carrying capacity of the local watershed significantly reduces the amount of energy and money that is required to transport water long distances for drinking water, crops, and industrial uses.

Reworking transportation options is going to play a major role in redesigning neighborhoods and cities. (See Chapter 13 for more information.)

Green building is going to play a big role in redesigning urban spaces. The Congress for the New Urbanism (CNU) has partnered with the U.S. Green Building Council (USGBC) and the Natural Resource Defense Council (NRDC) to create a set of standards for green neighborhoods called LEED for Neighborhood Development (LEED-ND). For more information about this rating system, check out `www.cnu.org/node/124`.

As more renewable energy sources are sited locally, each community will need to adjust its long-term land use plan to accommodate new technologies, transmission systems, and distribution hubs. Open space areas are likely to be targeted by utilities and developers for such projects. Finding the right balance for renewable energy sources, wildlife, and community members will require negotiation, knowledge, and finesse.

Sample job functions

- ✔ **Planning:** Regional planner, community development director, city planner, assistant to zoning manager, urban planning project manager, chief planner, associate planner, planning professional, senior planner, planning/sustainability director, urban designer, planning manager, planning technician, land use planner, planning consultant

- ✔ **Environmental planning:** Senior environmental planner, environmental planner, natural resource planner, conservation program director, natural resource manager, environmental impact assessment specialist

- ✔ **Economic development:** Economic developer, economic development manager, development director, economic development specialist

- ✔ **Transportation planning:** Commute smart program manager, high capacity transit project manager, aviation planner, senior airport planner, transportation planner, transportation bureau planning chief, urban transportation planner

- ✔ **Housing:** Urban housing planner, community development specialist, community planner

- ✔ **Specialized planning:** Coastal resources specialist, military planner, green building specialist, GIS specialist, occupancy/space planning manager

Greening of the financial industry

As noted in Chapter 2, money is a key factor shaping the green economy. Venture capital and funds from the American Recovery and Reinvestment Act of 2009 are allowing emerging companies and industries to gain traction as they research, introduce, and sell their green technologies and services. Without this funding, the green economy wouldn't be developing as fast as it is.

Looking at the larger financial industry, however, signs of support for the green economy are still a bit weak. Although research indicates a number of green financial vehicles have been offered since the 1990s, the financial industry as a whole has not jumped on the trend. Although there are stellar examples of companies in each of the following categories, professional associations or industry associations have not formed yet to support green financial institutions.

✔ Banking: Green banks are offering an array of services to help people purchase green cars, make energy efficiency retrofits, add solar, purchase green homes, or use credit cards that donate a percentage of charges to carbon offset projects.

✔ Personal investment: Over the last few decades, socially responsible investment firms have been growing. Now, with the growing emphasis on ventures that are environmentally sound, a new segment of the investment world, *sustainable investing*, is also gaining strength.

✔ Financial analysis: Investment companies are developing means to evaluate and compare companies' performance when it comes to sustainability, environmental, social, and corporate governance (ESG), and social responsibility.

✔ Micro loans: Piggybacking on the socially responsible micro loan trend, groups are beginning to fund green micro financing ventures, such as `www.greenmicro finance.org`, to help low-income communities around the world gain access to clean, renewable energy.

One sign of a concerted effort to transform the financial industry is the United Nations Environment Programme Finance Initiative (UNEP FI), which is a partnership between the United Nations Environment Programme (UNEP) and the financial sector worldwide. The purpose of this organization is to discover how the financial sector can invest in sustainable solutions that benefit the environment and social causes while creating solid financial results. Their Green Economy Initiative, also called the Green New Deal, was launched in October 2008. Since that time, they've published several reports that are worth reviewing at `www.unepfi.org`.

For more on green finance, check out the following Web sites:

✔ Principles for Responsible Investment: `www.unpri.org`

✔ RiskMetrics Group's Sustainability Solutions: `www.riskmetrics.com/ sustainability`

✔ *Green Money Journal:* `www.greenmoney journal.com`

✔ Sustainable Business: `www.sustainable business.com`

✔ Green Business Banking: `www.green businessbanking.com`

Industry association

American Planning Association: www.planning.org

Continue your exploration

- ✔ American Planning Association Career Development: www.planning.org/onthejob
- ✔ Smart Growth America: www.smartgrowthamerica.org/whatissg.html
- ✔ Congress for the New Urbanism: www.cnu.org/Intro_to_new_urbanism
- ✔ New Urban News: www.newurbannews.com
- ✔ Planetizen: Planning, Design, and Development: www.planetizen.com
- ✔ The Planning Universe: http://plannersweb.com/universe.html
- ✔ Transit-Oriented Development: www.transitorienteddevelopment.org

Politics and Policy

The people we elect and the legislation and policies they enact have a significant impact on the shape of the green economy, the pacing of its development, and the industries that are likely to flourish. The people and organizations that influence voters and those in government are diverse and play a number of roles in the process.

- ✔ **Researching and analyzing issues** provides in-depth information to government officials, industry leaders, environmental specialists, journalists, and others. Accurate knowledge becomes a critical component in campaigns, elections, policymaking, and advocacy.

- ✔ **Influencing** the public, politicians, and members of the government to act on a particular issue, cause, legislation, or agency rule, requires determination and action. Depending on the organization, the purpose, and the target, influencers may use education, activism, advocacy, and lobbying to get their point across.

- ✔ **Campaigning** is a complex process to influence voters to elect a particular candidate or pass an initiative. A variety of tactics are used to inform and persuade the public to exercise their right to vote.

✔ **Policymaking** is the process of developing legislation and regulations that guide appropriate actions. The entire multi-step process is collaborative in that many constituents, from voters to interests groups, have the right to influence what ends up in a particular piece of legislation. To find out more about this process, read `www.waterencyclopedia.com/Oc-Po/Policy-Making-Process.html`.

Industry's current status

To get a sense of the influence of the political arena, take a look at the following statistics gathered from experts in the field. The American Association of Political Consultants (`www.theaapc.org`) reports that more than 50,000 elections occur each year in the United States, not including elections for local and state initiatives. According to Lobbists.info (`http://lobbyists.info`) there are over 22,000 lobbyists and 2,500 lobbying firms in the United States. These lobbyists work with 12,000 client organizations to influence the bills and votes of 535 Congress members.

The day after his inauguration, President Obama announced new lobbying limits in an effort to make government actions more transparent. Several of the restrictions are meant to limit the revolving door that often exists between special interests groups and government officials. In late March 2009 additional limits were placed on lobbyist communications with administration officials regarding the American Recovery and Reinvestment Act funding decisions. For more on these topics see `www.washingtonpost.com/wp-dyn/content/article/2009/01/21/AR2009012103472.html`, `www.alldc.org`, and `www.whitehouse.gov/omb/assets/memoranda_fy2009/m09-24.pdf`.

The Center for Responsive Politics has studied how money influences politics since 1996. In addition to tracking donations to political campaigns, the organization has an in-depth database about lobbyists. A quick look at `www.opensecrets.org/lobbyists` illustrates that spending on lobbying ramped up dramatically between 1998 and 2008. As of this writing, the spending on lobbying and the number of lobbyists in 2009 appeared to be dropping, but to be sure, check the final 2009 numbers. This organization also tracks the work history of members of Congress and lobbyists to highlight any revolving door activity. Use the search function on `www.opensecrets.org/revolving` to pull up detailed employment profiles.

Rating

The process of creating and influencing policies is mature.

Future trends (and caveats)

The move against corruption and toward transparency in government is likely to continue. Many, including the American League of Lobbyists, are calling for reforms in the lobbying process. The key is ethics. What's the most ethical way to influence the legislative process? When new ethical standards are put in place, the next challenge will be enforcing the rules.

At a 2008 conference of the American Association of Political Consultants, political consultants completed a poll about the recent campaign season and campaigning practices in ten years. The poll results show a dramatic shift from direct mail and television advertising to Web-based campaign communications, using e-mails, online videos, social networking, and blogging. Those polled expected to see evidence of this shift as early as the 2010 elections. For a discussion of the results, see www.theaapc.org/press/state-of-political-consulting-poll.

Sample job functions

- **Advocacy:** Grass roots organizers, community organizer, public policy advocates, transportation policy advocate, grass-roots campaign manager, field representative, grass-roots advocacy coordinator, program organizer

- **Research:** Researcher, economist, scientists, environmental scientists, ecological economists, science-policy scholars, legal scholars

- **Public education:** Public affairs program assistant, outreach and communication coordinator, media coordinator, educator

- **Lobbying and legislative affairs:** Environmental affairs specialist, climate legislative director, legislative affairs director, government relations senior specialist, government relations manager, legislative assistant

- **Policy making:** Policy associate, policy analyst, financial analyst, policy adviser, legislative director

Industry associations

- The American League of Lobbyists (ALL): www.alldc.org
- American Association of Political Consultants (AAPC): www.theaapc.org

Continue your exploration

✔ Council on Environmental Quality: `www.whitehouse.gov/administration/eop/ceq`

✔ E.O. Lawrence Berkeley National Laboratory, Environmental Energy Technologies Division: `http://eetd.lbl.gov/einfo-policymakers.html`

✔ Environmental Law Institute: `http://eli.org/index.cfm`

✔ Nonprofit Advocacy: `www.npaction.org`

✔ Association for Politics and the Life Sciences: `www.aplsnet.org`

Regulation, Compliance, and Enforcement

After a legislative bill is signed by the President, the law spells out what's expected in a certain circumstance. Agencies within the executive branch of government or public authority must then develop regulations that help the country reach the goal spelled out in the law. Within the environmental realm, these regulations may cover pollution, water quality, air quality, toxic waste, or other issues.

✔ **Rulemaking:** When agencies develop regulations, they embark on a multi-step process called *rulemaking* to come up with the specific standards that industries and businesses must adhere to. Often during the process they rely on scientific and industry experts to provide the necessary details to make the original law workable. The rulemaking process is structured to ensure transparency. For an outline of the process, see `www.epa.gov/lawsregs/brochure/developing.html`.

✔ **Compliance:** As soon as the regulation is in place, the next step is to take actions to ensure that industries and businesses comply with the law. Several tactics are used to make this process as efficient and as effective as possible.

  • Compliance assistance uses workshops and training materials to educate the companies about the regulations and requirements.

  • Compliance monitoring entails inspections to help companies understand where they are in compliance and where they need to enhance their processes and standards.

  • Compliance incentives and auditing provide companies with the option of self-disclosing the problems they know about. Often the regulatory agency sets up an incentive program to encourage companies to fess up.

✔ **Enforcement:** When violations are discovered during compliance, authorities must act to enforce the law. The appropriate action depends on the situation. The follow-up may trigger a civil or criminal enforcement process. In other cases, as in a toxic spill or release, the focus will be on cleaning up the environment first and foremost. Penalties of varying severity are levied as necessary.

Industry's current status

`Regulations.gov` provides online tracking of the entire rulemaking process for all regulations issued by the 300 federal agencies within the U.S. government. In total they issue an amazing 8,000 regulations a year! The EPA is by far the most prolific rulemaking agency. To get a sense of the vast number of topics they address, scan the following Web pages:

✔ By topic: `www.epa.gov/lawsregs/envtopics/index.html`

✔ By industry: `www.epa.gov/lawsregs/bizsector/index.html`

✔ By state: `www.epa.gov/lawsregs/states/index.html`

✔ By law: `www.epa.gov/lawsregs/laws/index.html`

For more on the regulatory process at the EPA, visit `www.epa.gov/lawsregs`.

In 1970 the National Environmental Policy Act (NEPA) started a new era of transparency and collaboration between communities and federal agencies. All federal agencies were required to examine the impact of their proposals on the environment and prepare an Environmental Impact Statement (EIS). To gain a better understanding of this process, see `www.epa.gov/compliance/basics/nepa.html`.

When possible, the EPA looks for nonregulatory ways to achieve the goals of the laws they are required to uphold. The EPA can sometimes negotiate a voluntary partnership, create economic programs to encourage action, or enhance technological solutions through support and training.

Rating

The triad of regulation, compliance, and enforcement is mature.

Future trends (and caveats)

The government will create and enforce regulations for the foreseeable future. Although the EPA isn't the only agency that impacts the environment, it's the most prolific and instrumental when it comes to protecting the environment and hazards to health. Every five years the EPA creates a strategic plan. The plan with a blueprint for the EPA's actions for 2006 through 2011 is available on www.epa.gov/ocfo/plan/plan.htm, and the strategic plan for 2009 through 2014 is expected to be released in late 2009. Take a look at the April 2009 update, www.epa.gov/progress.

In the progress report, the EPA outlines plans to utilize the $7.22 billion dollars it expects through the American Recovery and Reinvestment Act. Most of the funds will go to water infrastructure projects and toxic cleanup projects. At the time of this writing, most states have received between 0 and 10 percent of the funds they have been promised by the EPA. Check out this map, http://134.67.99.241/stimulus/EPA_RecoveryApp.html, the coolest depiction of stimulus money by state that I've seen yet.

Sample job functions

- ✔ **Rulemaking:** Federal information policy director, program coordinator, consultant, environmental protection specialist

- ✔ **Compliance:** Chief compliance officer (CCO), emissions certification and compliance specialist, compliance engineer, global trade compliance sustainability manager, environmental engineer, quality assurance, environmental compliance program specialist, regulatory compliance analyst, regulatory compliance specialist, regulatory compliance manager, environmental and regulatory advisor, compliance counsel

- ✔ **Enforcement:** Environmental enforcement attorney, code inspection specialist, code enforcement officer, inspector, prosecutor, enforcement specialist, civil investigator, regional counsel, enforcement specialist paralegal

Industry associations

- ✔ American Bar Association: www.abanet.org/environ/committees/environcrimes

- ✔ International Network for Environmental Compliance and Enforcement: http://inece.org/overview/structure.html

Continue your exploration

- ✔ Environmental Business & Legal Reports: http://enviro.blr.com

- ✔ Environmental Protection Agency (EPA): www.epa.gov/lawsregs

Chapter 12

Inspiring and Motivating More Sustainable Actions

In This Chapter

▶ Keeping people informed and in the know about environmental issues

▶ Persuading people to change their ways through marketing and sales

▶ Consulting with businesses and organizations that want to be more sustainable

*F*or the green economy to grow, individuals and companies must change their ways. Generally speaking, people and organizations are more comfortable with the status quo than they are in taking new actions. Therein lies the rub.

Enter those who want to make it their work to motivate and persuade the world to act more sustainable. The process of educating and inspiring people and organizations to see a different, greener future is playing a critical role in the unfolding of the green economy. This work takes a number of different forms, from making sure people know how the environment really works to using marketing channels or the sales process to engage them in new behaviors.

Environmental Education

To move toward a sustainable way of life and business, all of us need to have a solid understanding of environmental issues and biological systems to be able to make sound decisions and take eco-friendly actions in own lives, with political issues, and in our business activities. Environmental educators — working in a variety of settings, from formal educational institutions at all levels to government agencies, corporations, and environmental organizations — strive to develop environmental literacy or eco-literacy in people of all ages.

Environmental educators don't push a particular solution or strategy. Instead, they focus on raising people's awareness of the environment, furthering their understanding of how nature functions, and increasing their ability to think through the issues involved in various environmental issues and the solutions and strategies put forth to resolve them.

The Tbilisi Declaration, created during the first intergovernmental conference on environmental education and convened by the United Nations Education, Scientific, and Cultural Organization (UNESCO) in cooperation with the U.N. Environment Programme (UNEP) in 1978, provides the most commonly referenced definition of environmental education. You can read the definition and a detailed description of common environmental education settings on this Web page: www.caee.org/CEEMP/ceempfundee.html.

Industry's current status

When the National Environmental Education Act (NEEA) passed in 1990, the Environmental Protection Agency (EPA) created the Office of Environmental Education to increase environmental education through training programs, educational materials, grants, and awards. This program to provide environmental educators around the country with accurate, well-designed materials and information to share with their students is alive and thriving within the EPA. To gain more insights about this work, read the short version of the original bill at www.epa.gov/enviroed/whatis.html, visit the EPA Teaching Center at www.epa.gov/teachers, and check out the EPA Environmental Education Resources: www.epa.gov/enviroed/resources.html.

Another facet of the NEEA was the founding of the National Environmental Education Foundation (NEEF), a nonprofit organization that functions independently from the government as a liaison between various levels of government, businesses, education institutions, and environmental organizations. Currently NEEF focuses its efforts on building public-private partnerships with organizations and professions that interact with the public on environmental topics on a daily basis, such as weather forecasters, land managers, and health professionals. By engaging these professions and providing them with well-researched, easy-to-share information, the organization is leveraging these moments when the public is already thinking about the environment. For details about the programs, check out this Web page: www.neefusa.org/programs.

The NEEF conducted an annual survey of environmental knowledge from 1995 until 2005. According to the report, available at www.neefusa.org/resources/publications.htm#neetfpubs, the general public is not well informed, and at times is misinformed, about environmental issues that impact policy, elections, and local decisions. That's the bad news. The good news is that the public is overwhelmingly interested in and supportive of environmental education. Results indicate that better education could "guide the public to simple actions that could save at least $75 billion annually."

Rating

The industry is mature and thriving. As environmental topics take center stage the need for environmental education becomes more evident and essential.

Future trends (and caveats)

Environmental educators are being called upon to provide educational programs in a variety of settings on a wide range of topics. Although they're trained and committed to providing quality education, they don't always know how impactful their programs actually are. Although conducting in-depth evaluations is the next logical step, many educators don't have the training or resources to conduct these evaluations themselves. The School of Education and Natural Resources and Environment Department at the University of Michigan partnered with the EPA and the Forest Service to spearhead the development of MEERA — My Environmental Education Resource Assistant (`http://meera.snre.umich.edu`). With this resource, more environmental educators have the tools they need to evaluate their own programs and review examples.

A recent study by the NEEF points to a new environmental education trend in businesses. As companies and organizations commit to sustainability and environmental initiatives, they are relying less on environmental specialists and more on the employees on the front lines. To engage their employees and ensure that they have adequate knowledge to contribute to changes in the workplace, they're turning to environmental education. You can read the executive summary or full report at `www.neefusa.org/business/index.htm`. If you're interested in this field, consider working for a third-party training organization that companies are turning to for employee training.

Sample job functions

- ✔ **Any setting educators:** Program manager, program coordinator, outreach coordinator, senior education project manager, senior director, environmental education instructor, environmental educator, science teacher, environmental educational specialist, education coordinator, educational programs coordinator

- ✔ **In-the-field educators:** Naturalist, resource manager, park ranger, interpretive programs director, interpretive programs supervisor, field teacher, teacher naturalist, outdoors ethics program director

See Chapters 8 and 11 for additional job titles.

Industry association

North American Association for Environmental Education: www.naaee.org

Continue your exploration

✔ EE-Link: http://eelink.net/pages/EE-Link+Introduction

✔ An extensive list of environmental education organizations: http://eelink.net/pages/EE+Organizations+and+Projects+-+General

✔ National Environmental Education Foundation: www.neefusa.org

Marketing

As a new green product or service makes its way to market, the marketing team must work out the best way to brand, package, describe, display, and advertise it. The key ingredient to the marketing in this scenario is describing to potential customers how green the product or service really is. This marketing conversation with the customer may include a description of how the product was produced, where the raw materials came from, how it was packaged and distributed, what can be done with the product at the end of its life, and how energy efficient it is. The green story is about far more than the green features; it's a description of the entire life cycle of the product.

If the company has a corporate social responsibility initiative, the marketing story may also include a description of the social impact of the product on the communities of the suppliers, producers, and end users. GenGreenLife refers to this expanded form of marketing as sustainable green marketing. See www.gengreenlife.com/environment_101.php?topic=17.

Industry's current status

Green marketing, also known as environmental or ecological marketing, has been evolving since the early 1980s with Ben and Jerry's Ice Cream and the publication of *Green Marketing* by Jacquelyn Ottman (2004, BookSurge Publishing). More recently the push toward sustainable green products has raised the stakes on green marketing. Grabbing and keeping the customer's attention and purchasing dollar has led some companies to stretch the truth or downright lie about the green characteristics of their products and services.

This so-called *green-washing* by some has put all green marketers under pressure to represent their products and services ethically and honestly. Even the Federal Trade Commission is concerned with the prospects of green-washing, as illustrated in this blog post by TerraChoice: http://blog. terrachoice.com/2009/07/14/government-hears-greenwashing.

If you want to familiarize yourself with the issues underlying the term, green-washing, visit TerraChoice's site and click on the Seven Sins of Greenwashing icon (www.terrachoice.com). Take some time to study the matrix in this GreenBiz.com article that describes four types of green-washing (www. greenbiz.com/news/2009/08/12/preventing-greenwashing-one-company-time) or the full report they are discussing by Business for Social Responsibility and Futerra Sustainability Communications (www.bsr.org/ reports/Understanding_Preventing_Greenwash.pdf).

The Direct Mail Association is making a concerted effort to green its industry with a Recycle Please campaign, an Environmental Planning Tool to help member companies rethink the life cycle of direct mail from design and production to distribution and disposal, according to their Green 15 bench-marking tool (www.the-dma.org/Green15/OverviewDMAGreen15.pdf). In addition, the organization has created a certificate in eco-responsible market-ing with a detailed list of courses at www.the-dma.org/cgi/disppress release?article=1238. It has committed to "reducing 1 million metric tons of carbon emissions between 2009 and 2013 through smart list and data man-agement, and resulting direct mail marketing activity."

Rating

Green marketing is a developing industry that is experiencing some growing pains as green companies compete for customers.

Future trends (and caveats)

One of the biggest challenges facing this industry is the fact that no one is quite sure what constitutes a green product. With no agreed-upon standards, companies are left to their own devices to evaluate their products and deter-mine the best way to communicate their green features. Although some are doing a better job than others, experts are searching for and debating a number of ways to create a consistent standard that is understood by busi-nesses, the government, and consumers:

✔ The Federal Trade Commission has guidelines for those making environ-mental claims about their products, packaging, and services. The guide-lines (www.ftc.gov/bcp/grnrule/guides980427.htm) include a number of case studies that illustrate and apply the guidelines to common terms, including *biodegradable*, *compostable*, and *recyclable*.

✔ The Global Ecolabelling Network (`www.globalecolabelling.net`) recommends a labeling system to assess the life cycle impact of a product or service by using rigorous, scientific standards established by an objective third party. Green Seal, `www.greenseal.org`, and EcoLogo Program, `www.terrachoice-certified.com`, are examples of programs that work with companies to ensure that their products and services pass muster.

✔ Others, such as GreenBlue (`www.greenblue.org`), believe that eco-labeling must be accompanied by transparency in reporting exactly how the product or service impacts the environment. In a post on this topic, `www.greenbiz.com/engage/blog/2009/07/30/real-opportunity-radical-transparency-b2b`, Jason Pearson, CEO of GreenBlue, explains his view.

One of the issues influencing the direct mail industry is the challenge of reducing its use of paper made from wood pulp. Although recycled paper is one option, some companies are looking to alternative kinds of paper. Tree Free Paper (`www.treefreepaper.com`) describes four different ways to make paper from non-wood sources such as agricultural waste, crops, fabric sources, and plants found in the wild. If you really want to go out on a limb, imagine paper made of stone. Although it may seem impossible, *Deliver* magazine reports that Johnson Paper LP supplies stone paper: `www.delivermagazine.com/case-studies/2009/04/22/the-new-stone-age`.

Sample job functions

✔ **Market research:** Market research analyst, market intelligence analyst, marketing analyst, data analytics manager, internet marketing analyst, media research analyst

✔ **Marketing:** Agency account planner, agency account coordinator, agency account executive, marketing director, marketing manager, brand manager, product manager, consumer products manager, e-mail marketing specialist, event planner, direct marketing manager, media buyer, media planner, online marketing manager, online promotions manager, online media buyer, online media planner, search engine marketer, event manager

✔ **Communications:** Communications editor, communications manager, communications specialist, online publicist, public relations account coordinator, media relations manager, Web content editor, Web content manager

✔ **Creative:** Animation designer, creative director, art director, copywriter, graphic designer, illustrator, producer, production artist, production manager, user interface designer, multimedia designer, Web designer, instructional designer

Green sales?

Every company with a product or service needs a sales team. Any consulting firm or business is going to need a sales team to do business development. Yet the sales profession doesn't appear to be offering training on how to become a better green salesperson or guidance about how to find these positions.

One sales position that has gotten a lot of media attention is solar sales. Training programs for solar salespeople are beginning to surface. Rich Hessler Solar Sales Training (`www.pvsolarsalestraining.com`) and The Art of Selling Solar (`www.4solarsales.com`) are examples of such training programs.

You may also be able to find independent sales positions with companies that provide green cleaning products and beauty supplies. But that's really just the tip of the proverbial iceberg. Every company is going to need a sales team when they are ready to sell. Although companies in the early stage of development may not have a product ready for market, you may be able to identify business-to-business sales positions as these emerging companies ramp up their production.

Solar sales and personal products aren't the only career options for those in sales. The key to finding a good sales position is to track industries that are a good fit for your previous sales experience and your passions. If you sold highly technical equipment before, look for a green company with a similar kind of equipment and a comparable sales cycle. If you sold building supplies, transition into green building supplies that leverages off your knowledge of the building industry.

To succeed, you must know how to sell and know about your target industry. If you don't yet know much about the target industry, take courses, attend conferences, and soak up as much information as you can. If you haven't done sales before, but have a strong background in a particular industry, take some sales training courses to build your expertise on the sales process. When you find an industry that looks promising, track its progress and be ready to join the team when someone is ready to hire a sales team. If it looks like you'll be waiting a while, get known in the industry, find work in a related field that will give you leverage within this industry, and get the training you need to be a sales star.

For more on sales in general, see the following Web sites:

- ✔ National Association of Sales Professionals: `www.nasp.com`

- ✔ The Sales Association, Professional Development for Business Development: `www.salesassociation.org`

Industry associations

- ✔ Green Marketing Coalition: `www.greenmarketingcoalition.com`
- ✔ Direct Marketing Association: `www.the-dma.org`
- ✔ Global Ecolabelling Network: `www.globalecolabelling.net`

Continue your exploration

- Green Biz's Marketing-communications section: www.greenbiz.com/browse/marketing-communications
- Direct Marketing Association Environmental Resource Center: www.dmaresponsibility.org/Environment
- *Deliver*, a magazine for marketers: www.delivermagazine.com/topic/green-marketing
- TerraChoice Magazine: http://viewer.zmags.com/publication/84d2b13d#/84d2b13d/1

Sustainability Specialists

The move from business as usual to sustainable business is underway. Although the specifics of the transition may differ depending on the actual focus of the organization, the process and approach remain fairly consistent, including the following components:

- Assessing an organization's social and environmental impact may include measuring the organization's carbon footprint and the extent to which the company impacts its community. With the shortcomings in mind, the next step is to create a multi-faceted action plan to reduce emissions and minimize the impact on the community. After implementing the plan, monitoring the results allows the organization to continue to refine its actions to meet overall goals for sustainability.

- Training and educating those involved in the process of evaluating current systems and finding more energy- and resource-efficient ways to perform the tasks of the organization are essential for employee engagement and participation.

- Communicating the impact and progress through a sustainability report allows various stakeholders to understand the organization's green efforts. Incorporating the initiatives and actions into the marketing plan and public relations is also key.

Industry's current status

As companies assess their impact on the environment and community, they must decide who will actually implement the initiatives associated with improving their sustainability status. Some organizations hire a consultant who provides the facilitation and structure to help the organization determine where they stand on a variety of environmental criteria.

Green media

The media has covered the environmental movement since its earliest phase in the 1960s and 1970s. In fact, the field of environmental journalism developed to report on and translate what was happening in the environment for the public. An ongoing debate within the environmental journalism field is whether journalists should stick to reporting current events objectively or take an advocacy role for the environmentalism point of view. For an overview of the media impact on the green movement, check out www. crinfo.org/booksummary/10380. Writers interested in the environment may also want to consider science writing, environmental interpretation, environmental advocacy, and green marketing as outlets for their talents. For a description of these genres, visit http://en.wikipedia.org/wiki/Environmental_journalism.

Although the news media has played an influential role in the environmental movement and the green economy, the industry itself isn't particularly green, though there are some early signs that the industry is moving in that direction:

- These days many media sources report on the green economy and environmental news, but often it's by a reporter who's been assigned to the green beat rather than a trained environmental journalist. The Society of Environmental Journalists strongly believes that the quality, accuracy, and depth of reporting on environmental issues must be enhanced.

- Well-known media sources such as *The New York Times*, *The Washington Post*, *The Los Angeles Times*, and *The Wall Street Journal* have blogs covering green economy issues.

- Sources dedicated solely to green topics are found in several new media outlets: From cable television (*Planet Green*, including *Focus Earth* with Bob Woodruff, http://planetgreen.discovery.com) to online video (Green.tv), to an ever-growing array of blogs written by online journalists, industry experts, and individuals committed to the cause. See the book's online Cheat Sheet (www.dummies.com/cheatsheet/greencareers) for a list of green blogs.

- The National Association of Broadcasters partnered with the EPA to create a booklet for broadcasters to disseminate relevant green facts, public service announcements, and ways to green their workplace: www.nhab.org/member_resources/goinggreen.html.

- A sustainability consulting firm called Reel Green Media (www.reelgreenmedia.com) helps the entertainment industry, from production companies to theaters, green up their act. They take a look at everything from the food on the set to opening night events.

- In 2008 the Digital Entertainment Group released a study of the home entertainment supply chain from home entertainment studios to retailers. Findings indicate that there are ways to build more efficiencies into the process of producing DVDs and getting them into the hands of customers: www.dvdinformation.com/News/press/031808.htm.

For more on green media, see the following Web sites:

- Society of Environmental Journalists: www.sej.org

- Association for the Study of Literature and Environment: www.asle.org

- National Association of Science Writers: www.nasw.org

- Whole Terrain: www.wholeterrain.org/resources.cfm

- National Association of Broadcasters: www.nab.org

In some cases organizations hire from within, finding a current employee who is interested in efficiency and environmental issues or who has line experience in a key area of the organization. This individual's title may range from sustainability manager to chief sustainability officer (CSO). The field is so young that the role of the CSO often varies across organizations as different companies figure out the best way to address their impact on the environment.

Sustainability is also influencing other sectors of our economy besides big business. Several nonprofit associations have been working toward sustainability for many years, such as the Association for the Advancement of Sustainability in Higher Education (AASHE — www.aashe.org) and ICLEI-Local Governments for Sustainability (www.icleiusa.org). Both sites offer a wealth of information about sustainability in general and as applied to their niche. Even small- and medium-sized companies are getting into the act with the help of sustainability consultants, such as Strategic Sustainability Consulting: www.sustainabilityconsulting.com/about.

Companies worldwide are making the extra effort to report on their environmental performance based on a widely used reporting system developed by the Global Reporting Initiative: www.globalreporting.org/ReportingFramework/ReportingFrameworkOverview. As more companies adopt this standardized reporting framework, companies are able to assess their improvement over time and compare their efforts with those of other companies.

Rating

The industry is emerging as more and more organizations transition to sustainable business practices.

Future trends (and caveats)

Although you've probably heard of sustainability initiatives in manufacturing, local municipalities, and retail stores, you may not have thought of sustainability efforts in the entertainment field (see the earlier sidebar, "Green media," for more on this topic), the medical field (www.practicegreen health.org and www.gghc.org/about.cfm), and your local brewery (www.greengrog.com/west-coast-dominates-green-brewing). Nearly every industry out there is exploring sustainability to some degree. Just because you (or I) haven't heard of it yet doesn't mean it isn't happening. Use your favorite search engine to discover how your target industry is going green. Enter **"your target industry"** + **green** to see what you find.

In March 2009 the Global Reporting Initiative released the Amsterdam Declaration of Transparency and Reporting, asking all governments to implement a policy that requires companies, public organizations, and the global financial regulatory body to complete an annual sustainability report, www.globalreporting.org/CurrentPriorities/AmsterdamDeclaration. Their assessment is that voluntary compliance is not enough. Transparency and the full costs of environmental and social impacts must be taken into account for the global economy to regain momentum.

Sample job functions

Chief sustainability officer, sustainability account manager, sustainability integration director, resource architect, business sustainability consultant, sustainability coordinator, corporate sustainability manager, sustainability outreach specialist, director of sustainability, director of sustainability advocacy, environmental program manager, life cycle practitioner, sustainability analyst, sustainability assistant.

Industry associations

- ✔ International Society of Sustainability Professionals: www.sustainabilityprofessionals.org
- ✔ Association for the Advancement of Sustainability in Higher Education (AASHE): www.aashe.org
- ✔ ICLEI-Local Governments for Sustainability: www.icleiusa.org
- ✔ World Business Council for Sustainable Development (WBCSD) www.wbcsd.org

Continue your exploration

- ✔ AASHE's Climate Action Planning Wiki: http://www.aashe.org/wiki/climate-planning-guide/contents.php
- ✔ The Natural Step: www.naturalstep.org, www.naturalstepusa.org and www.transformagents.org
- ✔ Strategic Sustainability Consulting: www.sustainabilityconsulting.com
- ✔ Corporate Social Responsibility Newswire: http://www.csrwire.com

Chapter 13

Providing Green Products and Services

*A*lthough much of the green economy focuses on large scale changes to our world such as transitioning to new energy sources, revamping the transportation infrastructure, and creating new laws and policies to regulate said changes, the green economy also touches our lives at a much more personal level.

This chapter explores the green products and sustainable experiences that bring the green reality up close and personal. Whether you want to have a role in creating natural products, planning exciting travel experiences, managing large-scale events or helping people with their real estate transactions, there are plenty of opportunities to make your mark.

Ecotourism

Traveling the world to see and experience the sights and sounds draws people to natural spots, from beaches and mountains to jungles and meadows. Unfortunately, mass-market tourism has a detrimental impact on the very environments that draw tourists to travel. The ecotourism industry has evolved over the past 20 years to allow people to travel to nature destinations more responsibly. According to the Mohonk Agreement of 2000 (www.rainforest-alliance.org/tourism.cfm?id=mohonk), ecotourism is "tourism that seeks to minimize ecological and sociocultural impacts while providing economic benefits to local communities and host countries."

The International Ecotourism Society (TIES) (www.ecotourism.org) describes ecotourism as being built on the principles of minimizing the impact of travelers on the environment, increasing peoples' awareness of both the environment and the local culture, creating positive experiences for both travelers and the locals, finding innovative ways to make conservation and local involvement financially beneficial, and raising awareness of the local areas' political and social realities.

The ecotourism industry consists of three main functions:

✔ Assessing and developing sustainable tourism destinations

✔ Managing ecotourism destinations sustainably

✔ Marketing the destination

For more information about these functions and related topics, check out the online courses listed on www.ecotourism.org under Learning Center.

Industry's current status

According to the Rainforest Alliance (www.rainforest-alliance.org), the travel industry helps more than 900 million people travel each year. In addition to being one of the largest sources of income and employment for many developing countries, the travel industry can have a detrimental effect on local environments if not managed properly.

Although ecotourism has only amounted to 3 or 4 percent of the travel industry in the past, international travel has motivated local residents in stunning destinations to conserve and maintain their corner of the world. The trick is finding the right balance between using ecotourism as a way to motivate and fund conservation and minimizing the carbon footprint of transporting people halfway around the world to visit these natural areas. For more information on this dilemma, read: www.guatemala-times.com/environment/946-can-ecotourism-be-more-than-an-illusion.html.

According to the United Nations Environment Programme (UNEP) Sustainable Consumption and Production Branch, www.unep.fr/scp/sc, nature tourism is growing by 10–12 percent each year. The World Tourism Organization also reports that nature-based tourism is the fastest-growing tourism sector. There are also signs that the mass-market travel segment is beginning to see the benefits of becoming more sustainable.

Ecotourism destinations have taken it upon themselves to become certified in recent years to demonstrate their efforts to become more sustainable. More than 60 certification programs, with a grand total of 4,500 different criteria, exist worldwide. To help key stakeholders make sense of all the different certifications, a group of 27 travel organizations joined together as the Partnership for Global Sustainable Tourism Criteria (`www.sustainable tourismcriteria.org`) to create a global sustainability certification standard.

Rating

The industry is maturing and reaching for new goals.

Future trends (and caveats)

The World Travel and Tourism Council (WTTC), a group of the largest travel and tourism companies in the world, released a report entitled Leading the Challenge on Climate Change in which 40 of the largest tourism companies in the world committed in 2005 to reducing their carbon emissions by 50 percent by 2035, with an interim milestone of a 30 percent reduction by 2020. For more information about this commitment and the report, visit `www.wttc. org/eng/Tourism_Initiatives/Environment_Initiative`.

The next step after certification is continued monitoring. If establishments fail to be monitored for performance and adherence, they may well lose their sustainable status. Methods for monitoring must be implemented along with the certification process.

Education and marketing the benefits of sustainable travel is crucial to the industry's success. Countries blessed with rich biodiversity may be able to restore and conserve local ecosystems and habitats while also strengthening local economies. Tourism businesses can use ecotourism and sustainability to build their brand with travelers by making them aware of the benefits of ecotourism. One of the ways travelers can enhance their impact is to use part of their vacation to make a difference in the local community by working on a restoration, wildlife conservation, or other local improvement project.

A new trend in ecotourism is establishing a presence on various social networking platforms such as Twitter and Facebook. You can help out your favorite ecotourism establishments by following and friending them. Share their updates with your friends. Who knows? You may find yourself on vacation thanks to a special deal.

For the ecotourism industry to thrive, the airline industry must strive to lower the carbon footprint of air travel. Several airlines are testing various biofuels and fuel combinations to determine which ones are most effective.

Sample job functions

- ✔ **Development and management:** Tourism development specialist, sustainable tourism business development manager, sustainable development consultancy, ecosystem management and development, ecosystem management and development officer, tourism and human resources advisor

- ✔ **Operating ecotourism locations:** Heritage tourism officer, sustainable tourism manager, ecotourism project manager, rainforest station manager, ecolodge manager, cultural tourism project facilities manager, rural tourism officer, sustainable tourism operator, ecotour leaders, green caretakers of tropical island, coastal tourism and conservation program officer, sustainable consumption and conservation manager, conservation expedition country coordinator

- ✔ **Managing natural lands:** Nature tourism ranger, nature tourism park manager, parks and recreation director, wildlife visitor center advisor, reserve director, conservation program manager, conservation project manager, preserve manager, naturalist programmer, conservation expeditions field positions, conservation program assistant (see Chapter 8 for related job titles)

- ✔ **Scientific roles:** Conservation scientist, nature center research technician, biodiversity specialist, wildlife research assistant (see Chapters 7 and 8 for additional job functions)

- ✔ **Promoting ecotourism:** Guidebook writers, protected areas communications officer, responsible tourism communications manager, adventure travel promotion manager, responsible tourism marketing manager (also see marketing job titles in Chapter 12)

Industry associations

- ✔ The International Ecotourism Society: www.ecotourism.org

- ✔ Sustainable Travel International: www.sustainabletravel international.org

- ✔ Adventure Travel Trade Association: www.adventuretravel.biz/about.asp

- ✔ International Tourism Partnership: www.tourismpartnership.org

Continue your exploration

✔ Green Travel Market: www.sustainabletravelinternational. org/documents/op_green.html

✔ Rainforest Alliance: http://www.rainforest-alliance.org/ tourism.cfm?id=main

✔ The International Ecotourism Society Learning Center: www. ecotourism.org

✔ World Travel and Tourism Council: www.wttc.org

Event Planning

Conferences, trade shows, weddings, and other large gatherings are generally energy-consuming, waste-producing ventures. Whether planned by internal staff or external consultants, creating events with the lowest possible carbon footprint and highest possible waste diversion is the goal of green meetings.

Each meeting is a confluence of vendors and venues. According to BlueGreen Meetings (www.bluegreenmeetings.org), each of the following groups has a role to play in greening events:

✔ **Convention and visitors bureaus:** Professionals trying to bring large conventions to town must be able to demonstrate what the city and region are doing to become more sustainable. They may also be asked to recommend venues, hotels, and activities in the area that meet the green initiatives of the meeting planner/sponsoring organization.

✔ **Accommodations:** Hotels have an array of actions they can take to reduce their impact on the environment. From guest services to hotel-wide systems, changes can be made. For details see the "Lodging and restaurants" sidebar.

✔ **Meeting/event venues:** The meeting site itself has special challenges and opportunities. Feeding, engaging, entertaining, and cleaning up after a large group for several days is intense. Special care must be taken to find sustainable ways to achieve each desired outcome.

✔ **Transportation:** The vendors that provide ground and air transportation to and from the event must also be brought into the loop. By doing research upfront, the meeting planner can suggest the greenest alternatives to the attendees.

> ✔ **Food and beverage:** Sourcing, preparing, serving, and disposing of left-overs several times a day for the duration of the meeting requires coordination and creative thinking. Working with the venue's catering staff can bring innovative solutions to the situation.

> ✔ **Exhibition production:** The exhibit hall brings its own set of challenges as each vendor arrives with its own handouts, giveaways, signage, and displays. Providing recommendations and guidelines can ensure that the exhibit hall activities reflect the green initiatives of the event.

Industry's current status

The final set of standards of the Convention Industry Council's Green Meetings and Events Practice Panel were released in late 2009. For more about this set of standards, read: `http://meetingsnet.com/checklist showto/green_meetings/0701-developing-meeting-standards`.

On Earth Day 2009 the Green Meeting Industry Council (GMIC) launched the Million Tons of Trash Challenge, asking hospitality, travel, and meeting planning companies to divert one million tons of waste in one year. *Diverted waste* means waste that doesn't make its way to landfill because it is reused, recycled, or composted (`www.greenmeetings.info`).

As the industry ramps up sustainable meeting practices in a tight economy, industry suppliers, such as hotels, caterers, florists, and the like, are highlighting their sustainable and socially responsible solutions to gain business from meeting planners. For examples of these innovations, read `http://meetings net.com/checklistshowto/green_meetings/0701-companies-managing-budget-cuts`.

Rating

This industry is mature and taking new steps to become more sustainable.

Future trends (and caveats)

The future holds several likely outcomes. As the field of sustainability evolves, the industry's standards will be upgraded to match the new benchmarks and technological advances. In addition, a training system will be put in place to bring meeting planners and suppliers up to speed on the standards released in late 2009.

As soon as training programs are in place, a certification process is likely to be implemented to verify that the standards are in fact being met by various venues, suppliers, and meeting planners. As this system takes hold, meeting planners will be able to use quantifiable results to demonstrate that they've met their corporate clients goals for sustainability and achieved a certain amount of cost savings as a result. In addition, suppliers will use their scores in their marketing materials to prove their viability to meeting planners.

Sample job functions

- ✔ **Meeting management:** Meeting planner, meeting coordinator, registration coordinator, conference assistant, conference manager, events manager, membership and conference coordinator, programs and meeting manager, government event planner, event center coordinator, corporate event planner, event planner/finance manager, senior event planner, special event planner, meeting planning consultant, conference setup attendant, trade show specialist, conference services manager, convention services manager, travel coordinator, meeting assistant, meeting coordinator, meeting assistant, meeting director, event operations

- ✔ **Marketing and sales:** Marketing coordinator, senior marketing communications manager, global account manager, sales manager, outside sales manager, group sales manager, marketing specialist

- ✔ **Communications:** Communications specialist, advertising coordinator, promotions assistant, public relations specialist

- ✔ **Supplier services:** Catering and events services manager, catering manager, catering coordinator, director of banquets, audio/visual film technicians, florists, convention and visitors bureaus representative

Industry associations

- ✔ Green Meeting Industry Council: www.greenmeetings.info
- ✔ Destination Marketing Association: www.destinationmarketing.org (Formerly International Association of Convention & Visitor Bureaus)
- ✔ Meeting Professionals International: www.mpiweb.org
- ✔ Convention Industry Council's list of member associations: http://www.conventionindustry.org/aboutcic/members.htm

Lodging and restaurants

In the hospitality industry, job titles are likely to be nearly identical in green and traditional properties. To find a position in this industry, focus your efforts on establishments that are actively moving toward sustainable business practices. Creating a sustainable hospitality industry requires reworking four segments of the industry:

- **Hotels:** Powering, maintaining, decorating, cleaning, lighting, and managing waste all create expensive challenges for large chain hotels, boutique hotels, and bed and breakfasts. Becoming more sustainable allows establishments to cut costs significantly while minimizing their impact on the environment. To see what's entailed in greening a hotel, see `www.green lodgingnews.com` and `www.ahla.com/green.aspx?id=24560`.

- **Restaurants:** In addition to finding new food sources that are more organic, local, and sustainable, restaurants must also evaluate their water and energy usage. Becoming more efficient in their use of water and energy and installing renewable energy sources shrinks both costs and carbon footprints. Waste from food preparation and leftovers, as well as paper products, has quite an impact on landfills. Finding new solutions, such as composting and purchasing biodegradable containers made from tree-free sources, can transform this industry's impact. For more details: `www.dinegreen.com/restaurants`.

- **Supply manufacturers:** Companies that manufacture products and cleaning supplies for restaurant and hotel use also have an opportunity to clean up their act. The Green Restaurant Association (`www.dinegreen.com/manufacturers`) and the Green Hotels Association (`www.greenhotels.com/appvvend.php`) endorse environmentally sound products that are manufactured sustainably.

- **Distributors:** Companies that distribute products in the restaurant industry must review their offerings, own work systems, and transportation systems to find more environmentally sound ways to do business. See `www.dinegreen.com/distributors/default.asp`.

For more about green restaurants, visit the following sites:

- **Green Hotels Association:** `www.greenhotels.com`

- **Green Lodging News:** `www.greenlodgingnews.com`

- **Green Restaurant Association:** `www.dinegreen.com`

- **National Restaurant Association's Web Site, Conserve–Solutions for Sustainability:** `http://conserve.restaurant.org`

Continue your exploration

- Green Meetings' Get Informed Section: `www.greenmeetings.info/Get_Informed`

- Environmental Protection Agency's Green Meeting Initiative: `www.epa.gov/oppt/greenmeetings`

- BlueGreen Meetings: www.bluegreenmeetings.org
- Green Hotels Association: http://greenhotels.com/question.php

Natural Personal Care and Cleaning

Customer demand for environmentally sound products and services is fueling more natural products in the areas of personal care, beauty, health, dietary supplements, pet products, and cleaning. Consumers want to know that the products that are touching them, their babies, and their pets are safe, effective, and natural in their ingredients and their formulation.

As this broad industry responds to this market-driven trend, companies are coming up with natural products that appeal to their customer base.

- **Personal care and beauty:** Everything from basic soaps and toothpastes to hair products, skin care, fragrances, and makeup
- **Cleaning:** Household and industrial cleaning products
- **Health:** Supplements, treatments, remedies, and herbs

Often the business or individual selling such products also provides a related service that is marketed to be natural, organic, and sustainable. Think makeup artists, hair salons, spas, cleaning services, and alternative health providers. In each of these scenarios, the professionals providing the service must rethink how they perform and advertise their services. For example, a green cleaning company must not only purchase the appropriate cleaning products, but must also have the proper equipment, tools, and knowledge to clean a house, commercial building, or hotel in a way that uses fewer cleaning products and less energy and disposes of waste properly.

Industry's current status

The sale of natural products is growing by leaps and bounds. According to In-Cosmetics, the natural personal care market has experienced "double-digit growth annually" since 2003. Natural cosmetic products and those inspired by nature (more on that in a moment) are 6 percent of the market.

Throughout this multi-faceted industry there is a debate, namely: How does the industry define the terms *organic, natural, nature-inspired,* and *natural extracts*? How does it educate consumers and fulfill marketing promises? How do consumers know that what they are buying is what they think they're buying?

Although the U.S. Department of Agriculture (USDA) regulates cosmetics for organic ingredients, it doesn't evaluate how natural cosmetics or other personal care products are. In an effort to self-regulate its industry, the Natural Products Association has created a definition consumers can use to evaluate the personal care products they purchase: "Natural products should contain only ingredients that come from a renewable/plentiful source found in nature — in other words, flora, fauna or mineral sources. Any synthetic ingredient must only be used in a natural personal care product when there is no viable natural alternative ingredient available and only when there are absolutely no suspected human health risks." Read their one-page description: www.naturalproducts foundation.org/clientuploads/WYSKA_Natural_Personal_Care_ Products.pdf.

To support this standard, certification programs are being put into place. For example, the GreenSeal certifies soap and shower products and personal care products (www.greenseal.org/certification/environmental. cfm#6). The Natural Products Association (NPA) bestows the Natural Seal on natural products (www.thenaturalseal.org), while NSF International, the public health and safety company, certifies organic products (www. nsf.org/business/quality_assurance_international/index. asp?program=OrganicFooCer). Quality Assurance International/NSF and NPA are agreeing to recognize each others' certifications, allowing cosmetic companies to offer their products across borders more readily.

Some cosmetic companies are expanding their line to include products created from natural ingredients harvested from environmentally vulnerable areas in an effort to encourage locals to nurture their natural flora and fauna. By setting up fair trade agreements, the company gives an economic boost to an area of the world that needs it. In return, the company is able add to additional value and marketing appeal to their product.

Rating

Growing in response to consumer demand for more natural products.

Future trends (and caveats)

The push in natural personal care and cleaning products is for common standards across borders and across product categories. Terms such as organic and natural should have standard, agreed-upon meanings for all the players, from consumers to retailers, marketers, distributors, manufacturers, suppliers, scientists and educators. Integrating these definitions into existing certification organizations is going to be challenging at best.

Industry experts express concerns about the trend toward genetically engineered products, cosmetics produced with nanotechnology, cosmeceuticals (cosmetics blended with drugs for topical application) and nutricosmetics (products ingested orally). For more details see www.nanowerk.com/news/newsid=1505.php and www.gcimagazine.com/marketstrends/segments/nutricosmetics/42535102.html. Given that these products are relatively new and untested, it's worrisome that the Food and Drug Administration has no standards in place to evaluate the efficacy of products in these categories.

Sample job functions

- ✔ **Research and development and product development:** Senior product development chemist, cosmetic chemist, project manager, senior R&D researcher, R&D engineer, chemist formulation, analytical chemist
- ✔ **Operations:** Operations manager, logistics coordinator, logistics manager
- ✔ **Product lines:** Brand manager, brand assistant manager
- ✔ **Marketing and sales:** Consumer and market knowledge associate manager, market intelligence manager, beauty sales (see Chapter 12 for more information about marketing and sales)
- ✔ **Service providers using natural/non-toxic/organic/green products:** Hair care professional, stylist, house cleaner, commercial cleaner, housekeeper, spa manager, spa assistant, spa director, nail technician, beauty consultant, makeup artist, alternative health practitioner, health care consultant, perfumist

Industry association

Natural Products Association: www.naturalproductsassoc.org

Continue your exploration

- ✔ Global Cosmetic Industry: www.gcimagazine.com

  Don't get lost in here! An amazingly rich site.
- ✔ Organic Consumers Association: www.organicconsumers.org
- ✔ Natural Products Foundation: www.naturalproductsfoundation.org
- ✔ INFORM: http://informinc.org/project_cleaning_health.php

Fair trade commerce

Fair trade is an economic partnership to create an international trading system that is just and sustainable. Fair trade organizations work directly with artisans and farmers to create an equitable exchange of goods that enables them to create independent businesses that are financially viable. Fair trade partnerships that work lead to positive changes that ripple throughout the community, including bringing back nearly forgotten cultural techniques, conserving the biodiversity of the region, and creating communities that value the contributions of women.

The Fairtrade Labelling Organizations International (FLO) (www.fairtrade.net) reviews the supply chain from point of origin to the point of sale to ensure that all steps in the process meet fair trade standards. In North America, the organizations that certify fair trade products are TransFair Canada (www.transfair.ca) and TransFair USA (www.transfairusa.org). Each organization tracks certain products, many of them food related.

The bodies that evaluate organizations for their commitment to fair trade principles include the World Fair Trade Organization (www.wfto.com) and the Fair Trade Federation (FTF) (www.fairtradeorganization.com) for North America. Retailers and importers generally focus on food products, accessories, crafts, packaging, and gifts. Members of these organizations commit to a set of principles to make sure that they are selling free trade products that were grown or manufactured by people who were paid equitably.

Part IV
Using Green Job Search 2.0 Techniques

The 5th Wave   By Rich Tennant

Dear Ms. Heppner,
I look forward to my interview for the position of Conservation Coordinator. I think my position on recycling stands on its own merit.

In this part . . .

Before you officially launch your green job search, take time to prepare yourself to be the best job candidate you can be. In this part you discover ways to explore potential green industries, build your green network, and strengthen your knowledge and skills. Using what are called Job Search 2.0 strategies — such as social networking, blogging, and online portfolios — you create an online presence to enhance your visibility for your job search. As your path becomes clearer and you become more confident about your skills and competitive advantage, you create a clear, concise statement of your unique contribution that captures the attention of the company that hires you.

Chapter 14

Getting to Know Your Target Industry

*T*he green economy is an ever-changing sea of opportunity. Every day brings new information. If you attempt to explore every green industry to figure out where you fit, you'll likely be overwhelmed. The key to finding your green career is to focus your attention on one or two industries that intrigue you most. These *target* industries become the rudder you use to keep yourself on track during your exploration phase.

In this chapter you discover a number of ways to investigate your target industries to confirm that they are viable and a good fit for you personally and professionally. Although you may be tempted to launch into a series of informational interviews as soon as you identify your target industries, take some time to explore your top two industries online first. With your initial research, you gain a basic understanding of the field, which you can then build upon through conversations with people who work in the field.

 For now, focus your attention on gathering information about your top two target industries. Your goal is not to make a decision at this point, it is to develop an objective understanding of your targets without interjecting your hopes and worries into the mix. You have plenty of opportunities later on to decide which you want most.

Gaining a Solid Foundation Online

The Internet offers a vast array of resources you can use to explore any and every topic under the sun. Use it to strengthen your understanding of your target industries, as well as your profession or trade. Although you may be tempted to click off in a number of different directions, keep your focus on your top two targets for now. Depending on your own personal style, you may want to set aside some time to investigate one field first and then do the other.

As soon as you have a basic grasp of a target industry, you have a foundation to build on. As you begin your research, be on the lookout for resources you may want to come back to if you decide to pursue this target career.

Refining your keywords

Keywords — the terms you enter into search engines to find information — are your friends. By using keywords strategically you enhance your ability to gather meaningful, content-rich material about your favorite topics. Throughout this chapter, as you build your research toolkit, you find keyword combinations you can use each step of the way.

To create a list of keywords for your industry, think about the words that are commonly used when discussing it. Jot down industry descriptors as you come across them in your research. Review the following keyword lists for a few green industries to grasp the kinds of terms you're looking for.

- ✔ **Smart grid:** Unified smart grid, microgeneration, co-generation, energy transport, energy information technology, smart appliance, emeter, smart meter, smart device, energy transmission

- ✔ **Solar:** Solar energy, solar nonprofit, solar installer, photovoltaic, PV, thin-film PV, Copper indium gallium (di)selenide (CIGS), solar cells, solar panels, photovoltaic conversion efficiency, concentrating solar power (CSP), building-integrated photovoltaics

- ✔ **Cleantech:** Clean technology, sustainability technology, energy productivity, cleantech design, greentech

- ✔ **Energy efficient:** Energy-efficient design, energy efficiency policy, energy-efficient buildings, transportation efficiency, industrial efficiency, energy efficiency assessors, negawatt (energy saved through efficiency), Energy Efficiency Resource Standard (EERS), energy efficiency resource standards

- ✔ **Environmental science:** Environmental impact assessment (EIA), biodiversity, water quality, groundwater contamination, soil contamination, use of natural resources, waste management, sustainable development, disaster reduction, air pollution, noise pollution

Creating an overview of a target industry

To make the best use of your time, begin by getting a general idea of your industry. Use the following keyword combinations in your favorite search engine to discover Web pages with straightforward descriptions of your target field. Just replace the word *keyword(s)* with the best keyword(s) for your target industry. And use quotation marks as I do here if your keyword contains more than one word. Putting quotation marks around words tells the engine to find pages that contain exactly that phrase, rather than pages that contain all three words in any order. You may need to experiment with keyword selections to determine which ones are most productive for you.

```
"keyword(s)" + "what is"
"keyword(s)" + industry
"keyword(s)" + history
"keyword(s)" + profile
```

It's quite likely that your initial searches will bring up Wikipedia resources. Although Wikipedia pages are written by the public, they often provide well-organized, easy-to-read descriptions. You always want to corroborate what you discover there. Think of Wikipedia as the starting point of your research, not the final word on a subject.

You may also run across industry overviews on a variety of other sites. As you come across sites for professional associations, industry associations, training, and certification programs, keep track of the Web site addresses for future reference. Either bookmark them or paste the URLs into a document.

Read at least three to five industry overviews, or until you notice that your sources are repeating the same information. You might want to open each overview in a new browser tab to move between the pages for easy comparison. Although you're likely to find more detailed information as you continue your research, repetition is a good sign that you've gotten to the core of your topic.

If questions come to mind as you read the overviews, jot them down. You may find answers later in your research. You can also use your questions to develop a strategy for informational interviews later in your research process.

Professional associations

Your next goal is to identify the associations that are most closely aligned with your target industry. Depending on your target, you may be looking for an industry association, a trade association, or a professional association.

If you found a profile of your target industry in Chapters 7 through 13, see if there's an association Web site listed there. If you didn't find a profile of your industry or if you're interested in a specialized part of an industry, you may need to search some more to find the association that's most relevant to you. Try the following search strategies to locate an appropriate association:

- ✔ In Wikipedia, review the content again to see if the main text, sidebars, or fine print at the bottom names any associations. It's often found in the External Links section near the end of a page. If you find the name of an association, click the link or search for the association's Web site.

- ✔ Use a keyword(s) search: "**keyword(s)**" + **association**.

- ✔ Check out the categories on Weddle's Association List (www.weddles. com/associations/index.cfm).

Bookmark association Web sites. You're likely to return there frequently. If you locate several associations, compare them to see which is most closely aligned with your career goals. While you're on each site, sign up for newsletters. If the newsletters are only available to paying members, wait until you know which direction you're taking before you subscribe.

Industry-specific terminology

Another challenge when you begin to explore a new industry is getting the hang of the lingo and jargon. Each industry has its own terminology that you must understand to be successful in your investigation.

Wikipedia articles can be a good place to start getting a feel for the terminology of a new industry because most terms are linked to another page for that keyword. You may also be able to find a glossary dedicated to your industry by using the keywords: "**keyword**" + **glossary**. Don't be alarmed if your search brings up a glossary for students. Often these glossaries are concise enough that you can read them within minutes. Then you can look for more in-depth glossaries to further your knowledge.

Key players to watch

Identifying the people who are very involved and instrumental in shaping your target field can be critically important. As soon as you recognize a few names, your understanding of the nuances and dynamics of the industry picks up a notch. Suddenly a blog post that didn't mean much to you becomes a rich source of information because you understand the players and their perspectives. Read and bookmark several blogs that focus on your industry or profession to become familiar with key players. Not sure which blogs cover your industry? Search these terms: **"keyword"** + **blog**.

Another powerful source of names is the Web site for your industry's main conference. If you've found your professional associations, look to see if they have a link to a recent or upcoming conference. Review the names of keynote speakers, breakout speakers, moderators, and exhibitors. It may take a while to decide which names to follow closely, but you're likely to be able to make some connection from this information. With time, you'll notice patterns that point you toward the people to watch in your profession. If you can't find a conference listed through an association, search: **"keyword"** + **conference**.

Publications to read

As you conduct your exploratory research, notice the titles of publications you should add to your must-read list. Most associations publish an annual report on the state of the industry or a description of new advancements in the field. Given that green industries are changing quite rapidly, these reports are often the most current description of trends, warnings, and future directions.

Another source for up-to-date information on your industry is the media. Typically, blogs and online news sources are great ways to get updates as changes unfold in your field. Enter keywords in the Google News search box at http://news.google.com or use keywords to find news vehicles:

```
"keyword" + blog
"keyword" + news
"keyword" + report
```

Confirming That the Industry Is Right for You

Before you invest more time in exploring your target industries, consolidate what you've discovered thus far by considering the following questions:

- ✔ **Is your target industry viable?** From the reading you've done thus far, what is your sense of the industry? Are you comfortable enough with what you're reading to continue the process of exploring the industry?

- ✔ **How does your target industry match your interests and skills?** If you've read Chapters 4 and 5, take another look at your notes. Can you see your favorite skills and interests coming into play with your target industry? If you're missing a skill, is it one you'd like to develop?

✔ **Will this industry allow you to work the way you want to?** Take another look at your notes from Chapter 6 to assess whether this piece of the puzzle is a good fit for you.

✔ **Given what you know about yourself and this industry, can you see yourself working in this field?** Imagine how you would feel if you were working in the field. Would you feel engaged and energized? Or would the work environment or topic drain or overwhelm you?

At this point, you're primarily looking for red flags that might cause you to question your decision to pursue this target industry. Essentially this is a gut check based on your current understanding of your target industry.

✔ If you feel comfortable enough with your assessment, move on to the next section of this chapter. You know that you have more details to discover and you're excited about what you've uncovered.

✔ If you aren't comfortable with what you've found so far, ask yourself:

• Are your concerns based on assumptions you're making about your target industry? If your preconceived notions about the industry are skewing your thinking, continue your exploration to determine whether your assumptions are valid or not.

• Are your worries stemming from what you don't know about your industry? Perhaps you wonder about pending legislation or technology developments that will make or break your industry. This isn't a time to back off, this is a time to dig in to discover as much as you can from industry experts.

• Is your discomfort based on facts you've uncovered while gaining an understanding of the overall industry? If so, you may decide to pass on this industry and choose a different one.

Given the fluid nature of the green economy and all the factors that must come together to build a thriving economy, it's possible you'll need to switch your focus at some point. You may decide that your interests are taking you in another direction or that the industry isn't looking as promising as it once did. The key is to stay alert and nimble. Honor your sense of your direction.

Deepening Your Understanding of the Industry

After verifying that you want to pursue a career in your target industry, it's time to dig deeper to gain more insights into its current state and future. Your focus is on understanding the opportunities and threats facing your field. In addition, you want to know the problems your industry faces at this time.

With this foundation of knowledge, you can now assess the career options within the industry to determine which job titles you want to explore. Avoid the temptation to latch onto a specific job title early in your research. The more you know about the overall industry, the better you'll understand your career options within the industry.

Recognizing industry opportunities and threats

Keep your eyes open for discussions of issues that may have a long-term impact on your career. As the green economy takes shape, a number of pieces are being put in place that can have a dramatic effect in the short term and long term. Although you may not know enough detail yet to unravel the full impact of new policies or the expiration of an incentive, identifying that these issues exist is your primary goal for now. Later, as you talk with people in your field, you can ask them for clarification on the issues you identify.

The best places to look for trends are the blogs, news media, industry associations, and conferences you've already found. If you've identified key players in the industry, pay attention to what they are saying about the industry's future. If you aren't spotting trends there, search "keyword" + trends.

When you scan for opportunities and threats, consider the following factors:

- ✔ **Goals:** Policies, treaties, and laws that spell out new, more environmentally sustainable goals shape the green economy. Fuel efficiencies and renewable energy standards are just a few of the policy goals that are in place to inspire industries to find innovative ways to address their business. Depending on the industry, these goals could cause your industry to boom or falter.

- ✔ **Incentives:** Often early-stage industries get a boost from refunds or tax credits for consumers or investors. If you notice existing incentives are set to expire, pay attention. The expiration of incentives can impact an industry, especially if it is still emerging.

- ✔ **Disincentives:** Capping carbon is a tool to dissuade companies from emitting greenhouse gases. For some industries, it's going to play havoc with business-as-usual. Opportunities may appear as a result.

- ✔ **Definitions:** In all these factors there are definitions that determine which side of an incentive or disincentive your industry falls on. Sometimes definitions set up by the government don't coincide with how proponents of the industry see the impact of a technology. You must pay attention to how this discussion unfolds for your target industry.

✔ **Funding sources:** Follow the money to see how your industry is funding its growth. Look for discussions about grants, subsidies, venture capital, and joint ventures. When funding is flowing, your industry is likely to go through a growth spurt. If funding looks like it's drying up, stay alert, as your industry may need to consolidate or restructure to survive.

✔ **Technological improvements:** Enhancements in technologies used in your industry also influence its future. If you're working on one technology and breakthroughs happen in another technology, you may feel the impact in your business. Always be aware of developments in your general industry category, not just your specific segment.

Defining current problems

As you read about your target industry, notice the issues the industry is wrestling with right now. Think through the entire value chain, from identifying raw materials to manufacturing the product to end-of-life processes. Where in the process is your industry facing the most challenges?

✔ Is there a bottleneck in finding sustainable raw material?

✔ Could the product be designed more efficiently to reduce manufacturing costs and steps?

✔ Is the current distribution channel sustainable?

✔ Are branding, marketing, and sales helping the product's success or not?

✔ What happens to the product at the end of its life cycle?

Use your own expertise in the field or a related field to identify gaps, inefficiencies, and redundancies the industry must identify. Although you may not know all the ins and outs of the industry yet, apply what you do know. You may see things from a different perspective that will uncover opportunities the industry itself may not be aware of. Your ability to resolve these issues makes you attractive to potential employers, especially when you can clearly and accurately articulate the issues.

If you're not looking at a product-focused industry, think through the issues associated with providing your service, knowledge, or information. How can your industry streamline its efforts to fulfill the needs of customers?

As you identify potential issues, note them. When you talk with people in the field, ask about the issues to gain insights and perspective.

Identifying careers within the industry

With your current understanding, take a look at the careers that exist. Don't just look at the job functions that fit your skills and interests. Take the opportunity to get a full picture of how work gets done in your industry. You have several options for researching job functions:

- ✔ If your professional association has a job board, do a general search to pull up all the jobs on the list. Scan job titles to get a sense of the range of jobs. Click through to read the full job descriptions as well.

- ✔ Search for information about job titles and careers related to your industry: "**keyword**" + "**job title**" or "**keyword**" + **career**.

- ✔ Explore LinkedIn (www.linkedin.com) for people who have jobs in your industry. Take advantage of the company profiles to find companies within your target industry. (See Chapter 15 for more.)

- ✔ If you find a job function that interests you, enter the job title in a general-purpose job board or a job board that caters to a specific profession. Read over the job listing, paying close attention to task, skill, and education requirements.

Don't be overly concerned if you don't find a job description that's a perfect fit for your skills. Other positions may exist that you aren't aware of yet. You may discover a peripheral position that is a liaison between two industries or departments. The job that's a good fit may be a consulting position, which won't necessarily show up on a job board. Or you'll create your own position based on your unique set of skills, interests, experience, and education.

If you're targeting an emerging industry that is primarily in a research and development phase, you may not find a defined set of job titles. You may need to use what you know about the industry and infer the positions that are likely to evolve as the industry matures. When companies within your target industry begin to hire depends on where it is in the maturation process.

Taking Your Research to the Source

When you have a good sense of your target industry, turn your attention to talking with people who work in it. The more you interact with potential peers, the better. Those working in the field you want to work in are your best source of information about its current status, local trends, and problems.

Identifying whom to talk to

Review your personal contacts, friends, colleagues, former professors, former classmates, and family friends. Who do you know who may know something about your target industry or who may know people in the industry? Networking in person can also lead to productive connections. If your professional association has local chapters, attend a meeting to begin building relationships with people who know about your field.

Use social networking connections to identify people within your target industry. You may want to do some preliminary research on your own to target those you'd like to talk with. Check out your network on LinkedIn and Facebook. Try joining a LinkedIn Group for your profession. And pay attention to people tweeting about your industry (www.twitter.com). If your efforts aren't producing the results you'd like, consider reaching out to the people you know to see if they can introduce you to anyone in your field.

Not sure how to use these online networking tools? Worried you don't have an established network? Refer to Chapter 15 for details about how to build your network by using in-person and online strategies.

Being comfortable and confident

When you begin talking with professional contacts, you may feel unsure of yourself and your purpose. You may slip into a rabbit hole that could bury not only your current conversation but future ones as well.

Your contact is not your coach or your therapist. They can only help you if you're clear enough about where you want to go that you can describe your needs clearly and concisely. If you appear anxious or confused or ask them to figure out your career direction for you, you've shifted the dynamic of the conversation. If your contact feels uncomfortable with your confusion or drama, they may not be willing to share what they know or refer you for an opening. The key to a successful meeting is to come prepared and focus on what you know about your own direction. It's perfectly normal that you don't have all the answers about your next career. Your contacts understand that. Avoid is the temptation to turn to them to determine your future.

No one understands every aspect of the green economy. Not me, not anyone. Your contacts know something about their slice of it. What they don't know is how well you'll fit. *You* are the best expert on who you are, what you want, and where you're headed. You must determine which career is the best fit for you and what steps you will take to reach your green career goal.

Conducting an informational interview that builds your credibility

As you prepare to talk with your contact, focus on questions regarding the issues that are at the top of your mind. Begin by creating a clear statement of your direction and your goal for the appointment. As you proceed with your interview, demonstrate that you've done your homework by articulating what you know about a subject and then asking your contact to deepen your understanding, broaden your perspective, or correct your assumptions.

When Joel was ready to launch his search for a green job, he asked contacts if they knew of any openings. Instead of asking, "Do you know any local green companies that are hiring?" he was more specific in his requests:

- ✔ I know about green companies X, Y, and Z in my industry. Do you know any other local green companies I've missed?

- ✔ I know company X is hiring people with my skills. I'm doing research on companies Y and Z, right now. Are you aware of any openings within these three companies?

- ✔ I'm also exploring career options in city L. So far I've identified companies A, B, and C. I know you used to work in city L. Do you know of any other companies I should be aware of?

By stating the information he has already researched, Joel is demonstrating that he is actively pursuing his own job search. He's not relying on others to do the legwork for him. In addition, he is able to ask his contacts very specific questions to expand what he knows, which allows them to provide him with information that is targeted to meet his immediate needs.

As you prepare for your informational interviews, use the following list as a starting point to create your own list of questions for your interview, but don't limit yourself to just these questions. For a 20- to 30-minute informational interview plan you'll probably be able to ask only five questions. Put the important questions at the top of your list.

- ✔ **Understanding your industry in general**
  - "What is the long-term outlook for this industry?"
  - "What are the pros and cons of working in this industry now?"
  - "What areas are likely to grow in the next few years?"
  - Create a question to clarify what you've discovered about a trend, technology, or regulation that is likely to impact the industry.

✔ **Exploring a particular job title**

- "What is your day like?"

- "What are your key responsibilities?"

- "What kinds of projects do you work on?" or "What kinds of problems do you solve for your organization?"

- "Who do you interact with most in your position?"

- "What are your most favorite and least favorite parts of your job?"

- "What kind of training did you have to land this position? What kind of training do you recommend?"

✔ **Researching an organization**

- "What do you enjoy about working for your organization?"

- "What job did you hold when you first started working here?"

- "What do you like most about the company culture here?"

- Ask about a company project or initiative you've discovered.

✔ **Identifying your training options**

- "I want to move into _____ career. I understand that one of my options for training is _____. Do you have other training suggestions to prepare me for this career?"

- "I'm exploring schools S and T. Do you know of others schools I should explore?"

- "I'm familiar with this certification, but I haven't run across any others. Are there certifications you'd recommend?"

If you can pull up reasonably good information on a topic by using Google, you'd be better off doing that research on your own. After you've reviewed the material online, you'll be in a much better position to ask more-detailed and considered questions of your contacts.

Chapter 15

Connecting with the Green Movement

· ·

· ·

*I*t's all in who you know, especially in the green economy. Whether you are exploring your green career options, looking for a green job, or advancing your green career, having a network in place improves your results. Thanks to various social networking tools you can now expand your networks in ways you never could before.

Experts estimate that only 15–30 percent of jobs are filled as a result of online job postings. A full 70–85 percent of jobs are filled through networking connections. In tough economic times, this discrepancy becomes even more extreme. Fewer jobs are filled through official job postings, and more jobs are filled through networking.

By building a community of individuals who share your values and goals, both online and offline, you have more access to key resources, local job openings, news of local companies, and knowledge about the green economy in general.

In this chapter you discover several ways you can build your online network and your in-person network. Don't feel you need to implement every single idea in this chapter. Focus instead on the activities that align with your style and goals.

Even after your career exploration and your job search, your network becomes your lifeline as your career continues to evolve. Keeping in touch with your network, online and off, helps you gain visibility in your field, in your companies or organizations, and in your region.

Growing Your Network Online

These days, your online professional network is a critical asset as you manage all aspects of your career. Although it takes a bit of motivation and dedication to get these online networking systems set up, after they are in place, they become an integral part of how you cultivate your network.

The good news is you can have some fun while building your network. Set aside 15 to 20 minutes a day to create your profile and begin connecting with current colleagues and people you knew in previous jobs, through school, or in volunteer organizations. Before you know it, the process of checking your social networking sites and engaging in conversations becomes second nature.

Always control your image

Think before you post. Always pay attention to what you say on your social networking pages. What you say — about yourself, your coworkers, your employers, and your work — will remain online for a very long time. If you'd be embarrassed to explain an update, photo, or comment to a prospective employer, don't post it. Bottom line, be as professional online as you are when interacting in person.

Be careful not to let your attitude leak into your posts as well. If you've had a bad day or you've had it up to here with your boss or a coworker, it's probably not the best time to post an update. Remember that your comments give prospective employers a view into your personality and your work habits.

Never post comments about a bad interview or a bad job offer. If you choose to do so, keep the name of the company or the person you interviewed with out of the comment. But remember, it's entirely possible that your prospective employer is linked up with you or someone in the office is, and they will be able to connect the dots to determine you are talking about the offer they just made you. That's probably not the tone you want to set for your next interaction with a prospective employer.

Continue to watch the content and the tone of your online posts even after you've become employed. People have been fired for speaking too freely about proprietary information on blogs and social networking sites.

Ultimately, it is up to you to manage the impression people have of you through your online profiles. In addition to tracking your own posts as you make them, you may also want to monitor what others are saying about you. If you are concerned about what may be on the Web about you, do a search on your name with your favorite search engine. Consider variations of your name as well. Review the first ten pages of links to see what's being said about you. If there is something you find offensive, do what you can to erase the damage. If you aren't able to get the offensive material removed, read this Newsweek article (`www.newsweek.com/id/109612`) to understand your options.

Linking into LinkedIn

LinkedIn is the main social networking application people use to create, maintain, and enhance their business relationships. The 47 million contacts registered on LinkedIn represent more than 100,000 companies, 170 industries, and 200 countries. When you register and build your network, you have immediate access to your own contacts, your contacts' contacts, and those contacts' contacts. On LinkedIn, these three levels of contacts are referred to as first, second, and third degree contacts, respectively.

You can join LinkedIn by pointing your browser at `www.linkedin.com`.

1. **Create your own LinkedIn profile.**

   • **Set up your professional headline.** This may be your current job title or a description of your strengths. In this section, you also select your industry from a drop-down menu. Your professional headline and your selected industry appear under your name any time your name is shown to your contacts and contacts who are reviewing your profile.

   • **Create a summary of your professional experience and your goals.** This is a free-form text area that allows you to describe what you've done in the past, what you are doing now, and what you are interested in doing in the future.

   • **Enter your work experience.** Start with your most current position. Enter your title, company, industry, dates, and a description of your position. Then repeat the process for your other positions.

   • **Describe your education.** In this section, provide the name of your schools, your field(s) of study, dates you were in school, your activities and societies, and any additional notes you'd like to add about your studies.

   • **Add additional information.** List your Web sites, blogs, and interests in this section.

   • **Decide how you want people to contact you.** You choose whether you just want introductions or introductions and InMail messages, which are proprietary messages sent within LinkedIn. You also indicate the kind of opportunities you want to receive and the best way for contacts to communicate with you.

- **Upload your photograph**. Profiles without photographs make it harder for people to connect. They may not recognize your name, but if they see your face, they know they met you at the conference last month. Make it easier for people to find you and recognize you by adding your photograph, preferably a photo with a professional image or an image that speaks to your personal brand. A graphic designer might get away with a caricature of themselves, but the rest of us would have a hard time pulling that off.

2. **Add contacts to your profile. Begin by searching for and inviting colleagues you know and trust into your network.**

   Keep in mind that you may be contacted at some point in the future by someone in your extended network requesting an introduction to your first-degree connections. If you don't know your contacts well, you may feel uncomfortable making the introduction. That said, how closely you monitor your connections may depend on your goals. Some only invite people they have worked with or known for a long time. Others have more of an open-door policy and will invite people they met at a meeting or conference (or hotel bar, as the case may be) to join their network.

   Use a combination of the following three methods to build your network.

   - Type in the name of a colleague into the search bar in the upper-right corner of your screen. Review the list of names to locate your colleague. You can narrow your search by using the fields on the right side of your results. Click on the person's name to see their profile. In the upper-right corner, click the link Add ___ to Your Network. On the next screen, indicate how you know your colleague, personalize the invitation, and click Send Invitation.

   - If you know a person's name and e-mail address, you can invite them directly. Click on the Contacts link on the left navigation bar. Then click the Add link in the upper-right side of the header. Although there is a form to add several contacts at the same time, you get a better response if you customize your invitation for each person you invite. Enter one contact's first name, last name, and e-mail. Then click on the Edit/Preview Invitation Text link and personalize your message to your contact.

   - When you receive an invitation from a contact, you'll receive a notification via e-mail (unless you've modified your settings). Click through to the invitation from the e-mail. If you know the person and want to add them to your network, click *Accept.* If you would prefer not to connect, Click Archive. Don't click the link that indicates you don't know the person because doing so impacts their ability to connect with others. If your contact has just sent you the default invitation, you may want to reply to their message to ask them how they know you. With more information, you may be willing to accept their invitation.

If you're concerned about who will contact you if you are listed in the network, don't be. You can set up your preferences in a way that allows you to access the network and control the amount and kind of inquiries you receive from others in the network. Actually, it's recommended that you don't share your direct contact information, but rather rely on the InMail system that's built into the network. You can receive messages without anyone ever knowing your personal contact information.

3. **Begin exploring LinkedIn to get a sense of how powerful the tool is for your career exploration, job search, and building your network.**

    • To search for people based on current or previous title, company, industry, location, and interests, click the People tab in the top navigation bar. When you have a list of contacts, you can then sort the list based on how close their relationship is to you, how often they are recommended, how many connections they have, and how relevant they are to your keywords. You can perform these searches for the entire network or one of your LinkedIn groups (more on groups later in the chapter).

    • Find job openings by clicking the Jobs tab on the top navigation bar. Enter your target keywords and your preferred location information, click Search, and the list of matching job opportunities shows up. If you are a member of a LinkedIn group, you can also click the Jobs link within that group to see what jobs are listed.

    • Use the Questions tab on the top navigation bar to put out queries to particular contacts or everyone on LinkedIn. Use your questions to get an overall view of a particular industry or resolve a stumbling block. You can also answer questions to build your credibility around the topics you respond to.

    • The Companies tab allows you to search for companies by using company name, keywords, geographic location, or industry category. From the list of companies you can determine where the company is located and how many employees work at the company. By clicking the link to the company, you find a description of the company and their specialties, as well as lists of people on LinkedIn who currently work at the company or did work there at one time. Sidebar information provides links to related companies and key statistics about the company.

4. **Explore your own presence on LinkedIn.**

    • The left navigation bar gives you immediate access to a status page that lists updates your contacts have made to their profiles, your groups, your profile, your contacts, and your LinkedIn inbox. You can also explore reading list possibilities, events, and blog posts by your network under the Applications heading on the left navigation bar.

Elsewhere in this book you'll find additional information about using LinkedIn to research your target industries (Chapter 14), finding job openings (Chapter 19), and taking your green career to the next level (Chapter 20).

Tweeting on Twitter

If you think Twitter is just about sharing what you ate for lunch or what your child said at the grocery store, think again. With the right tools, Twitter can become a treasure trove of contacts, information, and resources to help you establish yourself in your target industry.

First you must be clear about your reason for being on Twitter. Is your plan just to chat with folks and have fun? Or do you want to use Twitter to explore green topics, connect with people in your field, or find valuable resources for your career quest? You'll use the tool differently depending on your answer. For the sake of this section, I assume that you are using it to gain new insights and connections within your target industry and the green economy in general.

Begin by going to Twitter.com (www.twitter.com) to register and set up your profile. This doesn't take much time at all.

1. **Join Twitter.** Fill out the form with your full name, your username (which will be included in your Twitter Web address and will accompany all your twitter posts), your password, and your e-mail address.

2. **Set up your profile using the Settings button. The more information you fill out, the more likely people are to follow you.**

   - **Confirm your name and username.** Make sure that they are the way you want them to be.

   After being on Twitter several weeks, I ended up changing my *name* to Green Career Central and keeping my *username* as CarolMcClelland so that people coming to my Twitter page would make the connection between my personal name and my business name. Watch your tweets and invitation e-mails for a while to determine how you want to establish your own Twitter brand.

   - **Enter your location.** If you feel more comfortable, use the name of your region rather than your hometown. Having some geographic anchor helps people get a sense of who you are and how you relate to their world.

   - **Add a Web site link.** If you have a Web site or a blog that relates to your professional goals, choose one or the other. You can also use the link to your LinkedIn profile.

- **Write a 160-character biography**. Be as informative and concise as you can in your description of who you are and what your focus is. This is the only information people have about you when they decide whether to follow you or not.

- **Upload your photo.** Or if you must, a professional-looking logo or icon. If you are using Twitter professionally, this is probably not the place for your Second Life avatar to make an appearance.

- **Keep your updates public.** That's the whole point of being on Twitter.

3. **Tweak your page.** You can play around with the look and feel of your profile page by going to Settings/Design. Ideally, you want to use your Twitter profile to communicate your personal brand. To get started you can choose one of the designs offered by Twitter. You can return any time to customize your profile by uploading a background image. As you connect with people, notice which profiles you want to use as inspiration for your own background.

As soon as you have your profile set up, it's time to get started with your Twitter life! You probably already know that a language has developed around this particular social networking tool. Familiarize yourself with the following list of terms as you get your feet wet. Before too long, these words will become part of your everyday speech. Yes, really!

- ✔ **Tweet:** A tweet is a 140-character message through your Twitter account, your iPhone, or through your TweetDeck. You can set it up so that your tweets (the messages you post) also show up as your Facebook status update (see more about Facebook in the next section). What should you tweet about? It's perfectly acceptable to tweet about what you are doing (especially if you are doing something exciting, interesting, or funny), or to jot down inspiring quotes, informative resources, links to things you find interesting, recommendations, your thoughts on a topic, and things you are celebrating. Let your excitement and passion come through your tweets.

- ✔ **Follow:** Building your network on Twitter is a two-way street. You want to follow people who are interesting to you and you want people to follow you because they are intrigued by what you tweet about. If you see someone tweeting about something you are interested in, click their username to check out their profile and other tweets. Then make a decision about whether you want to follow them or not. You don't have to follow everyone who follows you.

  Follow strategically. These people are your early-warning system for breaking news. They are your research team to help you spot trends and find meaty articles about your topic of interest. They are your sounding board when you have a question. Be selective so that the tweets you receive are relevant to you and worth your time to read. You can always unfollow someone without them knowing you've left their list.

✔ **Reply (@):** By putting the @ sign in front of someone's username in a tweet, you are sending them a message that all those on Twitter can see. You can use a reply to compliment, thank, or congratulate another person. You can also reply to ask a question or engage them in a conversation about one of their tweets or a common interest. Remember, others see these tweets and you want them to because this is one of the ways you become known. Someone new may see your reply, like what you have to say, and then choose to follow you.

✔ **Direct Message (DM):** Use direct messages sparingly, with people you truly know, when you want to converse privately. Some people set up an automated direct message to thank new followers for following. Others find these messages to be a bit over the top. You need to decide where you stand on this issue after you become more familiar with Twitter.

✔ **Retweet (RT):** If you see a tweet that engages you, retweet it to your own followers by putting an RT in front of the original sender's username. Retweeting is much appreciated by the original tweeter as long as you are forwarding information the original author wants to share with the world.

✔ **Hashtags or Twitter Memes (#):** If you find a hashtag, a # with a word or series of letters following it, you can do a Twitter search (see details that follow) to pull up all the tweets that include that tag.

Some organizations create a hashtag for conferences, classes, or other shared events so that everyone tweeting from the event can follow everyone else's tweets. This is especially helpful if you can't attend a conference and want to enjoy the conference vicariously. If you are at a conference, find out what the hashtag is so your tweets can demonstrate your expertise and show the world you attended the event.

Others establish a hashtag to track comments about a particular topic. Watch for #green or #greentweets, which indicate the associated message is about a green topic. Remember, you can use these as a search term to bring up a complete list of these tweets.

Twitter Memes look like hashtags but carry a special meaning and inspire people to tweet in a certain manner on a given day. The first Twitter Meme was #followfriday (sometimes shortened to #ff), used when people send tweets with the usernames of those they enjoy following. A newer Twitter Meme is #ecomonday when people forward the usernames of people who tweet about green topics. Google "Twitter Meme" to uncover the meaning of other common memes.

Twitter tools make your Twitter experience more productive and focused. In fact, they completely transformed my thinking about Twitter. With the right tools you can follow topics, search for key terms, and connect with people who follow the topics you follow.

- **TweetDeck** (www.tweetdeck.com)**:** This free software provides you with a personal browser you can use on your desktop for your tweeting pleasure. You design the browser to show what you want to see. In addition to seeing the tweets from your followers, you can also set up search terms such that any tweets that include your chosen terms show up on your TweetDeck. It's a great way to make connections with those in your field of interest. (Setting up this tool completely changed my experience of Twitter, for the better.)

- **Twitter Search** (http://search.twitter.com)**:** This search engine for Twitter allows you to enter a couple of keywords or hashtags. The results display all the tweets that include those terms in real time. This function is helpful if you want to gain insights about a particular topic, to get a quick update on a current event, or to find other people who are tweeting about the topics that are near and dear to your heart.

- **Twellow Pages** (www.twellow.com)**:** This site is called the yellow pages of Twitter, for good reason. You can add your own listing, identifying your other social networking applications and your chosen categories. In addition, you can search categories for people you want to connect with.

- **Twellowhood** (www.twellow.com/twellowhood) **and LocalTweeps** (www.localtweeps.com)**:** Take your search local. Use either of these sites to search for tweeps (people who tweet) in your local area.

- **WeFollow** (www.wefollow.com)**:** Enter a keyword tag in the upper-right corner of this Web site to pull a list of tweeps who are interested in that topic. A great tool for finding people you may want to follow. You can add yourself to WeFollow as well. As you set up your account, you select three tags you follow so people can find you.

Don't attempt to activate all these Twitter-related services in one sitting! Start with the basics by setting up your account, creating your profile, tweeting, and following. The next step is to download TweetDeck. TweetDeck makes it easier to find people to follow. From there it all begins to snowball.

Networking with Facebook or MySpace

Facebook (www.facebook.com) and MySpace (www.myspace.com) are primarily set up for connecting with friends. As a result, much of what gets posted is very social in nature, with photos, family activities, and partying. MySpace has a tendency to focus on the social side of life even more than Facebook.

You can use Facebook to connect with individuals you know and those you meet. By tracking people's updates, you gain an understanding of your friends' passions and interests. When you discover a shared connection, reach out to them by commenting on their updates or adding a comment on their wall. Use these conversations, whether public or private, to strengthen your relationships.

Although you can't search for people who are interested in a specific topic or those outside your network who work in a specific company, you can browse their profiles and their groups to discover their interests and affiliations. This level of research is not as easy to do on Facebook as it is on LinkedIn and Twitter.

Use your own posts to reflect your green career quest. Are you exploring an industry? Researching a particular company? Investigating a certain green job title? As part of your post you might put out queries or requests for resources to your friends periodically. Be sure to link to your LinkedIn profile so your contacts can read your full professional background when they want.

Beware: Your social networking profiles aren't just for your family and friends to see. According to a recent survey by Careerbuilder.com, 20 percent of employers search online networking profiles for information about prospective job candidates. The good news is that 24 percent of the hiring managers in the study found content on social networking profiles that helped them decide to hire a candidate. Lesson here is to make sure that your social networking profiles and posts project your professional identify.

On the flip side, employers may run into information that's not so flattering. If you or your friends tend to post photos of your social activities on a Friday night or they provide too much information about your behavior or their own, you may need to rethink your social networking strategy.

Review and test your privacy settings to make sure that only your friends have access to your personal profile. Consider starting a networking page on another site to build your professional network.

If you want to step out of the traditional job search box, consider using Facebook to do an ad campaign to target your ideal company or industry. Although this is a fairly new use of social networking sites, the participants in this study, a study by One Day One Job (`www.onedayonejob.com/blog/use-facebook-ads-to-make-employers-hunt-you-down`), **report a number of wins** as a result of their targeted ads. Check out the article for more details.

Discovering Like-Minded People

In addition to using social networks to build your own community, each networking tool has a system to connect with people who share the same values and interests. To expand your network and stay connected to those in your field, consider adding groups to your social networking mix.

Groups are a particularly good way to dip your toe into a potentially interesting industry. You can always drop out of the group if it doesn't match your interests after all.

✔ **LinkedIn Groups** (www.linkedin.com/groupsDirectory): After setting up your LinkedIn profile, click Groups in the left navigation bar of your account. Use the Search Groups fields to pull up groups that relate to your interests. You can sign up for up to 50 groups. Groups let you connect with others, ask questions, review job listings, and read news.

✔ **Twibes** (www.twibes.com): You have probably already guessed that this group is related to Twitter in some way just by the funny name that begins with *Tw*. Use your Web browser to access the Twibes Web site. Then click Twibe Groups to browse the list of twibes. A number of green twibes are listed under Ecology/Green, including one on green careers. If anyone in the twibe uses the group's keywords in their tweets, their tweets are reposted on the twibes profile. This is another effective way to find people you want to flock with.

✔ **Facebook Pages** (www.facebook.com): The best way to access the group search area is to put a topic in the search box on the upper-right corner of your screen. From there you can use tabs to select pages (typically organizations and businesses, groups, and events). Click on each tab to find the entries for your keyword. Another handy and sometimes more effective way to find groups you are interested in is to notice which groups your friends belong to or post about. When in a group, you can connect with others in the group, join chats, post on the wall, and more.

Quality is more important than quantity. Explore your options and then select the groups that are most closely aligned with your needs and interests.

Meeting in Person

Although building an online network allows you to create a broad reach, you can leverage it by building face-to-face relationships that bring your network home, to your local community. Having a strong local community helps you understand your local green economy.

As you prepare to meet people face to face, create a business card you can hand to people who want to stay in touch. Keep it simple with your name, contact information, and a short title or tagline about your interests. Remember, the first impression is what sticks. Investing just a few dollars in a card with a simple design element and professional printing is worth it.

Volunteering

Volunteering is one of the most effective ways to build your local network because you have a role to play, and in that role it's easy to reach out to talk with people you might not otherwise connect with. Through your activities, you are able to build skills that are relevant to your career goals, add leadership experiences to your resume, share your strengths, gain valuable hands-on knowledge, and grow in areas you want to develop.

Volunteer for a cause you believe in, whether it is community based, environmentally focused, or socially responsible. Don't just volunteer because it will look good on your resume. Give your time because it feels good to make a difference *and* it builds out your resume. If you can identify a project or group that aligns with your values and career goals, all the better.

The stronger your personal connection with the cause, the more you can demonstrate your passion and excitement. The people you work with — organizers, sponsors, and other volunteers — will notice and recall the extra zing you brought to the project. You want them to remember you when opportunities come up for media coverage, meeting with a prospective funder, interacting with an elected official, or taking on a larger, paid leadership role.

Set up your volunteer work so it works for you. Perhaps your schedule dictates that you work on a series of individual short-term projects. Or you have the ability to arrange your schedule around a regular volunteer shift on a weekly basis. Whatever you commit to, be prepared to follow through. Do all you can to demonstrate that you are reliable and dependable.

Christine has volunteered for more than 60 different organizations over the last 30 years. She has such a desire to give that she can become overextended if she's not careful. Recently she created a set of criteria to evaluate how she wants to get involved in the organization. First, the organization needs to be close to where she lives so she doesn't expend a lot of time, energy, and money traveling. Second, the group must align with her values, passions, and interests. Third, the opportunity must help her reach her goals in some way, whether it's helping her gain experience, build a new skill, develop a new network, or give her new insights about the field. Taking this more strategic approach to her volunteering efforts has allowed her to focus on the opportunities that allow her to give in a way that also feeds her future.

One of the biggest benefits of volunteering is being able to plug into an existing network of people who share your values. Take the opportunity to get to know the people you are volunteering with. Be available to talk when opportunities present themselves. Be strategic in who you meet by being prepared. Do your homework so you know who is affiliated with the organization. If you discover one of the funders, executives, or sponsors would be a good connection for you, introduce yourself at events, or request an introduction after you've been part of the organization a while.

Although Jonathan was out of work and struggling to build his own consulting business, he remained active and volunteered for environmental groups in his area. During a creek cleanup in his community, the sponsor for the event came over and introduced himself. Turns out he was the president of an engineering consulting firm in the area. He picked up on Jonathan's passion about the environment and the task at hand by watching him interact with volunteers during the day. After a meeting or two, Jonathan accepted a full-time position at this engineering firm. How sweet is that!

When you leave the volunteer organization, ask for a written recommendation for your records. Or have someone from the organization add a recommendation to your LinkedIn page for all to see.

Wondering where to find volunteer organizations in your area? Use the following volunteer categories as a starting point. Exploring your community may bring additional opportunities to light.

- ✔ **Green teams:** Check to see if your city or region has an active green team that is sponsored by the city or has grown from a grass-roots effort. Green teams are very active programs to encourage residents and businesses to go green. Get involved and you'll meet individuals committed to the environment and community. Check to see if your city has an environmentally focused commission where you could play a role in your city's future.

- ✔ **Cool Cities** (www.coolcities.us): Cool Cities is a Sierra Club campaign to turn North America green, one city at a time. Click the map to discover Cool Cities teams in your area.

- ✔ **Environmental nonprofits:** Do some research in your area to discover organizations working on environmental projects or issues. You may find hands-on projects, activist campaigns, or fundraising opportunities.

- ✔ **Volunteer center:** Search the Web for a volunteer center in your area. These centers are designed to match volunteers with projects.

- ✔ **Idealist** (www.idealist.org): Use this search engine to find volunteer activities in your area that match your target keywords and focus.

- ✔ **Networking groups:** Networking groups often need volunteers to keep the meetings going. Another opportunity exists if your region doesn't yet have a green/sustainability networking group. Take the lead to build a group in your community — you'll get to know everyone in the area and they will see you as a leader. Check out the networking groups listed in the section "Taking part in local networking meetings" later in this chapter.

If you aren't able to volunteer in person due to your travel schedule or personal responsibilities, look for volunteer activities you can do virtually. Whether the volunteer organization is in town or across the globe, you do all your work from your own computer. Check out Volunteer Match (www.volunteermatch.org) or Idealist (www.idealist.org) for possibilities.

Attending eco-friendly fairs and festivals

Fairs, festivals, and job fairs also bring people together who believe strongly in issues of sustainability. Watch for local advertising, especially around Earth Day, April 22. You might also do a Web search for green fairs or festivals in your region. While at the event, take advantage of the opportunity to immerse yourself in all things green:

- **Speakers:** Scan the program to discover who is speaking when. Mark the talks you want to attend. Listen carefully, take notes, and ask a question. If you have the opportunity, connect with the speaker after the presentation.

- **Exhibitors:** Review the list of exhibitors before the event to identify any potential employers, interesting associations, or nonprofits. Take advantage of the opportunity to gain new insights about each organization. Pick up their literature or note their Web address for future research. Strike up a conversation about getting involved. Be prepared to express your interests clearly and concisely. You never know who they know or what needs they have. Collect business cards.

- **Sponsors:** Although you may not have an opportunity to interact with sponsors of the event, you can still glean some important clues that could be useful to you in the future. Often larger companies are sponsors. Perhaps you notice one of the largest employers in town is a sponsor of the event. If you didn't know that they had green interests before, you may want to investigate that company more closely in the future.

- **Other participants:** During the day, notice the participants who ask meaningful questions during the presentations or are having lengthy conversations at the booths. If the opportunity arises, strike up a conversation while waiting for a talk to start, grabbing a bite to eat, or waiting to talk with people at a booth.

- **Volunteers:** Those donating their time to support the event are likely to be just as passionate about green topics as you are. If you have enough lead time, find out how you can volunteer at the event and then get to know your fellow volunteers. If you miss the deadline, pay attention to the volunteers that are engaged and happy to be there. Ask them how they became involved. Inquire about what they do in their profession or how they became interested in sustainability.

If you can't attend the actual event, glean as much information as you can from the sponsors, exhibitors, and speakers listed on the event Web site. Use Web searches to explore these groups online. If you find something of interest, call up the organization. Mention that you found their information through the festival Web site. Swing by the Web site after the event to see if they've posted any photographs or videos from the event.

Participating in conferences

Attending a conference for your profession, industry, or trade can also be a powerful experience. Imagine arriving at a meeting where every person in attendance is interested in and passionate about the same topics you are. New ideas, opportunities, and connections often surface throughout the conference.

As the meeting begins, set the intention to soak up as much information as you can about the industry and profession. Listen to keynote speakers, attend breakout sessions, and check out the exhibitors. Pay particular attention to information about cutting-edge trends, technological advancements, and any changes to the business climate due to regulations or incentives.

At times you may feel like you are drinking water out of a fire hose. Use the following strategies to make the most of the conference:

✔ Take copious notes so you can integrate all the details later.

✔ Notice the key players throughout the meeting. Who is running the show? Who is being honored for their contributions over the years? Catch the names of these players and connect the dots as you discover more about the organization.

✔ Meet your peers during breaks, receptions, and meals. If you plan to attend year after year, this part will become easier because you'll be able to build on the relationships you started the first year you attended.

✔ As the conference winds down, take stock of what you've discovered. Is the industry viable? Is it moving in a direction that matches your goals? Do you have the skills you need to succeed in the industry? Or, if you don't have the skills, what should you do to prepare to enter the field?

✔ Do you feel at home with this group of people? Do they think the way you do? Is their assessment of problems and situations similar to yours? Do you understand and laugh at their jokes?

Although it may sound crazy, the last question is more important than you may think. Every profession has a certain sense of humor that doesn't always transfer well. If you found yourself laughing at the humor during the meeting, chances are fairly good you feel comfortable with those in this profession. If their humor doesn't sit well with you, take a hard look at the industry as a whole to understand where the disconnect is. It may be that your underlying goals are different.

If you can't attend a conference, study the Web site for as many clues as you can about the industry as a whole, the key players, and the trends. If there is any indication that they plan to stream any of the talks, return to the Web site to watch them. You may also be able to purchase recordings of the presentations after the conference. Check to see if they've announced their next conference and explore the option of volunteering at next year's conference.

Taking part in local networking meetings

Engaging in networking groups in your community is another effective strategy to build your local network. The recurring nature of a networking group means that you are likely to recognize more and more people each time you attend a meeting. In addition, there's some likelihood that people you know through your volunteer efforts will also attend these meetings. Seeing familiar faces in the room makes networking far more enjoyable and more effective.

Check out your professional association's Web site to discover whether it supports local chapters. Although you may feel a bit uneasy as you enter your first meeting, give it a chance. Let the people at the registration desk know that it's your first meeting so they can introduce you to others. Give yourself a few meetings before you determine whether or not it's for you. Combat your uneasiness by inviting a friend to attend the meeting with you or by becoming active in the organization. Taking on a role gives you a task to do at meetings and allows you to talk with people for a specific purpose.

Local green networking groups are another option. Check out the following organizations to determine if there is a group meeting near you:

- ✔ **Eco Tuesday** (www.ecotuesday.com): This networking forum is for those interested in sustainable business. The group meets on the fourth Tuesday of the month in several major cities and is growing. You can apply to be an ambassador to bring the network to your city.

- ✔ **Green Drinks** (www.greendrinks.org): People in the environmental field from NGOs, academia, government and business, gather for drinks once a month. This group grows organically in many countries and cities around the world. Find a gathering near you on the site.

- ✔ **Net Impact** (www.netimpact.org): This global network is for those using business to change the world as students, graduate students, and professionals. Use the Find a Chapter option on the site to find a map of all the international and United States–based groups.

- ✔ **Business Alliance for Local Living Economies** (www.livingeconomies.org/netview): These meetings are for local businesses, government officials, economic development professionals, social innovators, and community leaders who are building local economies. Check the link for meetings in your area.

If you are receiving outplacement support, check with the organization to see if there's an informal subgroup that has formed to explore green, cleantech, or sustainable career options.

Enrolling in classes

Taking classes or attending presentations gives you ample opportunities to meet people locally. Check your local adult education program, community college, or university for classes or speakers that add to your knowledge about green, environmental, or sustainable topics.

Whether you attend an evening talk or a semester-long course, use the opportunity to expand your network. Make an effort to introduce yourself to the instructor or speaker facilitating the event. Ask a question about the presentation or follow up on a point made during the session. If possible, collect contact information so that you can thank them for their presentation.

Your classmates are likely to share your goals and interests. Be open to engaging in conversation. Participate actively in discussions, study groups, and team projects. Find ways to connect with those who share your commitment to the class, the cause, and their own future. See Chapter 16 for more tips on how to find the best classes for you.

Leveraging the Contacts You Make

Meeting people once does not a network make. A network is a collection of people you can reach out to with questions about your target field, requests for referrals, and information about your local green economy. To create a strong network, you must nurture the relationships as soon as you've made the first connection. After making contact, invite your contact to meet with you one-on-one, develop a strategy to follow up with your contacts, and keep them up-to-date with your progress.

Your first step is to enter your contact into your personal database and to find your contact on your favorite social networking applications. If you can't locate them immediately, check your contact's e-mail signature and Web site for indications about which social networking applications he or she is using.

Scheduling one-on-one meetings

When you meet someone of interest at a networking event, conference, or volunteer activity, contact them to set up a time to get together. If you live near each other, getting together for coffee, lunch, or even a walk may work well for both of you. In-person meetings tend to be enjoyable and establish a strong bond. If you aren't able to meet in person due to geographic distance or scheduling conflicts, set up a time to talk by phone. Don't despair, you can definitely develop meaningful connections through phone meetings.

Planning for your meeting

As you prepare for your networking meeting, take some time to identify your main goals for your conversation. Look for how your needs overlap with your contact's work experience and interests.

Begin by discovering as much as you can about the person. Recall anything you already know from your previous conversations. Then read your contact's LinkedIn profile. (If you haven't done so already, send an invitation to your contact to connect via LinkedIn.) Google their name or company to find newspaper articles or online descriptions of his or her work. You might also explore YouTube to discover videos they've done as part of their work.

When you have a sense of the person, look at your goals for the meeting. What do you want to discover through your conversation? Pinpoint the topics that you think the person will be qualified to answer based on their training, work experience, education, current position, and personal interests. Create a list of three to five questions based on the following goals that meet your needs:

✔ Understanding your target industry in more depth

✔ Identifying the trends, opportunities, and problems facing industry

✔ Exploring possible job titles within the industry and confirming that they match your skills

✔ Determining training requirements to work in the industry

✔ Finding local companies that hire people in your field

✔ Pinpointing potential job openings that would be a fit for you

Refer to the comments about how to use the interview to increase your credibilityin Chapter 14 for specific questions you can ask your contacts.

Remember, first impressions count. Be respectful of your contact and their time. Keep your conversation focused and enjoyable at the same time. Be sure to ask engaging questions that allow them to share who they are. You might ask what they like about their job and how they got involved in the green industry. Listening to their answers will give you insights and help you frame your questions more effectively.

Making the most of your meeting

Use the following guidelines to envision your networking meeting. Generally, this pattern will be productive for most situations.

- ✔ **Spend some time getting to know each other.** Through your conversation, find interests, people, and organizations you may have in common.

- ✔ **Gain more insights about something related to your target industry.** Perhaps you want to discover more information about an organization, a project, or a profession that your contact has experience with.

- ✔ **Toward the end of the conversation, ask your contact for referrals.** You may ask a general question, such as, do you know anyone else I should talk with? Or you may want to be more specific. You could ask for referrals in a particular organization or professional association.

- ✔ **Ask if your contact is aware of any companies that are hiring or may hire in the near future**. Don't ask this question if you are unclear about your career direction and never lead with this question. Build a rapport first. You may even want to wait until a subsequent conversation to get into the conversation about job openings.

- ✔ **Ask how you can be of service to your contact.** Do they need information you may be able to provide? Are they wrestling with any work problems you may have insights about?

Focus on what you know about your direction. Review comments about how to use your interview to increase your credibility in Chapter 14.

Following up after your meeting

After your meeting, be sure to follow up with your contact. Write a thank-you note or e-mail in appreciation of their time and insights. In your note be specific about how your contact helped you.

If you promised to research something for them or to send them a resource, be sure to follow through on your commitment. Your overall goal is to build a strong relationship with this person so you can return to them as your job search develops. You want to demonstrate that you are on top of things, that you are on time, and that you follow through on your word.

Strengthening your relationships

As your journey continues, communicate your status to your entire network. If you change your direction in response to your networking meetings and your own online research, let your contacts know your current goal. Thank them for whatever role they played in helping you gain more clarity.

Be sure to connect with your contacts regularly through your social networking applications. Comment on their posts, congratulate them on developments in their lives, and contribute to questions they may pose online. When you see something that will be of interest to one of your contacts, reach out to them with that information.

When you land your new position or achieve another major milestone, be in touch with your contacts. Networking contacts love to hear about your progress. Continue to thank your contacts as you celebrate your achievements.

Your network continues to play an active role in your career even after you've found your next position. Contacts can help you think out-of-the-box when you are wrestling with a problem at work; they can mentor you as you stretch into new roles, and they can offer support as you move through various professional, and perhaps personal, transitions in your life.

Keep in mind that a networking relationship is always a two-way street. Just as they are helping you progress in your career, you can contribute to their professional development as well.

Chapter 16

Advancing Your Green Education

*W*ith the green economy growing and changing as it is, you will most likely need to update your skills and knowledge periodically throughout your career. Use the suggestions in this chapter whether you are taking classes to test out a new career idea, preparing to move into a new career, adding green know-how to your resume, or maintaining your edge in an existing career.

If the thought of getting additional training makes your skin crawl or your stomach sink, don't give up on your green career goals just yet. Green education options come in all shapes and sizes, from local one-time classes to online courses, from certificate programs to full-fledged degrees. Keep an open mind as you explore your green education options. You may discover a solution that works surprisingly well for you.

Identifying What You Need to Know to Succeed

One of the questions I hear most frequently is what training should I get to enter the green economy? There is no single answer to that question. The training you undertake depends entirely on the green career you target. Refer to Chapters 4 through 6 for information about how to identify your green career goal.

Keep in mind that the training requirements for many green careers are likely to evolve as the green economy develops. As green industries and professions mature, more regulations and certifications are likely to follow. Continue to track education and training requirements as you move into your career to ensure that your skills stay competitive.

Discovering the key topics

As you focus on your target field, develop a list of the skills you need to perform on your job and the topics you need to understand to succeed. Be as thorough and detailed as possible as you create your list.

As you prepare this list, your best sources of information include your notes from the informational interviews you've conducted with your contacts, research you've done online, and requirements you've gleaned from your professional association's Web site. Use the following categories to organize your training list:

- ✔ **Industry knowledge:** What do you need to know about the overall industry?
- ✔ **Professional topics:** What topics and skills are unique to your profession?
- ✔ **Sustainability issues:** What do you need to know about sustainability in general and as applied to your career?

Review your growing list of training and education needs. Look for keywords that seem to define the information you must know to succeed in your chosen profession. You will rely on these keywords later in this chapter to perform online searches for informal and formal education opportunities.

Although you may think you should be able to find a list of training topics online somewhere, most green professions aren't developed enough to have a completely defined list of training objectives available to those entering the field. As various professions mature, these lists are likely to become more available.

Establishing your must-have level of training

In addition to knowing what topics and skills you must gain in preparation for your green career, you must also determine the level of training you ought to obtain. For some industries and professions, the requirements will be fairly obvious. For others, you may need to do a bit of hunting to find the answer you are looking for.

Is it possible to train yourself through a collection of informal opportunities or are you required to earn a certification or a degree? As you evaluate this question, consider the following nuances as well.

✔ Is there one specific path to enter your chosen profession? Must you earn a specific certificate or degree or can you choose from several possible paths to reach your goal?

✔ Does making a slight change to your career goal impact the amount of education you must obtain? Perhaps there's a related profession that doesn't have the intense training requirements.

✔ If you are in a related field already, what do you need to add to your previous education to make the leap to your new profession?

 Understanding the level of training you need to have to enter a green career is important. Before you jump to conclusions about whether you can handle the preparation, be sure to check the facts with several sources. Your first source may or may not have the story straight.

Discovering What Works for You

Green training is available in a variety of formats. The format that works best for you depends on your personal style. By understanding how you prefer to develop your skills and knowledge, you can use your training time more effectively and productively.

 Forcing yourself into a training modality that isn't a good fit for you adds a lot of unnecessary stress to your life. In such a case, training is likely to take more time and effort. You'll have to force yourself to study or work on projects that don't feel right to you. You may not even develop as many skills as you might have with the right training system.

Consider the following questions to gain insights about the kind of training format that's going to be best for you:

✔ **Under what circumstances are you most likely to gain skills and knowledge?** While you were in school was there a particular kind of project or assignment you enjoyed most? On your first few jobs, what helped you become proficient at your work? When you want to increase your knowledge about something on your own, how do you approach the topic?

✔ **What is your primary learning style?**

• Are you a visual learner? Do you gain information by reading about a topic, looking at illustrations or pictures, or taking notes?

• Are you a kinesthetic processor? Do you develop your skills through experience by doing a task, using trial and error, or practicing?

• Are you an auditory learner? Do you comprehend information best by listening to instructions, attending a lecture, or hearing someone describe what you need to do?

✔ **Where do you think, concentrate, and study most effectively?** At home, at a public library, in a café, outside, at your office, or at school?

✔ **Where are you likely to learn best?**

- At a school with a live instructor
- Observing an instructor via video
- At home via a teleclass (a class by phone)
- At home via the Internet
- Through a self-paced course
- By video or DVD
- On-the-job

In addition to understanding how you gain knowledge and skills, take a look at how education is going to fit your lifestyle. What form of education is more likely to blend with your lifestyle?

✔ Full-time school

✔ One course a semester

✔ Evening or weekend classes

✔ Intensive courses that last three to five days

✔ Self-paced classes in a school setting

✔ Internet courses on your own schedule

✔ An internship or apprenticeship

✔ On-the-job training

✔ Mentoring from a successful individual in your field

Use what you've discovered about your own personal style to determine which training options are a good fit for you. If you must tackle an education program that's not a perfect fit for your style, think through the kinds of support and structure you'll need to be successful. Be honest and realistic.

Creating Your Training Plan

As you consider the topics you need to explore, the depth of training you need, and the style of education that works best for you, you are ready to prepare your plan. Your personal plan is going to depend on your immediate purpose.

If you are still exploring your green career options, your immediate goal is to gain more insight about your target career. In addition, you want to confirm that your career direction is a good fit for you. During your preliminary training, you may discover a specific area of your field that you would like to study in more depth.

To achieve your goals, you may want to take a few courses, listen to some lectures, attend a conference, and read a few books. If you feel better with a plan in place, research your options and write out a specific plan to follow. If you prefer to develop your plan as opportunities present themselves, make a list of the topics and skills you want to focus on over the next six months and then take advantage of opportunities that align with your goal.

If you've determined your target green career and you are confident about your decision, your training goal may be more specific. You may need to complete a certification program or get a degree to allow you to move into this new field.

Regardless of your goal, use the remainder of this chapter to explore the range of informal and formal green education options that exist. You may find solutions you didn't know existed or you may discover a combination of ideas that allows you to customize your training plan to meet your specific needs.

Exploring Ways to Gain New Knowledge

Although established degree programs are beginning to take shape for some topics, they don't exist yet for every topic. Depending on your target career goal, you may find you need to create your own training syllabus based on independent study and exploration.

Although you may feel you have limited options due to your geographic location, don't despair. In the following list of training options you'll find several online training solutions that are available to all.

Taking in expert presentations

Hearing an expert speak about a pertinent topic can be a thrilling opportunity. Not only do you gain solid information about an interesting topic, but you also get to experience the expert in person.

Take an inventory of local organizations that offer presentations. You might find a particular bookstore has a regular schedule of book signings. Green or sustainability centers or environmental organizations may be another source of expert presentations.

Don't limit yourself just to in-person events. Look for virtual presentations in the form of *teleclasses* or *webinars* (Web seminar) as well. Your professional organization may offer this kind of event for their members who live throughout the nation.

You may also find interesting presentations on the following Web sites:

✔ Arnold Creek Productions (`www.arnoldcreekproductions.com/SustainabilityShorts.htm`) offers a collection of short clips of speakers talking about sustainability topics. If you find a speaker you want to hear more from, search Google for additional presentations or publications.

✔ GreenBiz (`www.greenbiz.com`) offers periodic webinars on a variety of topics. Enter **webinar** in the search field on the Web site. Then scroll to the bottom of the list of webinars for current offerings.

✔ TED (`www.ted.com`), which stands for Technology, Education, and Design, is an organization that sponsors an invitation-only event where the world's leading thinkers and doers come together to find and share inspiration. Use the list of keywords at `www.ted.com/talks/tags` to identify the videos you want to watch. Be prepared to be inspired!

When you find a source with interesting and relevant presentations, make note of it. Return periodically to check out their calendar or sign up for event announcements to ensure that you don't miss an important presentation.

Reading books

It's said that if you want to know more about a topic than the vast majority of the general public, read at least three best-selling books on the topic. By reading books by several different authors, you gain different perspectives on the same topic.

First, do a thorough survey of the green topics collection at your local library. Whatever you can find at the library is one less book you have to buy. And don't forget to check out the periodicals while you are there.

Check out Amazon.com to determine which books in your field qualify as bestsellers. You may want to read several books on the overall topic of sustainability and then three more books on your specific industry or profession. Use the keywords you discovered at the beginning of this chapter to bring targeted books to the top of your searches.

Read the books mindfully, making connections between issues addressed in each book. Use your favorite study tools to make sure that you retain the key points from each book. You might want to use a highlighter, take notes, or write a summary of each chapter as you work your way through the book.

If you have better comprehension when listening to someone read the book, watch for audio versions of your target books. Listening to a book in your car while commuting or on your iPod while walking the dog are great ways to use time efficiently.

Consider starting with a selection of these books about sustainability. With a strong foundation in the issues involved in sustainability, you'll be able to see your own industry from a new perspective.

- ✔ *Hot, Flat, and Crowded: Why We Need a Green Revolution — and How It Can Renew America* by Thomas L. Friedman (Farrar, Straus and Giroux)

- ✔ *Our Choice: A Plan to Solve the Climate Crisis* by Al Gore (Rodale Books)

- ✔ *Cradle to Cradle: Remaking the Way We Make Things* by William McDonough and Michael Braungart (North Point Press)

- ✔ *Natural Capitalism: Creating the Next Industrial Revolution* by Paul Hawken, Amory Lovins, and L. Hunter Lovins (Back Bay Books)

- ✔ *Green to Gold: How Smart Companies Use Environmental Strategy to Innovate, Create Value, and Build Competitive Advantage* by Daniel Esty and Andrew Winston (Wiley)

- ✔ *The Sustainable Enterprise Fieldbook: When It All Comes Together* by Jeana Wirtenberg, William G. Russell, and David Lipsky (Editors) (Amacom)

Make an active effort to connect the dots between the various books you read. How does your industry approach sustainability? Are there any aspects of sustainability that are being missed within your industry? Any issues that are being handled more efficiently than in the mainstream? As you identify potential links between books, record them. You never know what will prompt you to have an idea that makes you attractive to a potential employer.

Exploring online courses

Whether you want to take a single course or you want to earn a certification on a particular topic, online courses may provide you with new possibilities. Suddenly you don't have to worry about where you live or what your work schedule is. You can take these courses in your pajamas or on vacation.

To deepen your understanding of sustainability, you may want to take a course that gives you a solid foundation in the terminology and philosophy of sustainability.

- ✔ **Sustainable Measures** (www.sustainablemeasures.com) is a site with a variety of information and resources for communities moving toward sustainability. Although not necessarily geared toward the corporate world, you can begin to understand the world of sustainability by reviewing the materials on this site.

- ✔ **Green Supply Chain** (www.greensupplychain.org) provides online sustainability training for individuals, schools, businesses, and governments. You can sign up for an individual course or take a series of online courses to become certified by this globally known company.

- ✔ **Natural Steps** (www.naturalstep.org/en/elearning) provides several online sustainability courses based on the Natural Step Framework that has evolved over 20 years of experience. To gain an overview of the framework, review (www.naturalstep.org/our-approach).

You may also find online courses that are specific to your industry. Use the guidelines in the section "Locating Informal Opportunities That Match Your Needs" later in this chapter.

Attending conferences

As soon as you identify your target green industry, visit the industry association Web site to determine the schedule for the annual conference. Whether you find that the conference has just passed or it's coming up in the next few months, pore over the posted information you find.

Review the agenda, read the theme of the conference, and notice the names of the speakers. This initial scan can provide you with valuable information about your industry that will serve as a foundation you can build on as you explore your target industry.

If at all possible, make plans to attend your industry conference. If pre-conference or post-conference training opportunities are listed, evaluate whether the additional expense will provide you with valuable training and networking opportunities. Scan the conference schedule and make note of the sessions you want to attend. Always note your top two preferences just in case your first session isn't available or doesn't meet your needs as closely as you thought it would.

As you await the next conference, take the time to do some preliminary reading about topics that are critical within the industry. With this foundation, you'll make more sense of the conference sessions. If the sponsoring organization offers any telephone previews of the conference, sign up to get an overview of the conference.

During the conference take advantage of any and all networking opportunities. Visit the exhibit hall to meet the exhibitors and understand their businesses and offerings. You may discover surprisingly helpful clues about your target industry. Meals, breaks, and receptions can be wonderful opportunities to meet other attendees as well.

As you attend the keynotes and breakout sessions, take comprehensive notes even if you don't completely understand what's being said. Each talk is likely to help you fill in blanks from previous presentations. You never know how you'll fill in the gaps. You may find clarifying clues months later as you read a book or talk with one of your contacts.

Enrolling in classes

If you want to take a class in person, check your local adult education system, the community college, or sustainability organizations in your area. It's likely you'll be able to search for these classes online. Rely on your collection of keywords to identify classes that match your interests. Refer to the section "Locating Informal Opportunities That Match Your Needs" later in this chapter for more detailed information about how to locate classes like this.

Another benefit of taking individuals courses is that you can explore a topic of interest without having to sign on for a full degree or certificate program. In fact, taking a course or two can be a great opportunity to confirm that you want to commit to a full program.

Becoming certified

In some professions your measure of success includes the certifications and licenses you hold in your field. To determine whether you need to earn a certification for your chosen field, refer to your professional association, trade association, or the training institute for your profession. You might also do a keyword search **"keyword(s)" + certification** or **"keyword(s)" + license** to find articles or blogs about relevant requirements within your field.

Keep in mind that some certifications are for established professionals to gain more credibility and to demonstrate their expertise. Depending on your field, it may take a few years to earn such a certification. In other fields you must be certified or licensed to do the work without supervision. You'll need to ascertain the facts surrounding your profession's requirements.

The following list of licenses and certifications is just a sampling of the programs available to professionals and trades people:

- ✔ **Certified Environmental Auditor** (www.beac.org): The professionals with this designation evaluate industry operations to determine environmental impacts and compliance issues.

- ✔ **Certified Water Treatment Plant Operator** (www.abccert.org): Those working as operators, analysts, and technologists in the water treatment industry can participate in this voluntary certification program to enhance their career and demonstrate their competence.

- ✔ **EcoBroker** (www.ecobroker.com/eb): Real estate professionals who complete a specific training program earn the EcoBroker designation and help their clients make more energy-efficient and environmentally sound decisions about their property.

- ✔ **Electrician:** Contact your state to find out more about this licensing program.

- ✔ **Greenhouse Gas Accounting and Management** (www.ghginsititute.com): The Greenhouse Gas Management Institute provides several certificates for those who complete one or more courses in greenhouse gas accounting and management, trading markets, offset projects, and verification.

- ✔ **LEED-AP (Leadership in Energy and Environmental Design)** (www.gbci.org): This prestigious certification is for building professionals who have a thorough and current understanding of green building practices. Several LEED AP designations are available.

- ✔ **Professional Engineer (**www.nspe.org/Licensure**):** This license is obtained to demonstrate one's competence in the field of engineering, whether in civil, electrical, mechanical, or chemical engineering.

Be aware that certification and licensing standards may evolve as the green economy takes hold. Keep in touch with your professional association for the latest news on this topic. If new certifications are required, the association may have a grandfather clause that allows current professionals to obtain the certification without meeting all the requirements. If you have this opportunity, jump on it without delay.

Earning a degree

If you are entering a completely new field or wanting to enhance your skills in your current field dramatically, you may find the most efficient way is to earn some sort of degree in it. Your target profession and where you are in your career are likely to dictate the educational path you choose.

✔ **Community college:** At your local community college you may find an environmentally friendly program that fits your interests. It's likely you'll be able to earn an Associates in Arts or Sciences or a certificate based on the number of courses you complete. If you already have a college degree, you'd most likely focus on earning a certificate in a particular topic area rather than a full Associates degree.

✔ **College or university:** If you want to take your education to the next level, consider an undergraduate or graduate degree in your chosen field. Review the list of degrees at your local university or expand your territory and search for the program that matches your goals.

✔ **Masters in Business Administration (MBA):** A number of MBA programs are springing up around the country that have a special emphasis on sustainable, green, or corporate socially responsible philosophies. Many schools offer a mix of programs to meet the needs of full-time students, part-time students, and executives. A few programs even offer a completely virtual experience. To evaluate whether various MBA programs meet your needs, refer to Net Impact's *Business as UNusual* publication (www.netimpact.org and click on Resources and then Publications) and the Aspen Institute's *Beyond Grey Pinstripes* report (www.beyond greypinstripes.org).

Locating Informal Opportunities That Match Your Needs

A combination of courses, presentations, videos, and conferences can provide you with a rich, multi-faceted understanding of your field of choice. The key to staying focused in this approach is knowing exactly what you are trying to achieve with your exploration.

✔ **Create your own educational path.** In some cases, the best way to develop your skills and your knowledge is to create your own training program. Think about what you want to achieve and then build your own syllabus to reach those goals. Tap into a variety of informal training opportunities to develop your knowledge and your skills. Give yourself a bit of room to evolve your plan as you discover more about the field.

✔ **Fill in key gaps in your resume.** Talk to your contacts to determine the kind of courses, conferences, or reading you must do to prepare you for your target career.

✔ **Test out a potential career before taking the dive into a formal degree.** Before investing the time, effort, and money to apply to a university for a degree, take some time to confirm that the field is what you think it is and that you enjoy exploring it. If the course of study isn't matching your expectations, it's much easier to make a course correction when you enrolled in a class or two than when you have been accepted into a four-year program.

After identifying what you want to achieve, your next task is to identify informal training opportunities that match your interests and occur in your region or are available online. Use the following keyword strings in your favorite search engine to pull up a wide variety of opportunities. *Note:* Replace **"your region"** with **online** to discover online training opportunities.

✔ **"keyword(s)"** + **training** + **"your region"**

✔ **"keyword(s)"** + **course** + **"your region"**

✔ **"keyword(s)"** + **conference** + **"your region"**

As you begin to find opportunities, create a list of Web sites and organizations you want to study in more depth. Bookmark the pages of interest so you can return to them when you have the time to review them. You may find it helpful to begin to categorize your finds in some manner. Unless you see an opportunity for tonight or this weekend, give yourself a chance to survey the territory before you plunk down your credit card to register. Although it may feel like you've hit a vein of gold, no one is going to take these opportunities away from you. You have plenty of time to sift through your options and make the best decisions for your short- and long-term future.

Searching for Formal Education Options

There is a wide range of educational opportunities in the green space. To avoid being overwhelmed, define what you're looking for before you begin your search.

✔ **What level of education is required to succeed in your chosen field?** Based on what you've discovered through your research and your conversations with your contacts, are you looking for a certificate, an undergraduate degree, or a graduate degree?

✔ **What area do you want to study?** Identify the keywords that are likely to describe the kind of program you want to attend. Each school may have a slightly different name for their program. In fact, the programs you are interested in may be found in different departments at different schools. Visit several school Web sites before you decide which keywords to use in your search.

✔ **What geographic area are you willing to consider?** Although you may be tempted to focus on educational options in your immediate area, keep your options open as you begin to search for opportunities. With distance-learning options, extension programs, and courses designed for working adults, it's possible you could find a way to attend a school that is outside of your immediate area.

✔ **How much can you spend on your education?** Before you close the door on your education, take a good look at your financial options. If you need some help identifying your options, look at this Web page that describes a variety of funding options for nontraditional students (www.freschinfo.com/strategy-nontrad.php).

Identifying potential degree programs

Start by creating a list of all the programs you know about. Don't worry if they're out of your area or feel beyond your reach financially. You can narrow down your list after you get a sense of the programs that exist.

Begin by reviewing your notes from your initial research of your target field. Remind yourself what your contacts shared about training for the field. Review the professional association's Web site one more time for clues. Add any institutions or programs you discover to your master list.

Then do a keyword search to find programs that you may not be aware of. Use the following keyword configurations to identify programs. Replace **"keyword(s)"** with the keywords that describe your target area of study.

✔ **"keyword(s)" + education**

✔ **"keyword(s)" + degree**

✔ **"keyword(s)" + certificate**

To limit these searches to a specific region, add another term to these search strings: **"keyword(s)" + education + "your region."** Replace the word **education** with **degree** or **certification** to pull up additional options.

If you'd like to explore your online training options, use this search string: **"keyword(s)" + education + online**. Remember, you can replace the word education with **degree** or **certification**.

Don't make any decisions on the fly. Just take all your results and add each program you find to your master list. Include a Web address so you can return later to study the program more thoroughly.

If you're having a hard time finding an education program, reach out to your contacts or professional association again. Be specific in your request for information about educational or training programs that would prepare you for your field of interest. It's also possible that there are no programs in your career area yet. If you are at the cutting edge of your field, you may be ahead of even the educational organizations. If this is the case, return to the section "Locating Informal Opportunities That Match Your Needs" for information about searching out courses, conferences, and presentations.

Evaluating degree programs

Depending on the number of schools you're considering, selecting the best program out of the list may be an overwhelming process. Between the amount of information you receive and the number of possibilities you are trying on, your mind may spin in all sorts of directions trying to figure out a workable plan of action.

Take your evaluation one step at a time. Use the following step-by-step process to stay focused as you move forward:

1. **Get an overview of each program.** When you have a collection of possible programs, read over the material in detail to get a sense of each one. Pay attention to the program description while taking note of any special features that are particularly relevant to your target career. Keep track of the faculty research interests as well. This information is important because most faculty members prefer to guide students who have interests similar to their own, so if you expect to do research as part of your degree program, make sure that their research is relevant to your goals. Double-check that the program prepares you for any additional licenses or certifications you may need.

2. **Compare and contrast the various programs.** Each school is likely to use a slightly different format to describe its program, so you may want to make a chart for each program to keep the details straight. Determine what you want to know about each program and then fill in the details. Don't be surprised if your chart has some blanks. You can fill in those answers in Step 4.

3. **Get a sense of which programs interest you most.** Tune in to your intuition as you study each program. Your sense of excitement, or lack thereof, is a clue worth paying attention to. Make note of what appeals to you about your top picks.

4. **Check out interesting programs.** If you are considering a traditional school, visit the school in person if at all possible. Call ahead to make an appointment to meet with a professor or an admissions counselor. Ask to talk with current students. See whether you can sit in on a class. Prepare questions ahead of time based on the blanks in your detailed spreadsheet. This is a good time to ask about prerequisites and any anticipated faculty changes.

   If you are considering a distance learning format and haven't taken an online course before, take a single course through the school to see what it's like before you commit to an entire program.

5. **Apply to your top choices.** Leave yourself enough time to complete each application with thought and care. For any required recommendations, choose people who have some clout in your target field or a related field. The people you ask should also know your talents and abilities, have a sense of your ability to complete an education program, and be able to affirm your character. Create a packet for each reference that includes a description of what each school wants, including any forms they must fill out, a copy of your professional resume, a list of courses you've taken with them, a list of projects you've worked on with them, a list of extracurricular activities that you've participated in (such as professional association memberships, volunteer activities, related course work, and leadership roles), and an explanation of why you are applying to the program. Be sure to thank your references and keep them informed of your progress.

Applying for a degree program, whether undergraduate or graduate, can be stressful. Reach out to others who have been through the process to help you through the maze. Having a mentor during the application process can make quite a difference. In addition to helping you understand the steps, your mentor may be willing to read over your essays and coach you to develop your vision statement.

Finding Creative Ways to Fit Education into Your Life

Making the commitment to take classes or earn a degree is a significant decision. To ensure your success, take some time to figure out the best way to integrate your education into your lifestyle:

- ✔ **Adjusting your priorities:** With school entering the picture, your life may change form. Make a list of your three top priorities. By being clear about your new priorities, you can make decisions in alignment with your current reality.

✔ **Giving your friends, family members, and coworkers a heads-up:** Tell the people in your life that you may not be as available as you have been and why. If you take care of this in an upfront manner, you're less likely to offend people who don't understand why you've pulled back or disappeared. Warn those you love when midterms and finals roll around.

✔ **Setting aside time to study:** Create a system to stay on top of your schoolwork. Keep up with reading assignments and begin thinking about projects as soon as they are assigned. You are investing too much time, money, and effort to shortchange your education by cramming before tests and rushing to finish projects.

✔ **Finding new ways to get things done at home and at work:** Simplify wherever possible. For example, if doing your hair takes you a half-hour each morning, get it cut in a way that takes you only five minutes. Eliminate tasks or delegate what you can by finding someone else who can accomplish the task.

Talk with friends and contacts who are currently in school or recently graduated. Ask them what strategies they use to maintain a reasonable balance in their life. They may also have tips to help you get acclimated as you settle into your new reality.

Chapter 17

Claiming Your Competitive Advantage

*Y*ou know what you want to do, but now you have to figure out the best way to communicate your value to your contacts, interviewers, recruiters, and hiring managers. This chapter helps you articulate your unique competitive advantage, create a strong resume, and develop your credibility.

If you feel a bit queasy at the thought of figuring this out, you are not alone. Everyone feels that way. It's not easy to take a microscope to your work history and your life to figure out which pieces and parts of it are unique.

The clearer you are about your desired goal, the easier you'll work through this chapter. If you're a bit fuzzy about what you bring to your job search in terms of talents, skills, experience, and knowledge, take a look at Chapters 4 through 6 before you attempt to articulate the value you bring to an open position. If you know what you want to do, but you haven't identified what green industry will allow you to use your skills, take a gander at Chapter 14.

Identifying Why a Company Should Hire You and Not Someone Else

As a job seeker, you are just one voice in a crowded room. The challenge is to figure out, before you begin your active job search, how are you going to stand out and be noticed. Taking the time to create this clarity step by step pays off as you launch your job search with confidence that will shine through to everyone you talk to.

Leveraging your unique background

Instead of slipping into the trap of thinking you are just like everyone else applying for your desired green position, give deep consideration to your unique background. How does your education, passion, work experience, service activities, and personality set you apart?

If you want some help bringing your unique qualities into focus, review Chapters 4 through 6 to remind yourself of your skills and interests, the processes you enjoy, and the problems you are able to solve.

Even if you think your individual accomplishments aren't anything to write home about, think about how your experiences combine to create the whole picture. Perhaps you've had two or three jobs that can be woven together to give you a unique point of view and an unusual set of skills.

Adam has discovered that all the clues he's collecting are pointing in one direction: planning large green conferences and trade shows. As he scans his work history, he realizes that his marketing work for a large company has given him valuable experience as an exhibitor. On occasion, he's also volunteered through his professional association to help organize parts of its annual conference. Working for a caterer in college gave him a unique perspective on the food services aspect of large events. His jobs selling advertising space in both the yearbook and for a large radio show station gave him the sales skills he'll need to pull off large events. He's amazed that his seemingly unrelated jobs are lining up to provide a very strong collection of experiences for his desired work — but he has some gaps in his background. With this insight he can take a few courses and take on a couple of volunteer positions to round out his background before he launches his job search.

It's unlikely that your unique competitive advantage is going to spring into your mind out of the blue. It's likely that you'll need to talk with people in the field, do in-depth research on your profession, and take time to mine your own history. As the pieces fall into place, reflect on the best way to position yourself as a distinct asset for the company.

If you aren't coming up with any brilliant insights about your own uniqueness, don't be alarmed. People often assume that they aren't that special — that everyone can do the things they're good at. It's likely you are so close to your own strengths (you live with them all day every day after all), that you can't make an objective assessment of where you shine. Turn to your family, friends, and colleagues and ask them what sets you apart from others in your field. It's likely that they'll be able to give you a quick answer because they see these qualities in you all the time.

If you're changing from one field or profession to another, you have an even bigger mountain to climb. Not only must you convince the hiring manager that you're a qualified candidate, you must also demonstrate how your unusual background is an advantage to the company. To succeed, you must know the green industry and the company and be able to point out why your experiences with a particular customer base, product, or distribution system give you a unique perspective on their core business. If you've thought this through in advance, you can share a few key points in your cover letter, and then eventually in your interview, that prove your point. The key is to match your strengths to their needs.

Naming your impact on a company's bottom line

In addition to describing how you are uniquely qualified for your target position, you must be able to articulate how your talents and services make a difference to the company's bottom line. After all, that's the question the hiring manager is asking: Are you going to be an asset to the business?

Review your work history to find ways your actions have contributed to your employers' bottom line. Quantify your contributions and tie them to the bottom line as much as possible. If you don't have precise numbers, it's acceptable to provide an approximate number. Just make sure that your references agree with your assessment of your work.

✔ Do you increase the company's income?

- If you're in sales, review your sales numbers for impressive evidence in terms of the number of sales you've made, the size of your sales, or your close rate.

- If you're in marketing, you might look to the effectiveness of your marketing campaign and how the campaign translated into dollars for your company.

- If you're in product development, look to the value of the product you designed. How much money did that product eventually bring your employer?

✔ Do you save the company money?

- If you're in quality assurance, estimate how much money you saved the company by fixing errors before the product was released.

- If you're a buyer, demonstrate how you cut the cost of key materials and parts for the company.

- If you're in customer service, estimate how much you've saved the company by reducing customer complaints.

If you aren't accustomed to thinking about your role as one that impacts your company's bottom line, you may need to spend some time working through this section. Reach out to others in your field to see how they articulated their value on their resume. You may also want to work with a career counselor or resume writers to develop this information.

Communicating Your Value Clearly

Knowing how you contribute to the bottom line is critical to your job search. Knowing how to communicate your value is even more essential. At every step of your job search you must be able to convey your value in person (informational interviews, networking, interviewing) and in writing (cover letter, resume, online portfolio). The sooner you pin down the most effective way to verbalize your target position and your value, the more successful your job search will be.

In many situations your description of what you're looking for is the first information your contacts, hiring managers, interviewers, and recruiters have about you. It's important that this statement is clear, concise, and compelling so you get noticed and get invited in for an interview.

 If you are unsure of your career direction, be mindful of how you introduce yourself. Remember, even if you aren't actively looking for a job, your network is building an impression of you. See Chapter 14 for important information about how to present yourself when you aren't yet clear of your direction.

Creating a powerful summary statement

Spend time developing your summary statement before you send out your first resume. Your *summary statement* should be at the top of your resume under your contact information and should tell hiring managers, interviewers, and recruiters exactly who you are, what you've accomplished, and what you bring to the position. Your statement must engage them immediately with its clarity, focus, and power.

If you're researching on the Web, you may find conflicting information about this topic. Here are some examples of what to do and what not to do:

- ✔ **Useless:** No introductory statement at all
- ✔ **Essentially useless:** Job title: Commercial Solar Sales
- ✔ **Next to useless:**
  - • Objective: Obtain a position at ABC Solar where I can use my sales skills.
  - • Objective: To secure a position with large solar company for a long-lasting position in sales.
- ✔ **Much better:** Dynamic Commercial Solar Sales professional with extensive experience selling large-scale solar power installations to companies with multiple locations. Experienced in all phases of the solar sales process, from commercial prospect identification and qualification to

signed contract, with consistent post-installation follow-up to identify additional opportunities. Collaborated with finance experts and design engineers to create custom large-scale solar power systems to achieve customers' unique goals.

✔ **Best:** Start with the previous paragraph at the top of your resume and add the following section with a bulleted list of expertise areas:

Expertise includes:

- Financing options including purchase power agreements
- Government and utility rebates and tax credits
- Utility certifications
- Commercial solar rules and regulations

As you can see, it's important to get your summary statement right. Your first draft of your summary statement isn't going to be your final product. Don't expect it to be. Begin by jotting down notes about your competitive advantage. Be sure to include your target position and why you are well suited for the position.

Keep refining your statement until you feel comfortable with it. Then test your draft in casual conversation with colleagues and your networking contacts. If they give you a blank stare or tilt their head in confusion, you know you have more work to do. If their eyes light up and they begin giving you stellar referrals and resources or asking you relevant questions about your goals, you know you are on to something. If you feel comfortable doing so, ask your contacts if they have suggestions or ideas to make your statement even stronger. When people understand what you want, they'll be able to help you much more effectively.

 As soon as you nail down your summary statement for your resume, you can use a variation of it as your 30-second introduction at networking events, your initial lead-in as you begin a conversation with a contact, your cover letter introduction, and your answer to the tell-me-about-yourself question during an interview.

Keep in mind that you need to update your summary statement as you identify specific job openings.

Developing persuasive accomplishments

The next important component of your resume consists of your accomplishments in each of your previous positions. To be effective, accomplishment statements must quantify your results in some way, whether it's how much money you made, the number of people you managed, the size of your budget, or how many patents you've worked on.

Notice how the numbers increase the value of the following accomplishment statements.

- ✔ "Managed a team" versus "Managed 100-person team during product launch due to unexpected departure of other manager."

- ✔ "Planned association's annual conference" versus "Planned 3-day annual association conference for 2,000 attendees with 50 exhibitors, completed project 8% under budget, and diverted 98% of waste generated."

- ✔ "Cut customer complaints" versus "Achieved 70% reduction in customer complaints through implementation of quality control measures."

Don't lose the result at the end of the statement — lead the bullet with the quantified result. Why? People read from left to right. Putting the number as close as possible to the left-hand margin is more likely to attract attention.

Before you even begin writing your resume for your target job, focus your efforts on building a database of accomplishments from all your previous jobs. Set a goal to write at least three accomplishments for each position. Don't worry about quantifying the statements as you are drafting your accomplishments. You can add in the numbers on your second pass if that's easier for you.

The key is to articulate how your actions boost the company's bottom line and minimize the company's impact on the environment.

When you have your complete database of accomplishments, you're ready to develop a customized resume for a specific position. Begin by pulling out the accomplishments that align with the responsibilities and tasks associated with your target position. If you don't have a clear sense of the target position, search for a representative job description online. Your goal is to use your accomplishments to demonstrate that you are a perfect fit for the job.

Highlighting your commitment to sustainability

Green, sustainable companies want to hire people who share their perspective. To communicate your commitment to the environment and social responsibility you must develop your resume accordingly.

- ✔ Look to your past jobs for evidence that you made a system more efficient, helped a company use less energy, or found ways to eliminate excess waste.

✔ Review your list of volunteer and service activities to find examples of ways you contributed to the environment or socially responsible causes.

✔ Highlight any leadership roles you've had. In the green economy everyone must have leadership capabilities to champion green efforts within the company and beyond.

✔ Make note of any classes you've taken to enhance your green expertise.

✔ List certificates, designations, or degrees you've earned in the process of greening your education.

✔ Assess whether your efforts to green your personal life are relevant to landing your target job. If you are moving into the solar industry, the fact that you've installed solar on your own home and your neighbor's house may earn you some points. If you want to work in the field of wildlife conservation, your dedicated efforts to relocate the family of raccoons that took up residence under your deck may prove to be a useful story to illustrate your commitment to wildlife.

Be prepared to describe your green, sustainable, socially responsible efforts in detail during your interviews. Although telling your stories may be entertaining, your primary goal here isn't to entertain but to persuade. Avoid describing every twist and turn of your story to make your point. Taking time to develop effective ways to describe your experiences concisely can make all the difference when it comes to making a positive impression in your interviews.

Incorporating relevant key words

Whether your resume is going to be reviewed by a person or scanned by a computer, you want to make sure that the language you use will grab their attention:

✔ Computer scanners are programmed to search for specific words. If your resume doesn't have those words, you won't get past that computer gatekeeper.

✔ Recruiters/interviewers need keywords because they are scanning many, many resumes in a sitting, trying to find the candidates that make the first cut. They literally scan each resume to find evidence that the resume is worth examining in more detail. If they don't see the words they are looking for, they too will toss your resume into the circular file.

If you use terminology from your old industry or terms you've created to describe what you do, you won't gain the attention you are searching for. To succeed, you must get inside of the head of the person programming the computer scanner or the person doing the scanning. It's your job to research and discern what they're looking for and how they'll find it.

To decide what keywords you need to incorporate into your resume, scan the job description if it is available. If you don't have a job description, search for a relevant job description or job listing online. Or do a search on LinkedIn to find people who have a similar job. Read these descriptions with an eye on the key terms. Then review all the descriptions to see which words repeat. *Those* are the words you definitely want to incorporate into your resume.

You need to have the right keywords in your resume each time you restructure it for a different job opening.

Preparing Your Resume for Prime Time

As soon as you're comfortable with the content of your resume, it's time to turn your attention to the format. Generally speaking, your resume should be formatted to highlight your key points with consistent spacing, bolding, bullets, and sufficient white space. I say generally speaking because you actually need to create several versions of your resume to be prepared for requests in various situations.

- ✔ **Creating a resume to hand to your contacts:** Always have a hard copy of your resume ready when you meet with a contact or attend an interview. This version of your resume must be printed on high-quality recycled paper with tasteful formatting that helps the reader scan the resume for key points.

- ✔ **Providing a resume via e-mail:** If your contact can accept attachments, create a PDF of your resume before sending the document to ensure that the formatting remains the way you want it. You can find free PDF converters online with a quick Web search. If your contact cannot accept attachments, you'll need to create a text version of your resume that will look good when your contact opens your e-mail.

- ✔ **Formatting the text version of your resume:** Your text resume should have little or no formatting — just simple line breaks, spaces, and headings. To convert your resume into text, copy the contents of your Word document into a text editor. (E-mail programs usually work as text editors — or if you use Windows, you can find Notepad or WordPad under Accessories in your list of programs.) The text editor strips out the formatting and leaves you with plain text that you can drop in an e-mail. Play around with the formatting until the headings are clear and spacing indicates the sections of your resume. Send your resume to yourself and a few friends to make sure it looks as good on the receiving end as it did when you clicked Send.

- ✔ **Designing an online portfolio:** If you have a specific skill you want to highlight, such as your design skills or technical expertise, you may want to consider creating an online portfolio. Check out `www.mycareerhigh lights.com` for sample portfolios. When you have your site set up, create links from your social networking profiles (LinkedIn, Facebook, Twitter) to your online portfolio.

For more guidance on resumes, refer to *Resumes for Dummies* by Joyce Lain Kennedy (Wiley) for the latest tips, sample resumes, and helpful hints.

Invest as much time as you can creating the best resume you can, but don't use your resume preparation as a reason to avoid your other job search activities. Although it is important to create a well-conceived, typo-free resume, don't get so hooked on perfection that you never hand it out!

Demonstrating Your Expertise

Another way to gain recognition and become known is to create your own content-rich watering hole where people gather to discuss your favorite topic. Although this strategy takes some time and determination to create, the payoffs may be worth the effort in your particular field. Not only do you gain exposure, build name recognition, demonstrate your knowledge, and create a living portfolio of your writing, you also become known as an expert in your field.

Creating your own blog

A popular strategy these days is to build a blog with well-researched, well-written articles about topics related to your target industry. Keep your focus on all angles of your target topic to create keyword-rich posts that keep the search engines coming back for more great content.

Building your own blog isn't hard. The key is to choose the blogging platform that fits your experience level. Here's a comparison of three common blogging systems: `www.bloggingbasics101.com/2009/01/choosing-a-blogging-platform`. And those systems are

- ✔ **Blogger (`www.blogger.com`):** Known as one of the easiest blogging systems to set up. Some may question the professionalism of many Blogger blogs.

- ✔ **Typepad (`www.typepad.com`):** For a reasonable monthly fee you can create a very professional-looking blog that's easy to use. The intuitive interface allows you to get started right away with the help of design templates.

- ✔ **Wordpress (`www.wordpress.com`):** Wordpress has a less intuitive interface, with lots of power in terms of add-ons and customizability. Also you need to find a host to house your blog. If you are comfortable with HTML coding and CSS stylesheets, you may want to consider this option.

Before you begin writing and posting random missives, take some time to define your purpose for creating the blog. Determine your primary topic and the scope of your blog. What is your mission? Do you want to explain a complex topic to general readers? Do you want to share the inside scoop on your target industry? Do you want to report on innovations in your field? Whatever you choose, stick with it. A hodgepodge of articles doesn't make the impression you are trying to create.

Whether you want to set up your own blog or not, begin commenting on the blogs that are well known in your network right now. You can build name recognition within your field relatively quickly by being known as the commenter with astute insights, detailed knowledge, and a contributing spirit. Don't be a know-it-all; be the expert everyone wants on their team.

Distributing your knowledge

If the blog format isn't for you, here are a few more ways you can build your credibility online.

- ✔ If you enjoy writing, consider developing a collection of articles on your topic. Then use an article submission system like www.submityour article.com to distribute your articles far and wide. This strategy is a viable way to build traffic to your blog or Web site as well.

- ✔ If you'd prefer to share your expertise by answering questions, consider becoming an expert on www.allexperts.com. Scan the array of categories to see where your expertise may fit. If you don't see the right topic, you can request that the topic be added to the site.

- ✔ If you like to tweet, build a Twitter account (www.twitter.com) with a professional background and profile. Tweet specifically on the topic you want to be known for. Set up TweetDeck (www.tweetdeck.com) to search for others who tweet about your desired topic. Begin to follow them, and before you know it you'll be part of the in-group.

Filming yourself in action

Images often speak louder than words. Consider sharing videos highlighting your talents, knowledge, and skills for others to see. Choose your topics and presentation style to match the industry you want to enter.

✔ **YouTube:** To prepare, register with YouTube (www.youtube.com) and create your own video channel. As you fill out your profile and set up your page, keep your purpose in mind. If you're highlighting information, remember to set yourself up as a guru. To build traffic to your video channel, designate your favorite videos and connect with friends within YouTube. Making a video is fairly straightforward. Start with your computer camera or a simple camera like the Flip camera (www.theflip.com). Depending on your goals, you may want to interview experts, demonstrate a skill, or create a slideshow with narration.

✔ **LinkedIn:** If video production is more than you want to take on, consider adding a slide presentation to your LinkedIn profile. To post your presentation to your profile, go to Edit Profile and scroll down until you find the Featured Application area. Click See All Applications and look for Google Presentations or SlideShare in the list of applications.

Regardless of where you post your productions, you need to spread the word to get noticed. Include a reference to your YouTube channel or LinkedIn Presentation in your e-mail signature, in your social networking profiles, and on your announcements whenever you create a new piece.

Part V
Activating Your Green Job Search

The 5th Wave   By Rich Tennant

"I'm here to interview for the job of alternative transportation director. I would have been here earlier, but I got lost in your parking lot."

In this part . . .

After setting the stage for your green job search, it's time to take action! In this part you develop strategies to identify target companies that fit your career goal and job openings that match your talents. In addition, you discover strategies you can use in your new green job to prepare you for your next career step.

Chapter 18

Targeting the Right Eco-Friendly Companies

- -

In This Chapter

▶ Deciding why you are researching companies

▶ Creating a list of green companies

▶ Figuring out the best way to gather information about green companies

▶ Exploring your favorite green companies in more depth

- -

*O*ne of the challenges of the new green economy is figuring out which companies in your area are green and sustainable. Although this is a somewhat useful question when you're exploring your green career options, it becomes even more critical when you're searching for a local job opening.

In this chapter you discover how to identify potential companies that match your criteria and how to determine what role you can play in helping them meet challenges and grow.

 When I use the word *companies* in this chapter (and the rest of the book), I'm referring to any kind of organization you might want to work for. You might see yourself working for a public or private company or you might prefer to work for a government agency, nonprofit, educational institution, small business, or consulting firm. Although green job opportunities are available in all these settings, it would be confusing to try to refer to every single one of these options repeatedly throughout the text.

Identifying Your Immediate Goal

You may think there's no need to research green companies unless, or until, you have an active job search underway. If you do wait, you may miss out on a great source of information about your future green career. Discovering which companies are thriving in your industry provides you with important insights about the direction of your industry and your profession.

Think about your immediate goals:

- ✔ If you're in the process of exploring a possible career direction, keep your company search geographically broad. By casting a wide net you identify more relevant companies. Glean as much information as you can by studying the companies' Web sites and other discussions of them online. This initial research enables you to uncover important clues about the kind of technology the industry uses, the associations companies belong to, the vendors they work with, and the customers they service. You can then use those clues to further your research.

- ✔ If you're in an active job search, your requirements for a green company become much more specific. You want a company within a certain commute, with a certain culture, working toward a specific purpose and — oh, yes — with a job opening! Although you may be tempted to focus all your attention on companies with active job openings, don't limit yourself. Keep your overall focus on the companies that are a great fit for you and your skills. With a detailed list of targeted companies in hand, you can leverage your networking connections and create a campaign to get in the door.

Most job openings aren't advertised or listed. The job you want may be open, but if you're only targeting companies with *listed* job openings you may miss the opportunity to apply for that job. To find out which companies have unadvertised jobs, you must tap into the knowledge of your network.

One sure-fire way to derail your quest for a green career is to narrow your focus too soon to only the green companies in your local area. Whether you're in full job search mode or not, take some time to understand the entire industry and its possibilities and trends *before* you start your local search. With a larger pool of companies to consider in the early stages of your job search, you have a better chance of seeing where your skills fit into the industry. Furthermore, your thorough understanding of the entire industry makes it easier for you to differentiate yourself from other job candidates in the interview process.

Clarifying the Focus of Your Search

One of my colleagues has a saying at the end of her e-mails: "If you don't know what you are looking for it is really hard to find it!" This is especially true when it comes to identifying green companies. Although you may be lucky enough to run across a list of the top 150 solar companies or a map of wind manufacturers, many industries don't come with a preexisting list of companies to choose from. Instead you must employ some detective skills to identify the companies within your chosen industry that exist in your geographic region.

Before you jump into searching for job openings, take a moment to create a clear description of what you're looking for. Your search criteria must include a concise description of what you intend to provide to an employer, the kind of organization it is, and your search radius. Having this list of criteria in mind helps you keep your focus as you embark on your search for companies.

Considering the work you want to do

To identify potential green companies, you must have a clear sense of what you can offer. Refer to Chapter 17 for guidelines on how to articulate the way your skills, experience, and education can help green companies meet the challenges they face.

As part of your own clarification process, examine which green industries are likely to need people with your skills. For the sake of focus, start with a list of one to three target industries. If one of the industries doesn't pan out, you can always swing back to the drawing board to pick up another one.

If you haven't yet established the best way to weave your skills, interests, and experience to identify your green focus, see Chapters 4 through 6. Having clarity about your focus is one of the keys to finding your green job.

Describing the organization

With your target industries in mind, your next step is to define the characteristics of the organization you want to work for. Review your past work settings and current lifestyle needs to identify which settings are more inviting to you than others. The clearer you can be about the specific characteristics of your desired organization, the easier it will be to keep your research target in focus.

Don't feel you have to limit yourself to just one picture. Think in terms of your top two or three choices.

To the degree that you can, include the following characteristics in your description of your ideal organization:

- ✔ **Kind of organization:** Do you want to work for a nonprofit, educational institution, or governmental agency? How about a start-up or private company? Based on what you know about your work style, what's the best kind of organization for you?

- ✔ **Company size:** What size company do you want to work in? You may want to consider the number of employees, the overall size of the organization, or their market share.

 ✔ **Company reach:** Do you want to work for an organization with a regional, national, or a global reach? Does your ideal company have a virtual presence or a brick and mortar location?

 ✔ **Company purpose:** Do you prefer to contribute to a particular purpose with your work hours? Perhaps you like to work in a research facility, for a manufacturer, or in an educational establishment.

Nicole knew from past experience that she felt more engaged and fulfilled when she worked in small offices and had the flexibility to work both in and out of the office. In figuring out where she wanted to use her talents, she decided to focus on nonprofit organizations, small companies, and education centers. She also decided that her ideal picture was to work for an organization that had an impact on her region and had less than 50 employees.

If you'd like more help sorting out your preferences on these factors, see Chapter 6 for more details and descriptions of these key concepts.

Setting your search radius

Location, location, location. A green job across the country or across the state doesn't do you much good unless you're willing and able to relocate. Before you begin your actual job search, take the time to determine the boundaries of your search.

Find a map of your area, ideally one you can actually unfold and place on the table in front of you. Take a good look at your region and make note of how far you are willing to commute. Do any of the transportation corridors have a mass transit system that would make a longer commute more feasible? To solidify your vision, literally draw the perimeter of your proposed search territory on the map. As you locate green companies, use push-pins or sticky notes to identify the companies' locations on the map. Having a visual representation of your search gives you a sense of where the key players are in your area.

If you're willing to relocate, think about where you would like to move. Of course, there's a bit of a chicken and egg dilemma here. Do you decide where you want to relocate and then find a green job there? Or do you decide what kind of green job you want and then figure out where you should live? The best strategy may be to work the questions from both directions. Where are the hot spots for your target industry. Of those areas, where would you most like to live?

If you do discover a company that is clearly outside your target area, either locally or in another region, you have the opportunity to make a very conscious decision about whether and how to proceed. The key is that defining your search territory allows you to sort through the trade-offs in a manner that keeps you in touch with your personal needs and desires.

Triple bottom line

Until fairly recently the main measure of a company's success was determined by its financial bottom line. Was it making a profit or was it sustaining losses? Although companies have been managing their activities by using their financial profits as their guiding light for a very long time, many stakeholders have sustained losses while the company's shareholders have celebrated their wins.

Times are changing, and the way companies measure their success is too. Now in addition to watching the financial profits, companies are assessing their impact on their physical surroundings and their community as well. When companies pay attention to the people they touch, the environment they impact, *and* the profits they make, leaders make more sustainable decisions overall. In fact, this way of doing business is causing companies to rethink how they produce their products and provide their services. In the process, the entire company system is becoming stronger.

Although the term *triple bottom line* may refer to specific reporting requirements, often it is used as shorthand for ventures that are socially responsible, green, *and* profitable.

As David researched companies that matched his target characteristics, he noted that several interesting companies were outside his geographic comfort zone. Before he pursued actual job openings, he evaluated how he'd proceed with each company. Working at one company would extend his commute by 15 minutes and the other would require that he relocate within the same metropolitan region. To further his evaluation, he did some additional research about each company and determined that the closer company was worth considering due to its one-of-a-kind technology. The other company was intriguing, but not interesting enough to take his kids out of their current school.

Finding Triple Bottom Line Companies

With your desire to work for a sustainable, triple bottom line company — one that pays attention not just to profit but social and environmental impact — and that matches your career goals, you now need a strategy to uncover companies in your area that fit the bill.

As noted earlier, there aren't many green/sustainable/triple bottom line company lists out there yet. To find the organizations of interest, you must do your own legwork. To put yourself in the right frame of mind for this project, retire your job seeker persona for now and step into your detective alter ego. During this phase, you must be driven to uncover clues and follow them up to find what you're looking for.

As you begin this process, create a spreadsheet and enter each potential company name as you find it. Include as much information as you can about each company's Web site address, location, and type of business. (Later in this chapter you add a few more columns to record more in-depth research findings and your impressions.)

As you search for companies that match your criteria, there's a tendency to want to figure it all out at once. As soon as you find a company name, you try, in that moment, to figure out whether there's a fit. That's putting a lot of pressure on a blind date! By dividing up the tasks you can gather a lot of company names quickly and then later take your time sorting through which companies you want to pursue in more depth. The next section is about how to research each company to evaluate whether it's a good fit for you and your needs.

Surveying media coverage

Media sources are valuable tools as you collect company names for your list. Consider the following sources:

- **Major media sources:** If you're looking for names of cutting-edge companies, look to lists of hot green companies put out by magazines and blogs. *Newsweek* (www.newsweek.com/id/215577) and *Fast Company* (www.fastcompany.com/fast50_07) are two media outlets that come to mind. Use these lists to spot trends, find company names, and take a fascinating look into the future.

- **Local media:** To find companies in your area, check local media sources to see if they've profiled any interesting green businesses or compiled a list of green companies in your area.

- **Niche media:** Web sites that cater to a particular demographic group or geographic region may also provide valuable lists of green companies.

- **Press releases:** Companies that have just launched, received funding, released a new product, or been included on a top green companies list are bound to distribute press releases to celebrate their achievement. In your favorite search engine, use terms such as "**target industry**" + "**press release**" to find relevant press releases.

Following the money

Financial news is also a source of information about green or sustainable companies.

- **Green investor information:** Companies that help individual investors make good financial decisions often provide information about the companies that qualify for their green lists. Some financial entities show you stock quotes (www.sustainablebusiness.com/stocks), whereas others tell you which companies are included in their funds (http://newalternativesfund.com/returns/returns_list. html). The Global 100 provides investors with a list of the 100 most sustainable corporations worldwide (www.global100.org).

✔ **Venture capital updates:** Where venture capitalists are investing gives you a broad sense of which industries are growing, staying stable, and contracting. If you dig into the blogs that report on companies that are getting new funding or additional rounds of funding, you can then track the company's progress as they move their product to market. See this book's online Cheat Sheet (www.dummies.com/cheatsheet/green careers/) for a list of blogs.

✔ **Stimulus fund distributions:** Until 2012, various governmental agencies will be awarding grants and distributing money to local governments, state governments, agency projects, and companies. The best places to track money from the American Recovery and Reinvestment Act are www.recovery.gov and www.recovery.org.

Finding the right lists and directories

Slowly but surely blogs and media sources are publishing lists of the top companies in various fields. When you find a list that matches your targeted industry, celebrate — you've just struck a vein of gold! To locate such a list for your industry, try a search using "**target industry**" + "**company list.**"

If you haven't found a targeted list, you may be able to find the kinds of companies you're looking for on a number of other lists:

✔ **Green energy/power lists:** Several organizations, such as the Environmental Protection Agency (EPA — www.epa.gov/greenpower/ toplists/top50.htm) report on companies that are purchasing the most green energy. This is actually a fairly good objective measure of a company's green mission. *Business Week* recently put out a list of the companies that have reduced their carbon footprint significantly (www. businessweek.com/magazine/content/05_50/b3963415.htm).

✔ **Green business organizations:** Another intriguing way to discover green or socially responsible companies is to identify associations where green businesses are members. Often these organizations, such as the Social Venture Network (www.svn.org), include a list of their members on their Web sites.

✔ **Green business directories:** Although some directories are like typical phone directories, where green businesses can purchase a listing, there are other green directories in which companies are screened to ensure that they meet the directory's standards for sustainability. The Green Pages Directory (www.coopamerica.org/pubs/greenpages) is a good example.

✔ **Job boards:** Although most people use job boards to find job openings, you can also use green job boards to research green/sustainable companies in a particular profession, industry, or geographic area. Most of the larger green/sustainable job boards include an advanced search function that allows you to filter results according to your criteria. (See the online Cheat Sheet at `www.dummies.com/cheatsheet/green careers/` for a list of popular job boards.) If your profession or field has a job board of its own, check that one out too.

✔ **Sponsors:** Another productive source of business names is to look at who is sponsoring your industry's conference or your local community's Earth Day celebration. Any company paying to sponsor an event is either brand new and trying to gain exposure or doing well enough to be able to afford the sponsorship fees.

Drawing on your social networking connections

After completing your own online research, reach out to your network. Be as specific as possible in describing your target company profile to your contacts. With a clear picture of what you're looking for, your contacts are better equipped to provide you with referrals that produce solid results.

✔ **In-person network:** Reach out to those in your network who are connected to your industry. You might send out an e-mail letting them know the research you've already done and asking them what you are missing or what other companies they'd recommend you contact.

✔ **Twitter:** If you've developed a group of followers in your field and related fields on Twitter, create a succinct tweet (what other kind is there?) asking for company ideas. You might ask for names of companies doing cutting-edge work in your industry or companies in your region. Do some homework on your own first so you know exactly how to describe the companies that will match your target range.

✔ **LinkedIn:** As a member of LinkedIn, you can do a fair amount of research yourself on various company profiles. You might search for people who are doing the job you want to have to figure out where they work. Then click through to the company profile to gain insights about the company itself.

See Chapter 15 for detailed instructions on using LinkedIn and Twitter.

Deepening What You Know about Your Target Companies

As soon as you have a list of companies that may meet your criteria, set aside time to research what you can about each one. Remember that these companies do not need to have active job openings at the moment.

Before you proceed, it's time to take your research tracking procedures up a notch. Think about how you process information from multiple sources. Are you better off working online or putting new information into a hard copy format? Or do you have a hybrid approach where you bookmark sites and write your impression into a notepad? Whatever you decide to do, keep doing it. Consistency is going to pay off when you need to look back at your notes later in your job search.

Consider creating a column in your spreadsheet or notebook to insert your rating of each company or organization. By setting up your own rating system, you have a quick way to assess how well each meets your needs. Something as simple as this can do the trick:

- ✔ +: Company is definitely worth more research

- ✔ 0: Company might be okay if there's nothing else on the horizon

- ✔ -: Company isn't worth pursuing

Finding the information you need

The key to gaining insight about your top targets is to keep your focus on your ultimate goal, whether you're exploring career options or searching for a job.

Use the following research strategies to gather the information you need to understand the situation in your industry:

- ✔ **Exploring online:** Start your research online. It's amazing what you can find out about a company by using some carefully crafted search terms. Refer to Chapter 14 for information about researching your target industry. Many of the same tactics can be used to find out more about your target companies.

- ✔ **Mining your network:** Your personal and professional networks are your next best strategy. Who do you know who may know something about the company as a current or former employee, customer, vendor, or colleague? The information each contact can provide varies depending on his/her relationship with the company. Think through your questions ahead of time to choose questions that are relevant, based on your contacts' relationship with the company.

- ✔ **Gathering information personally:** Your interactions with the company can provide a treasure trove of insights as long as you pay close attention during all your interactions. A phone call answered by the receptionist, a conversation with an employee at a trade show booth, and a walk to a hiring manager's office can all provide layers of clues about the company and what they are about. Record your impressions and discoveries so you can refer back to your notes as you try to assess how well the company matches your green career goals.

Understanding what the company does

As you begin exploring your target companies, your first goal is to get a grasp of what the company does and for whom. In this initial research, you want to determine the size and structure of the company and how established it is. In other words, is it in a research and development mode or does it have actual products and services on offer?

To find this information, use the following resources:

- ✔ **Company Web site:** Scour the company's Web site, reading everything you can find about the company.

- ✔ **Online search:** Use a search engine to search for the company name. Read any recent news accounts and their back story if you can find it.

- ✔ **LinkedIn:** Search for the company on LinkedIn by clicking the *Companies* tab. Review the summary of the organization and make note of any contacts you may know who currently work there or did at one time.

Before you move on, remember to record your initial impression of the company on your spreadsheet or notepad, based on what you've discovered thus far. Your quick assessments can tell you at a glance which companies are which and whether you want to pursue your research.

If you want to continuing gathering information about the company, set up a Google Alert at www.google.com/alerts with the company name. Having news items and media mentions dropped in your e-mail inbox is a great way to stay on top of what's happening with a particular company. If you plan to use Google Alerts consistently, consider creating a free e-mail account for these alerts to keep them all in one place.

Digging in to discover what you can do for the company

For the companies at the top of your list, it's time to pull out all the stops. Do what you can to discover the good, bad, and the ugly. To ferret out this information, you are going to have to use all the research skills you possess.

 If your target company is private, very small, or in research and development (R&D) mode, you may have a difficult time getting much information from the Web. If this is the case, turn to conversations with your contacts to garner additional insights. You may also want to invest time in understanding the current state of the industry as a whole to improve your chances of piecing together what you do discover about your target company. As you conduct your research, pay particular attention to the following three categories of information:

- **Unearthing the opportunities the company is capitalizing on:** You want to gain as much insight as you can about where the company is heading. Is it expanding services to a new customer base, adding a new technology, or broadening its offerings? Knowing this information gives you a sense of the future of the company. Keep your eye on industry news, press releases, and the word on the street.

- **Revealing the threats:** Given what you know about the industry, your target company's competitors, and the internal workings of the company, what strikes you as possible bumps in the road for this company? Are you picking up on anything that might derail the company completely?

- **Delineating the problems you can help solve:** After doing your initial research, take some time to outline the problems the company may be facing that you could help solve. Tap into your work experience, education, and training to bring your perspective to bear on the situation. What unique insights can you offer this company?

Evaluating the state of the company

Before you get too attached to working for a particular company, do your due diligence to obtain as much information as you can about its viability.

- **Is the company adequately funded?** Whether the organization is owner funded, investor funded, or donor funded, you need to know whether the company is stable enough to pay your salary on an ongoing basis.

- **Is the company ready for market?** Does the organization have a proven technology or process, an active customer list, and the ability to deliver the product or service to its customers?

✔ **What do you know about the quality of the products or services?** Can you find reviews online or talk to customers to get a sense of how well the company is meeting its customers' needs?

✔ **What's the company's history?** How long has the company been in existence? What do you know about its history?

✔ **Where is it positioned in the industry?** Is the company a front-runner or following along in the pack?

If you're thinking of working for an emerging company, go in with your eyes wide open to the possible risks. If the company is still figuring out what it's selling or is fine-tuning its technology, you have little guarantee that it will survive in the long run. Sure, the ride to the big time may be exciting, but it also carries some inherent risks. Understanding this reality going in helps you make the right decisions for you and your family.

Assessing the company culture

As part of your company research, be sure to pay attention to clues about what it might be like to work at this company. Companies generally don't provide much direct information about their culture. Do your best to discover what you can through your interactions with the company and through conversations with current employees, former employees, vendors, and customers. After gathering as much information as you can, read between the lines to develop a realistic picture of what's happening on the inside.

✔ **Work environment:** Discover what you can about how the office is structured. Where you spend a big chunk of each day has a big impact on your level of satisfaction. If you have the opportunity to visit the company on an informational interview or job interview, imagine working there. Be honest with yourself about your first reactions. If the work site resembles a college apartment, construction zone, or zoo, you may want to consider other options.

✔ **Team dynamics:** Notice what you can about the interplay between various members of the company. Do they have an easygoing communication style or are tension and formality in the air? During your interview everyone is likely to be on their best behavior, so rely on body language and the undercurrents in the office to make your assessment.

✔ **Management style:** Assess this by looking at the entire management team. Do you know anyone who has worked for any of these people in the past? Can they tell you what it's really like to work under them? Your immediate manager also has a large influence on how you experience the management style of a company on a day-to-day basis. As you get farther into the interview process, be sure to evaluate the management style of your potential manager.

✔ **Mission and values:** Read and reflect on any material you find that shares the focus of the company. Its Web site, marketing materials, and annual reports are good resources for evaluating its stated mission. Look for signs in the press and on the premises that the company is actually living up to its mission statement and values.

Confirming that the company walks the walk

You certainly don't want to start working for a company that is all talk and no action when it comes to greening the company. There's nothing more frustrating than going to work to make significant changes only to discover that you've been duped by a very effective green-washing campaign.

Yet companies work hard to project a certain image of their products and their reputation. As you review information about the company, your job is to compare its story with what you are actually discovering. In a nutshell, you want to know that the company is what it says it is. This vetting process is especially important regarding policies and results regarding sustainability, energy efficiency, and carbon emissions reductions.

Take the time to explore this topic as much as you can upfront. Although your efforts may not uncover the whole truth, hopefully you get enough of a realistic picture of the company that you feel comfortable working there or you see the writing on the wall before you sign the employment contract.

In the process of ascertaining what your target company stands for, you may want to look at third-party assessments of the company and its work:

✔ **Awards and recognition:** Do you see any evidence that the company has recent accolades from the media, its industry, or other organizations?

✔ **Affiliations with recognizable organizations:** Does the company have a green business certification icon or a membership with an association known for sustainability or social responsibility?

✔ **Ratings on sites that evaluate performance:** Climate Counts offers a score card on companies' efforts to address climate change. See if your target is listed: `http://climatecounts.org/scorecard_over view.php`. If you don't see your target company there, read up on other companies in the same genre to see what actions they are taking to become more sustainable. Then download the Climate Counts Criteria (`http://climatecounts.org/pdf/Climate_Counts_Scorecard. pdf`) to see if your target company is making any of the efforts listed.

✔ **Corporate social responsibility or sustainability reports:** A number of companies are now publishing reports about their efforts to become more sustainable or socially responsible. You may be able to find a link to this sort of report on the company's Web site. If you aren't successful, do a search by using one or more of these keyword options: "**company name**" + "**sustainability report**" or "**company name**" + "**corporate social responsibility report**" or "**company name**" + "**environmental report**" to pull up a report. You may also want to check out www.socialfunds.com/report to see if the site has a report for your target company.

Chapter 19

Finding Openings for Your Talents

....

In This Chapter

▶ Unearthing green job openings

▶ Getting your story straight for your interviews

▶ Becoming your own boss

....

*Y*ou are getting close to the prize now. You know what you have to offer potential employers. You know the kind of company that's likely to hire you and that fits your needs. Now it's time to make things happen.

Looking for a job is not like going shopping. You can't just pluck a job opening off the shelf and move to the register. It's more like a treasure hunt where multiple players are after the same prize. To have any chance to win you must actively search for clues and adjust your decisions based on the clues as you find them.

The dynamics of the current job market influence your experience. To understand why this is true, compare it to the real estate market.

✔ Too much supply, not enough demand:

- **Real estate market:** When there are too many houses on the market, sellers must work extra hard to snag a buyer. The buyers can make demands and requests, and often get accommodated because the seller is willing to play let's make a deal to move the house. This is called a buyer's market.

  Job market: When there are too many job openings and not enough job seekers, employers must find inventive ways to lure in qualified job candidates. This is referred to as a job seeker's market.

✔ Not enough supply, too much demand:

- **Real estate market:** When there are too few houses on the market, sellers are in the catbird seat. They can pick and choose to whom they want to sell their property. It's the buyers who must impress the seller. This is a seller's market.

- **Job market:** When there are too few job openings, employers don't have to work very hard to fill their positions. In fact, they get inundated by so many queries from highly qualified job candidates that they may not need to advertise their openings. In this scenario, it's the job candidate who must jump through hoops to get the attention of an employer. This is an employer's market.

In addition to understanding the dynamics at play in the overall economy, take a close look at the supply and demand issues within your target industry. If your industry is growing while the main economy is stagnant, or if people with your skill set are in short supply, you may have a lot more bargaining power than you might think. Pay attention to clues within your own industry to understand what dynamics are in play as you search for your job.

Tapping Unadvertised Positions

No matter what the job market dynamics are, the best way to find job openings is to interact with your contacts on a regular basis.

Although you might be tempted to reach out to everyone in your network and ask them if they know of any job openings, this direct question is actually one of the quickest way to shut your contact down. They may want to help you, but if they don't know of any openings or they don't really know you well enough to trust you, they'll avoid your e-mails and phone calls. In the end you'll lose out.

A more viable strategy is to build strong relationships with people who work in or interact with your target companies. As they get to know and trust you, they'll be more likely to share information about an opening when one comes available. You're more likely to receive solid job leads through this organic process than you are by asking directly about job openings in your first conversation.

To unearth viable job openings by building relationships with your contacts, take the following actions:

✔ Be clear about what you want.

- Know what you have to offer and be able to articulate it as clearly as possible (Chapter 17).

- Describe in as much detail as possible the kind of job you want to have (Chapter 18).

- Stay focused on the companies that best match your needs and interests (Chapter 18).

- Reach out to your contacts to find out more about your target companies. Most of your contacts will be happy to help you with your research by giving you solid background information. You want them to agree to this first request so you can build an ongoing relationship with them.

- Use your initial conversations with your contacts to find out what your target companies are doing in the industry, what their work culture is like, what sustainability measures they're taking, and who the top management is. The more you know about the company, the more prepared you are for potential job openings when they arise.

- Ask for referrals to people within your target companies. Search on LinkedIn for possible connections that can help you meet the people you want to meet. Continue your conversations about the company with new contacts you make.

✔ When you find a company that is a good match, take a close look at what they're doing to see how you can contribute. Review your experience and skills to determine how you might fit their needs.

Always be aware of the impression you're making. You want your contacts to know who you are and what you have to offer in terms of knowledge and experience. You also want them to trust you. To facilitate this process, you must build a strong rapport with your contacts.

When a position becomes available in your target company or even another company, your contacts will think of you because they've spoken to you about your interest in the company and know your strengths and talents.

You never know what's going to trigger the announcement of a new job opening. New funding or a new project are the obvious reasons for hiring a new person, but not all positions open up for logical reasons. A number of personnel changes happen unexpectedly from the organization's point of view. Someone may need to retire early due to elder-care issues, another may get promoted or need to relocate with a spouse, another may cut back her hours due to a difficult pregnancy. You never know what circumstances will create the job opening that has your name on it. Just remember that job opportunities do open up, even in a tight job market.

Keeping Yourself in Front of Your Target Companies

As you wait for a job to open up, you must do everything in your power to keep yourself in the minds of your contacts. This is not a time to sit back and wait for things to happen. You must take a very active role in your own future. Pay attention. Be very intentional as you make connections. Review your notes frequently to connect the dots between different people, organizations, and projects. The more you know about what's happening in your target companies, the more likely you are to be in the right place at the right time to take advantage of a new opportunity.

Use these methods to keep in contact with your contacts at your target companies:

✔ **Be helpful.** As you talk with your contacts in a company, contribute in ways that demonstrate your expertise and competitive advantage. You may be able to refer them to a potential partner, help them connect with a powerful strategic alliance, share a new technology, or give them detailed information about a policy that is going to be put in place. Demonstrate what you know in a confident way that is helpful and not annoying.

✔ **Find creative ways to get to know the management team**. Scan your local newspaper's business section and your association's newsletter for upcoming events. If your community has a newspaper that's dedicated to business news, check that calendar as well. If you notice someone from the company is going to make a speech, sit on a panel, or attend a conference, do what you can to attend. Listen carefully to pick up clues about the company's direction, struggles, and opportunities. If possible, arrange to have one of your contacts introduce you to the key player. If you do it right, asking a well-thought-out question during a session can also give you good exposure.

✔ **Share key information and resources.** As you scan the industry news, keep your eye out for articles and announcements that might be helpful to your contact. Send them a quick note via LinkedIn with the link and a short explanation of why you've passed it on.

Don't sabotage your success by putting all your eggs in one basket. Always, always target several companies at once. Even when actively interviewing for a job opening, keep uncovering leads at other companies.

For a while it may seem as though nothing is really happening. You're putting time and effort into making connections, building relationships, and sharing your expertise, but you don't have any job openings to show for your efforts. As long as you're continuing to make contacts and having solid conversations, work through your frustration and keep on keeping on. At some point, you'll reach a tipping point when a number of opportunities may pop at the same time. It's as though you reach a critical mass and suddenly things start shifting.

Employing traditional ways to find job openings

Generally speaking, only a small percentage of job openings are posted. In difficult economic times, when there's high unemployment, companies have no need to advertise their job openings because they have a constant supply of people who are searching for work.

Although it's not impossible to find a job through job boards or posted job openings, the chances are slim. When you look at job listings, don't just limit yourself to looking for openings — use what you find as more input to your research on target companies.

✔ **Searching for green jobs on general job boards:** Finding the right combination of keywords is the best strategy for finding relevant green job listings on general job boards. Although you may not be able to find a job that matches your skills, you may be able to identify companies in your region, determine which companies are hiring in general, and uncover information about job titles and descriptions that

you can apply in your other job search strategies.

✔ **Using niche job boards effectively:** If you can locate a job board for your specific profession, visit often. In addition to using the job board to understand the various positions within your field, you may also find viable job openings.

✔ **Visiting company job listings:** If you are targeting a specific company, check its Web site for job openings. Keep in mind that the career section on any company site is part of the company's PR machine. On this page the company is telling you what it wants you to know, and nothing else. Always double-check your facts by conducting your own research, using other online sources, and talking to those in your network.

Remember, the jobs you find listed on a job board are only a fraction of the openings that exist. Be sure to be in contact with your network to find the job opening you are looking for.

Refocusing Your Efforts When Necessary

Although you don't want to switch up your strategy every other day or week, you do need to be aware of the writing on the wall. If you're uncovering information that tells you that your current direction isn't going to work, you must take a hard look at your strategy to determine your next move.

If you aren't finding the kind of job openings that you'd like in your area of expertise or your region, you have a couple of choices:

✔ **Broaden your focus.** Take another look at your ideal job description. Explore ways you might broaden your vision.

  • Look to another industry. Perhaps your skills could be valuable in another industry that's in a growth mode.

- Emphasize a different skill. How might your job prospects be different if you highlighted a different skill?

- Explore other kinds of organizations. If you've been looking in the private sector, change your focus to look at your options in a governmental or nonprofit setting.

✔ **Relocate.** If you are open to some change, expand your geographic boundaries to see if job openings are available in another area. If you're looking for your first job out of school, it will be worth your while to be willing to go where the jobs are. If you're looking toward retirement, consider moving now to the place you ultimately want to live.

✔ **Rethink your approach.** Talk to a few trusted colleagues or advisors about your job search. Let them know what's working and what's not working. They may be able to offer suggestions to help you redirect your job search efforts.

As you look at your situation, lay out your best options and review the pros and cons. Then put your notes away for a day or so. When you come back to them, incorporate any additional thoughts you've had about the subject. Then notice which idea feels most comfortable to you. Take actions to implement that option.

Prepping for Your Interviews

When you receive the call to come in for an interview, you must be ready! The best strategy is to start preparing long before you even have an interview scheduled.

One of the benefits of prepping for your interview early is that you have ample time to practice describing your skills, talents, and accomplishments in casual conversation with your contacts. By testing out your points, you're able to refine and improve them before you need to use them in your interviews.

For more information about this topic, check out *Job Interviews For Dummies* by Joyce Lain Kennedy (Wiley, 2008).

Crafting relevant stories to back up your resume accomplishments

When you arrive at each interview, be prepared to pull up the details of each of the accomplishments listed on your resume and show the interviewer how your accomplishments prepare you to add value to the organization.

As you begin your preparation, look at the interview from both sides of the table:

- ✔ **Consider the position you are interviewing for.** What does the interviewer need to hear from you to recognize that you are a great fit for the position? If you were in their shoes, what would you want to know about you?

- ✔ **Evaluate your best strategy for demonstrating your value to the company in this position.** What are the most relevant accomplishments that you need to share in your interview?

  - Review the resume you submitted when you applied for the position. At a minimum, you need to come up with stories that illustrate the accomplishments they've already read in your resume.

  - Sort through the complete database of your accomplishments that you created in Chapter 17 (see the comments about how to develop persuasive accomplishments in that chapter) as you built your resume to discover any additional accomplishments.

- ✔ **Create a list of the accomplishments you want to have at the ready during your interview.** Then work with each one to come up with the best way to tell the story. Be sure that your accomplishments highlight your competitive advantage (see Chapter 17), demonstrate the impact you've had on the bottom line of your previous employers, and tie directly to the position being discussed. Be explicit in how you connect the dots for the interviewer.

Long, rambling, unfocused stories won't do you any favors during your interview. Tell the critical points in a few sentences. Practice, practice, practice. Record yourself telling the stories if possible. Notice whether the story is clear and your tone is right. When you feel fairly comfortable with each story, share it in conversation to see what kind of response you get from your contacts. Keep going back to the drawing board until you know exactly how to talk about your most outstanding accomplishments.

Don't even think about winging your interview. Imagine the impression you'll make if you don't remember what you have on your own resume or if you stumble while talking about your previous positions!

Share your accomplishments even if no one specifically asks you to during the interview. Find a way to weave each pertinent one into your conversation with the hiring manager or interviewer. "I think I know what you mean. Let me share what happened to me...."

If you don't share your value, the interviewer won't see you as a good fit for the position and will hire someone else.

Practicing for the big event

It's one thing to work out all the details of your interview presentation on paper or in a spreadsheets. It's quite another to speak about yourself in a clear, concise way. In addition to summarizing your accomplishments, you must be prepared to answer broader questions about yourself, including your strengths and weaknesses, your long-term goals, your passion about the field, and why you feel you are well suited to this position.

Although practicing in front of a mirror is a step in the right direction, it's unlikely you'll receive constructive feedback from your mirror. The best way to build your confidence and refine your pitch is to partner up with a variety of people to practice articulating who you are and to receive suggestions to help you strengthen your story. Consider connecting with the following people as you prepare for your interviews:

- ✔ Other job seekers, either individually or through a job search support group, feel your pain and are prepping for their interviews. Mutual interview prep support can lead to a number of insights and benefits.

- ✔ A mentor who has experience in the kind of work environment you want to work in can be invaluable. Whether they have a history of working for the government, in private enterprises, for educational institutions, or for nonprofits, they'll be able to help you set the right tone for your interview.

- ✔ A career counselor knows the most effective ways for you to present yourself in the current job market.

- ✔ A trusted friend knows you well and can see ways to articulate who you are that you may not see yourself.

- ✔ A colleague knows your work and believes in your talents.

Doing your homework for each company

Don't be caught off guard in the interview by recent news about the company. Make it your business to know what's going on for the companies you're targeting. As you prepare for the interview, review what you already know about the company from your sources. Then update your knowledge for the latest information.

If you've already done a fair amount of research on the company to include them on your list of target companies, you're in good shape. You just need to make sure that you have the latest updates. If an interview comes out of left field, you may need to do some catch-up work to get a good sense of the company and what it does. Refer to Chapter 18 for tips on how to research a company.

To find out information about the company's latest news, read recent press releases put out by the company, recent media stories, and whatever you can find about the company online. Scour the company's Web site for new information, and check out the company's LinkedIn profile as well.

As you scan the resource, notice changes in the following:

✔ Changes in management

✔ Any big announcements, from the launch of a new product to a report about a quality issue with last year's model

✔ New funding

✔ What its key competitors are doing

By demonstrating awareness of the current events of the company, you show that you're investing yourself in the industry and in your job search. Demonstrating your commitment to your job search shows the employer what you're capable of.

Building a list of powerful questions

You can show your interest in the company by arriving at your interview with a set of prepared questions. Instead of the typical tit-for-tat interview exchange, the interview can become an engaging two-way conversation that leaves both you and your interviewer feeling intrigued enough to want to have another conversation.

When you capture interviewers' attention in this way, they'll recognize that you aren't just another run-of-the-mill job candidate. As soon as they recognize your value, they'll want you and they'll start selling you on the value of the company and the position.

Building a list of thoughtful questions takes some time, so don't leave this task to the last minute. *Don't* include questions on your list that you could research yourself on the organization's Web site or Google. Think instead of questions that demonstrate that you already know something about the industry and the company or that reinforce your genuine interest in the company and the work.

✔ **Questions about the work:** What you'd do for the company is of utmost importance to you. Ask about the projects you'll work on, the team you'll work with, the resources you'll have. As you move into the interview process, you may have the opportunity to meet your team and see the work space. Pick up visual and nonverbal cues about what it's really like to work for the company.

✔ **Questions about the company:** An important part of the interview process is for you to gain a sense of the company and how it functions. You might want to ask about the work environment, the culture, the company's long-term strategy, and anything else that will help you determine whether you want to work there. If the company has a good description on its Web site, you could ask for clarification or further detail about some element that's important to you.

✔ **Questions about sustainability initiatives:** Hopefully you've been able to read about the company's efforts to become more sustainable. If it has a sustainability report of any kind, be sure to read it over before your interview. In your questions, indicate that you've read the document and then pose a question to clarify some portion of the report. You might also ask, if it's not already clear, how involved employees are in the process of moving the company to more sustainable practices.

Beware not to sound preachy or pushy about your own beliefs on sustainability. Your job interview is not the time or the place to push your agenda on this topic.

✔ **Questions about your team:** If you're being hired for a management position, ask about your team. You might want to know the size of the group, the experience levels, their morale, their current priorities.

Hold off asking about salary and benefits until those topics are raised by the interviewer in the interview process.

Creating Your Own Position

Under certain circumstances you may be able to create an opportunity in your target company. This is especially true if you want to be in a green industry that is just developing or if you have a skill that allows you to demonstrate to key decision makers what you can do for the company.

Don't get bogged down by what form the job might take. The key is to get yourself in the door to make a contribution that gets the attention of key members of the management team. Whether they hire you as an employee, retain your services as a consultant, or give you a stellar recommendation you can use to land your next gig, you'd be farther along than you are right now.

✔ **Investigating the industry:** The key to creating your own position is understanding your target industry inside and out. You must understand how the industry is structured, what opportunities the industry has as well as the challenges it faces. Although there's a learning curve involved with this option, you may be able to short-circuit the process if you can tap into an industry or function that is in some way related to your previous work experience.

✔ **Knowing what you have to offer:** Take a hard look at the work experience you have. Everything you've done before gives you perspective, insights, and innovative solutions. Leverage that information as you scan your new target industry for problems you can help solve.

✔ **Identifying a problem you can solve that impacts the company's bottom line:** Begin by thinking about ways you can help the company save or make money. With the current economic situation, I can't imagine a company turning away someone who has an idea to save it a sizeable amount of money. Business owners aren't crazy! If an idea makes sense from a business standpoint, they'll consider it.

  • Do you know, or can you come up with, a way to cut costs for energy, fuel, or water? Most likely the solution you discover will be green and help the company become more sustainable. Even if the company doesn't have an initiative to move in this direction, showing them the numbers may open their eyes to a new, more effective way of doing business.

  • Do you have ideas about ways to reuse, sell, or reduce waste in the company's manufacturing process or service? Solutions in this category may save the company money in terms of waste disposal while also cutting costs for new materials.

✔ **Pitching your solution to the key decision maker:** Get in front of the key decision maker and share the results you can deliver. They'll listen, especially if you meet them where they live: the financial impact of your solution. Be careful not to share how you'd implement your full idea. You want to get their attention, but you don't want to tell them so much that they can do it themselves without hiring you.

✔ **Negotiating the contract for your services:** Before you begin to negotiate your contract, be clear about the value of your solution. Talk to others in the field to determine how much impact your solution will have on the company.

You don't have to be approaching the biggest company in your area. Small companies are looking for ways to save money too. Look at the companies in your town or city to find opportunities. Test out your ideas in a small enterprise and use their story as a case study to gain more gigs. If you find a solution you can provide that matches the needs of several kinds of companies, your potential for finding opportunities can double or triple.

By moving in this direction, you are gaining valuable skills, experiences, and accomplishments that will continue to open doors as more and more companies become sustainable.

Making the Decision to Start Your Own Business

If you have a novel idea or know you feel more fulfilled working independently, you may decide to launch a start-up company, run an existing small business, or start a consultancy.

There are plenty of small business opportunities in the green economy:

- ✔ **Green an existing business in your area,** whether it's a printer, dry cleaner, cleaning company, local bookstore, bakery, or some other venture.

- ✔ **Become a consultant.** Leverage your existing experience and expertise to determine your best opportunity as a consultant. Ideas include, but are in no way limited to, becoming a sustainability consultant, energy efficiency consultant, organic gardening consultant — the list goes on.

- ✔ **Come up with a small business that is green from the start.** Take stock of your community. What opportunities do you see to help your area step up to more sustainable actions?

- ✔ **Purchase a franchise with a green focus or green element.** For more information about how to identify a franchise that fits your interests, values, and situation, visit www.frannet.com. Not all their franchises can be deemed be green, but more and more franchises have a green element. More solidly green opportunities are bound to follow.

- ✔ **Develop an online business that has a green mission.**

- ✔ **Launch a cutting-edge start-up based on an innovative idea or technology.**

If you'd like some help coming up with some ideas, check out *75 Green Businesses You Can Start to Make Money and Make A Difference* by Glenn Croston (Entrepreneur Press, 2008).

Evaluating your entrepreneurial temperament

Working on your own takes a certain kind of mindset. Some people thrive as entrepreneurs while others crumble. Nothing is guaranteed when you run your own business. It all starts with you, your vision, your commitment, your ability to manage risks, and your ability to persevere through thick and thin.

To succeed, you must be a self-starter, be able to manage your own time, work with and through a full array of emotions effectively, and know how to move yourself beyond feeling stuck.

Having a clear understanding of your personal style, temperament, and strengths is critical to your success as an entrepreneur. Purposefully choose or build your business to leverage what you do well. You must also know what you don't do well or what you are not well suited to do. Acknowledging these truths allows you to find team members, vendors, or family members to fill in the roles that you know you don't do well.

Sarah is a self-starter with a constant flow of ideas and visions. Although these skills helped her start a business, it's also left her with an array of half-finished projects. To succeed, she realizes that she needs to surround herself with an administrative assistant or business partner who is a finisher; someone who excels at creating and implementing systems, pushing projects to completion, and keeping her focused when she's excited by another new, completely unrelated idea.

To explore additional entrepreneurial characteristics, read this article: www. sideroad.com/Entrepreneur/become_an_entrepreneur_2.html.

Assessing the viability of your idea

Starting a business isn't something you do on-the-fly. You must research your idea, develop a plan, and then test it out. You may need to run through this cycle several times before you nail down your idea in enough detail that it's successful.

Review the following components of your business idea to verify its viability:

- ✔ **Customers:** Obviously your idea must appeal to customers to be successful. The fact that you see that they need what you have isn't enough. They must see that they need what you have and they must be willing to pay for it. Build a profile of your ideal target customer to refine your marketing pitch.

- ✔ **Business model:** As you explore your business idea, make sure that the numbers work. Explore different production and distribution methods to find the one that is most effective. Make sure that your business model is sustainable over the long haul.

- ✔ **Profits:** You must also estimate how your product or services prices out. What can you sell it for? What does it cost you to make your product or provide your service? How much will you need to charge to distribute your creation? All the numbers must line up so you end up with a profit at the end of the day.

- ✔ **Resources:** You must also figure out the materials and resources you need to put your idea into production. If you're going to market your product or service as green or sustainable, you must take the time to assess each input, source the best materials, and track developments as new, more ecologically sound materials come on the market.

If you've never started a business before, take a course on becoming an entrepreneur, work with a business coach, or hire a business consultant to help you evaluate the viability of your idea.

Taking the right steps to thrive

Building a thriving business doesn't happen overnight. Sure, purchasing an existing business or buying a franchise gives you a head start, but it doesn't guarantee full success.

As you explore the idea of creating your own business, build the following elements into your plan:

- ✔ **Define the vision for your company.** Think about the business you ultimately want to have and then lay out the steps you'll need to take to get there. Keep in mind that your vision may morph as you gain more insights about your industry, market, and customers.

- ✔ **Gather as much information as possible about your business topic**. You must be an expert in your field. Attend trade shows, take classes, read books, and stay on top of current news. Depending on the focus of your business and how rapidly your industry is changing, continuing education may be a part of your life from here on out.

- ✔ **Train yourself to run a business.** If you've never run a business before or if you've run a business that wasn't very successful, invest as much time grasping the ins and outs of being a business owner as you do finding out about your industry. Turn to the following For Dummies books as a starting point:

  - *Small Business For Dummies* by Eric Tyson and Jim Schell (Wiley)

  - *Starting an Online Business For Dummies* by Greg Holden (Wiley)

  - *Home-Based Business For Dummies* by Paul Edwards, Sarah Edwards, and Peter Economy (Wiley)

- ✔ **Take the time to develop a plan for your business.** Having a plan helps you keep your focus, stop possible problems early, and track your progress.

  - One Page Business Plans are a great place to start clarifying your thinking. If you aren't looking for external financing, it may be all you need: www.onepagebusinessplan.com.

  - *Strategic Planning For Dummies* by Erica Olsen (Wiley) helps you explore all the strategic, long-term elements that go into planning for your business.

✔ **Work out your financing and pricing.** Before you get in over your head, make sure that you have ample funding and that your pricing allows you to be profitable. If you aren't familiar with assessing the financial side of a project, don't lull yourself into thinking denial is the right answer. Reach out to financial professionals to get as clear as possible about this issue before you open the doors to your business.

✔ **Identify your brand.** Creating a clear way for people to differentiate you from other businesses owners is a critical step in building your business. If you're starting a new business that's never been done before, this part of the process can be challenging because you have to educate people so they understand what you do. You may need to start your business and revisit your brand after you have more experience in your marketplace.

✔ **Develop your marketing system.** Having several repeatable marketing campaigns that consistently create awareness, leads, and sales is crucial to your success. Finding these marketing winners may take some experimentation. Keep track of what you try and measure your results so that when you do find something that works, you know it.

✔ **Build a support system.** Running your own business is an intense experience. On any given day, you may be able to tackle exactly what's on your to-do list or you may be called upon to put out a series of fires. If you don't have a support system in place, being an entrepreneur can be completely overwhelming. Develop a mix of people you can connect with frequently:

  • Make a list of the people in your profession or industry that you can call to ask questions and keep it where you can easily find it.

  • Find other business owners who have a similar business model or business but don't compete with you directly. Be each other's sounding board and brainstorming partner.

  • Surround yourself with family members and friends who believe in your venture and support you unconditionally. Sometimes a friendly voice on the other end of the phone can smooth out the rough edges of the day.

If you find a business that's a good match to your skills, interests, and temperament, you can definitely impact your customers' lives with your vision.

Chapter 20

Taking Your Green Career to the Next Level

*Y*ou've been hired! Congratulations. All the best to you as you settle into your new green career.

Although you may be tempted to think you are done networking, volunteering, tracking your chosen industry, and gaining new skills, you'll be more successful if you keep up with those activities. Staying up-to-date and engaged in your community pays good dividends throughout your career.

This chapter gives you strategies to improve your performance on your current job, strengthen your knowledge, and prepare yourself for your next position when the time comes.

Staying Plugged In

Throughout your job search you focused on building your network. You spent time going to meetings, researching and networking online, reaching out to old friends, and connecting with new contacts. Hopefully you experienced the benefits of building this network of connections. Perhaps you even identified your green career or found your new position as a direct or indirect result of your connections.

Now that you are gainfully employed, you have a wonderful opportunity to deepen your network even more. Even though you may feel too busy making connections at work to keep up with your old networking activities, you should keep in touch with those who helped you get where you are today.

Continuing to nurture your network contributes to your new career by

- ✔ Getting you up to speed with the politics, key players, and priority initiatives in your new company
- ✔ Linking you up with resources you need to thrive in your new profession
- ✔ Identifying key educational or networking events for those in your field
- ✔ Staying up-to-date regarding changes in the local economy
- ✔ Tracking developments in your industry
- ✔ Being aware of personnel changes throughout your profession

Your connections are an asset for your long-term career success as well. Although it may not sound appealing at this moment, you are likely to make another career move in the future. Having an active, thriving network is likely to shorten your path to your next job. Instead of having to hunt down possible job openings, you are now in a position to be among the first to know about career opportunities. Imagine how nice it will be to be on the inside track of your profession during your job search rather than being on the outside trying to find a way in.

Keeping in touch with your network

As you settle into your new position, figure out the best ways to keep in touch with your existing network. Given your new schedule, you may need to modify your strategies just a bit.

Your first networking task is to share your big news with your entire network. Get back in touch with everyone you networked with during your job search. Share your story. Your contacts will love to hear how you landed your new position. Be sure to include your new contact information as well. You might want to connect personally, with a call or an in-person meeting, with anyone who had a profound impact on your job search process.

Your next step is to update your LinkedIn profile and any other professional profiles you have online. Remove any indications that you are looking for a position and add the description of your new position. Use the Update feature on LinkedIn to share news about your new position.

Then spend a little time coming up with a networking plan that will work with your new schedule. You might consider the following strategies:

- ✔ **Incorporating social networking tasks into your week:** Depending on your company and your position, some social networking activities may be seen as valuable on-the-job tasks. Take advantage of this opportunity if it is appropriate.

✔ **Identifying one or two relevant in-person networking events to go to each month:** Be strategic as you identify these opportunities. You want to find events that will help you in your current position and allow you to keep your connections with former contacts as well. You might want to select one group that focuses on your profession or industry and another group that is a general green networking group.

✔ **Finding a way to stay engaged in your community:** Explore volunteering opportunities that energize you and contribute in some way. You might look to organizations that you already belong to for possible volunteer opportunities. For example, helping your child's school, your church, your local neighborhood association, or your city go green could be beneficial to you on a personal and professional level.

Although you don't want to burn yourself out with too many activities, you do want to find ways to stay engaged and in touch with those outside of your current company.

Broadening your network

As a new employee in your company, you also have ample opportunities to extend your network in new directions. In fact, you'll be inundated with new introductions during your first few weeks at work.

Be proactive and strategic as you make connections at work. Look beyond your own work group to get acquainted. Reach out to meet people in your department, other departments you are likely to interact with, your customers (if appropriate), and suppliers and vendors. You also want to connect with people in your profession, especially if you've just entered your field, and with colleagues who have your role in other companies.

In addition to connecting with people on LinkedIn, be sure to collect contact information from those you meet. Maintain a database at work and at home so that you retain their contact information when you leave your current position.

One of the most effective ways to build strong connections with new contacts is to meet with people in person. When you find someone who would be good for you to know, invite them to lunch or coffee. Keep nurturing your key connections as you get established in your new role.

Remember that networking is always a two-way street. Although you may have been more on the receiving end of your networking relationships while you were in job search mode, now is a perfect opportunity to be available to help others who are out of work or looking for a way into a new field, new profession, or a new company. Giving to others now makes you more memorable to them when you need assistance in the future.

Expanding What You Know

The green economy is evolving every day. With every news cycle are announcements of new policies, new incentives, and new regulations. Company press releases announce new funding, new technologies, new processes, and new systems.

If you stick with what you know, you're going to be behind before you even start! The key to staying competitive is to continuously enhancing your skills and knowledge. As you settle into your new position, be aware of the skills you'll need to move to other positions within your current company. If you are not yet in your ultimate green career, continue to search for ways to prepare for your next green career as well.

On-the-job training

The most time-efficient and cost-effective way to expand your skills is to take advantage of training opportunities on the job. Watch for the following training options at work:

- ✔ If you're in a new position, you're likely to attend classes or get personalized training to master your current responsibilities.

- ✔ It's also possible that your company will send you to conferences, workshops, and training sessions for topics that are relevant to your current position.

- ✔ You may discover online training options or local training opportunities that your company might fund if you can tie the content directly to your current responsibilities.

- ✔ As you grow into your position, you're in a perfect position to reach out to others for more informal training. Set up conversations with co-workers in other areas of the company to see how their departments interface with your department. Getting a picture of how the organization works gives you a powerful foundation for your own development.

- ✔ If it makes sense for your chosen profession, explore certification opportunities. Talk to your manager to assess whether the company will fund this kind of development or if you need to finance it yourself. If the certification will open doors for you in the future, it may be worth obtaining the certificate even if you do have to pay for it yourself.

Exploring beyond the job

To develop skills or enhance your knowledge beyond what is required for your current position, you may want to invest your time in getting more training on your own:

- ✔ Reading books or listening to books on tape is one of the easiest ways to expand your knowledge. Take a book when you travel, read at night, or find a pocket of quiet time during the day for reading.

- ✔ A number of organizations are providing online courses on a variety of sustainability subjects. These self-paced courses offer a timesaving alternative to in-person courses.

- ✔ Check out courses at your local university, community college, or green organization. You may find an evening or weekend course you can take to add to your knowledge on a particular topic.

- ✔ If you prefer hands-on training, search for opportunities to volunteer on projects at work or outside of work. In addition to developing new skills, you'll have some accomplishments to add to your resume.

Scanning the Horizon for Opportunities

One of the best ways to demonstrate your value to the company is by keeping your eye on developments in your industry and profession and bringing word back to your employer about how those changes are likely to impact the company and the industry as a whole. Showing your company how to guard against problems looming on the horizon or act on opportunities makes you a very valuable employee.

Tracking new trends in your industry

To identify upcoming trends and isolate potential problems, you must take an active role in scanning news of your industry. Begin by implementing the tactics described in Chapter 14 to track trends in your industry. Be sure to use Twitter searches, Google alerts, and an RSS feed of your industry blogs to get real-time announcements of developments.

You may also have additional means available to you as an industry insider. Perhaps there's a discussion forum you have access to as a member of your profession. Your professional association or trade organization may have an alert system in place for announcements of key developments. Visit your professional portals sign-up for these announcements.

As you become more familiar with your industry and company, you'll develop a sense of who knows the field inside and out. Keep your eyes open for someone in your network who has a deep understanding of your industry. Get in the habit of taking them to lunch every six months to get the straight scoop and hear about the industry comings and goings.

Although professional conferences can be expensive, they can also be a treasure trove of information about upcoming trends, key technological developments, and long-term issues. Do what you must to attend these conferences. Split the cost with your employer if necessary. Be sure to bring back valuable insights and predictions to demonstrate that the fees were well spent. Use your time at the conference to build strong relationships that you can count on in the future.

Paying attention to changes within your company

Keep your eye on unfolding news within your company as well. If you're part of a small company, this task may not be very hard. If your company is large and multi-faceted, you might want to set up a Google alert or Tweet search for your company name and key products or services you offer. Having real-time news coming to your inbox will help you stay on top of what the media is saying, what customers are sharing, and what your company is announcing.

Make it a habit to check out your company's press releases as well. Someone in your PR department is busy making announcements that may have bearing on your work. Some of those announcements may be trickling down to you, but others may not.

Be aware of personnel changes in your company, as they may be the first signal of a change in strategy or emphasis within the company. If you link up with your contacts in the company, your daily LinkedIn updates may alert you to unexpected changes in their employment status or job title. You never know how subtle clues may shine light on a new development.

Don't just rely on your online sources to know what's happening within your company. Be a part of the conversation at the proverbial water cooler as well. You may connect with people outside your usual circle of contacts in the cafeteria, out at local lunch places, or at the gym. These connections can provide valuable insights about developments within your company.

Studying the moves of other companies

You may also discover valuable information by tracking your direct competitors and companies in your region. Many of the same tactics I describe in Chapter 14 can be put to use here as well.

You might want to develop relationships with colleagues at related companies as appropriate. Clearly, you don't want to give away any company secrets to your fiercest competitor, but you do want to have cordial interactions that provide insights about the direction, performance, and opportunities the other company is pursuing.

You may also find value in making connections within companies in analogous industries, vendors, or suppliers. Your networking meetings should give you opportunities to meet people from these organizations.

Plotting Your Next Career Move

Although it may not seem possible or probable right now, chances are good that you will want to transition into a new position at some point in the future. Whether you choose to switch jobs or you are forced to, change happens!

- ✔ If you're in the field you want to be in, your change may be a lateral move to another company in the same industry, doing the work you are doing now.
- ✔ If you aren't yet in your desired target field, you may choose to make another move to attain your green career goal.
- ✔ If your industry or profession changes in some way, you may find yourself looking for a job because the landscape of the green economy has shifted in an unexpected way.

Instead of being caught off guard by any of these potential changes, be aware of possible next steps in your career. As you build your network, always keep the needs of your current position in mind while also looking to your own future direction.

Positioning yourself for the future

Every six months or so take stock of your current situation. What's working in your current position? What could be working better? In what ways are you satisfied? In what ways are you frustrated?

Staying in tune with how you feel about your industry, your work, and your work environment allows you to make changes before you're locked into a bad situation. Although you don't want to create the impression that you're a revolving door employee, you do need to manage your own career and move to the next position when the time is right for you.

As you assess your current situation, whether it is good or bad at the moment, always think about where you'd like to go next. Revisit Chapters 4, 5, and 6 periodically to review your interests, skills, and possible career directions. Update anything that feels outdated so that your lists of favorite interests and strengths reflect who you are now. Brainstorm possible options within your current field or identify your next field.

As you connect with members of your network, talk to them about your interests in a casual, exploratory way. Begin to get a sense of the possibilities for your next professional move.

Finding creative ways to prepare

As soon as you identify a target or two, begin taking steps to prepare for your future. Review your resume and activities to determine what you need to add to move into your target field in the future. The sooner you identify what you need, the more time you have to put the pieces in place.

Be creative. Obviously your current job responsibilities are your first priority, but that doesn't mean you need to bury yourself in that role 24/7. Find ways to take strategic actions that help you gain skills, build your network, enhance your training, and strengthen your experience.

Look for opportunities at work or in your personal life to build out your resume. Participate on committees, volunteer to be a liaison to the department you want to move into, help plan a meeting that will put you in contact with people you want to meet, or head up a green project that's beyond your current job description and in alignment with your career aspirations.

When you put yourself out there, you never know who'll notice your initiative, your drive, and your creative spirit.

Part VI
The Part of Tens

The 5th Wave   By Rich Tennant

@RICHTENNANT

"Excuse me—is this the organization devoted to preserving our woodlands?"

In this part . . .

Landing your green career is a journey of discovery. In this part you find ten green career resources to help you move your quest forward. In addition, you discover strategies you can apply right now to green your resume while you green your current job.

Chapter 21

Ten Great Green Career Resources

*B*eing on top of the issues, trends, and innovations is the name of the game in the green economy. The more you know, the more you shine and the more valuable you become to potential employers.

In researching this book I identified far more than ten great green resources. To pass these gems on to you, I've placed the links into ten categories. Just scan the headings to find materials that can help you with your green career.

Making Sense of Global Warming

Although there are a number of good reasons to create a sustainable economy, one of the biggest motivators is the state of the Earth's climate. Familiarizing yourself with the issues of global warming, climate change, and related issues provides you with a strong foundation for your green career. In addition, having an overview of the general concepts and issues helps you determine where you want to focus your time, energy, and talents in your career.

By exploring these topics from several perspectives, you can pick up nuances and facts that strengthen your knowledge. Repetition is also a handy way to commit these topics to memory so that when others discuss them, you can follow the conversation and contribute in a meaningful way.

✔ National Geographic's Environment site has an in-depth section on global warming that includes discussions about its causes, effects, and solutions, plus science and alternative energy sources: http://environment. nationalgeographic.com/environment/global-warming.

✔ The Natural Resources Defense Council provides a detailed Q&A on Global Warming Basics (www.nrdc.org/globalWarming/f101.asp) and a five-step plan to solve global warming (www.nrdc.org/globalWarming).

✔ The National Oceanic and Atmospheric Administration's National Weather Service has produced an informative two-page brochure on climate change that addresses natural climate fluctuations as well as those influenced by human activity on the planet: www.weather.gov/om/ brochures/climate/Climatechange.pdf.

With a firm foundation of the basic issues under your belt, take the next step to discover how these issues are impacting different regions of the U.S. and the world. With this information, you may be able to discover a specific need that must be addressed in your area.

✔ The United States Global Change Research Program spotlights the key climate change issues and illustrates their impact on each region of the country and each sector of the economy. When you land on the home page, scroll down to the map to explore the impact of global changes on your region (www.globalchange.gov).

✔ In the book *Hot, Flat, and Crowded: Why We Need a Green Revolution and How It Can Renew America*, Thomas Friedman offers his perspective of how global warming issues (hot) interact with two other major trends (flat and crowded) to create a massive opportunity and need for innovation and a new way of doing business. This book will give you an appreciation of the global nature of the problem.

Tracking Legislative Actions

As you prepare to shift into a green career or manage your current one, you must keep your finger on the pulse of the green economy. With new policies, treaties, incentives, disincentives, and funding sources coming into play, the green economy is evolving each and every week.

Although it's easy to get complacent and believe that we've reached a status quo with all things green, that's not true. The factors shaping the new economy have the capacity to bring growth or contraction with the flick of a pen. To have a handle on your target industry, and more important your job status, you must invest time each week in tracking major developments.

- On Green Career Central I've created a Green Economy Timeline (www.greencareercentral.com/greeneconomy) to illustrate major developments defining the new economy.

- Green For All (www.greenforall.org) tracks green collar developments, from legislation to regional programs. This grass-roots movement has quite a bit of clout on Capitol Hill, so this site is a good one to find up-to-the minute actions you can take to move the green economy forward.

- The Apollo Alliance (www.apolloalliance.org) is a coalition that is working to bring about a clean energy revolution that creates green collar jobs for millions of Americans. A wide range of leaders contribute to the efforts of this organization. Visit this site to track legislative developments relevant to clean energy and green collar jobs.

 Your professional association is another important source of news related to your field. When asked to take action on pending legislation, do it!

Following Green Economy Developments

In addition to following legislative actions, you also want to be aware of financial investment trends. The old adage, *follow the money,* definitely applies in the green economy. Understanding which industries and organizations are receiving money helps you ascertain where to focus.

- Recovery.gov (www.recovery.gov) is the U.S. government's Web site to track where the funds from the American Recovery and Reinvestment Act of 2009 are landing. With a simple click you can slice the allocated funds by region, department, and category. Keep drilling down to reach the Web sites for each program.

- Recovery.org (www.recovery.org) is a private venture that illustrates where the recovery funds are heading in even more detail. By clicking your state on the home page map, you can see which projects in which counties are receiving funds. The panels on the home page direct you to the most recent projects, the most talked about projects, and recent news.

- The Green Career Central Blog (www.greencareercentralblog.com) runs two standard posts each week. The Follow the Green Money post highlights several projects that have recently received funding. The Green Career Trends post describes innovations, discoveries, technological advances, and industry trends that are likely to impact the careers in the green economy.

One final component of the green economy's progress is tracking how *green* green businesses really are. GreenBiz.com (www.greenbiz.com) publishes an annual *State of Green Business Report* that evaluates whether green businesses are, in fact, solidly green. One of the most interesting discoveries to date is how poorly our nation's statistics are designed to track green developments. This report shows what's changing and what's not. You may also find gaps that are begging for a solid, well-crafted solution. Perhaps you are the person who is meant to contribute it?

Scanning for Innovation

If you're inspired and motivated by the discoveries and innovations of others, use these sites as your muse. Set aside some time to explore these sites in detail. Clear your calendar. Although you may have a specific interest you want to explore, you can also use these sites to expand your vision of what's possible and discover what is happening right now.

- ✓ TED (www.ted.com) started out as a by-invitation-only conference where people from technology, entertainment, and design came together to share ideas. Now, thanks to technology, these presentations are readily available to all. Hover over the thumbnails on the home page until you find something that intrigues you. Click, listen, and be amazed!

- ✓ Planet Green (http://planetgreen.discovery.com/tv) and the Science Channel (http://science.discovery.com) are adding more and more programming about green, sustainable, and eco innovations. Check your local listings to discover what's available in your area.

- ✓ GreenBiz.com (www.greenbiz.com/browse/design-innovation) reports on innovative designs that bring environmental elements into the mix. Whether they're exploring the bio-inspired designs of biomimicry or the non-toxic creations of green chemistry, new ideas are sprouting.

As you explore new ideas, always dedicate a part of your mind to looking forward. How can you take what you witness and move it to the next level? How might you contribute to bring these innovations into the mainstream consciousness? When you experience the flash of an idea, record it immediately in a place you'll know to return to. A new vision may come to you all at once or you may collect clues from several places before you see the threads of connection. Just one new idea may be the spark you need to point your career in a new direction.

Grasping Green Business Concepts

To thrive in the new economy, it's essential that you familiarize yourself with the issues businesses are facing as they strive to become more sustainable and environmentally friendly. The following best-selling books provide descriptions and background information about key sustainability concepts:

✔ *Green to Gold: How Smart Companies Use Environmental Strategy to Innovate, Create Value, and Build Competitive Advantage* (www.eco-advantage.com) by Daniel Esty and Andrew Winston (Wiley)

✔ *Natural Capitalism: Creating the Next Industrial Revolution* (www.natcap.org) by Paul Hawken, Amory Lovins, and L. Hunter Lovins (Back Bay Books)

✔ *Cradle to Cradle: Remaking the Way We Make Things* (www.mcdonough.com/cradle_to_cradle.htm) by William McDonough and Michael Braungart (North Point Press)

✔ *The Sustainable Enterprise Fieldbook: When It All Comes Together* (www.TheSustainbleEnterpriseFieldbook.net) edited by Jeana Wirtenberg, David Lipsky, and William G. Russell (Amacom)

Refer to Sierra Club's blog (www.sierraclub.typepad.com) for a list of environmental, sustainable, and green book titles. Enter **book roundup** in the search engine to pull up hundreds of fascinating green titles.

Searching for Green Information

With the green economy evolving as it is, it's important to know how to find the latest information about topics that are of interest to you. Starting out, you use these tools to explore your target industries, green concepts, and more. Later, as you develop in your green career, you'll also rely on research to stay up-to-date in your field.

Use the following tools to gather information and additional resources pertaining to your target green industry and career:

✔ **Wikipedia:** If you're just starting your search for a green career, you may find it beneficial to read up on a topic or industry to get an overview before you begin your research in earnest. Wikipedia is a perfect tool for this application. Enter your **"keyword"** + **Wikipedia** into your search engine to find a general description of your topic. In addition to a definition, you may also discover an outline that describes the entire field, links to other pages of interest, key issues relevant to your topic, a historical background, and more. Using Wikipedia as a starting point for your research saves you time by helping you grasp the picture of the entire field in just a few minutes. From there you can drill down to discover the specific areas you want to research on other sources.

✔ **Google:** As you seek to understand green concepts, explore green industries, identify potential job titles, and find green companies, you'll discover Google is one of your best research tools. To make the most of your searches, enter your keyword into the search engine and then use a + sign to add a qualifier. For example, you might enter **"sustainability"** + **jobs** or **"solar manufacturing"** + **companies**. The more specific your keywords, the more useful your results become. Refer to Chapter 14 for instructions and specific examples of this strategy.

✔ **Green industry profiles:** Use the descriptions of green industries in Chapters 7 through 13 of this book as a jumping-off point for your own green industry exploration. Green Career Central (www.greencareer central.com/updates) provides updated information about the industries profiled in this book. Additional information about each industry is also available to members of the site, including links to conferences, job boards, news, education, glossaries, and keywords.

Identifying Green Networking Hubs

One of the most effective ways to move your green career forward is to build a strong green network. Connecting with people in your local area who are committed to sustainability and community action puts you in touch with a network of people who share your values and intentions.

Use the following resources to find green organizations in your area:

✔ **Green teams:** Communities around the country are forming to help cities make greener decisions and implement more sustainable programs. Check with your city hall. You may discover a city-appointed commission, city-sanctioned community organization, or grass-roots effort. As soon as you connect with the organization, start talking with the team members to figure out what role you can play.

✔ **Cool Cities Teams:** If you want to play a role in urging your community to take greener actions, take a look at Sierra Club's Cool Cities initiative. Use this map (www.coolcities.us) to find a Cool Cities group in your region of the United States or Canada.

✔ **Environmental organizations:** Use an online search, your local newspaper, or existing contacts to identify environmental organizations in your area. Depending on your community, you may find ways to volunteer at an organic farmers market, a land restoration project, a Habitat for Humanity effort, a wildlife conservation program, or a recycling education campaign. Find opportunities that fit your interests.

✔ **Professional networking groups:** Check out Eco Tuesdays (www. EcoTuesday.com), Green Drinks (www.greendrinks.org), and Net Impact (www.netimpact.org) for networking gatherings in your area.

In your efforts to connect with people in person, don't forget the value of building a green online network as well. Search the list of LinkedIn Groups (www.linkedin.com/groupsDirectory) or follow people talking about your target industry on Twitter. See Chapter 15 for more information.

Finding Green Companies

Identifying the companies and organizations that match your values is a critical part of your job search. Finding a list of companies that fits a particular criterion can be a great tool in locating companies you want to target.

- ✔ **Association membership lists:** On occasion, you'll find that an association lists its members on its Web site. Use that list as a starting point for your own research. For example, Social Venture Network (www.svn.org) provides a list of the socially responsible companies their members lead. Click the People link to find the list.

- ✔ **Lists of companies doing great work:** Books and Web sites often list companies who are doing extraordinary work in a particular area. For example, the Vault Guide to Green Programs (www.vault.com, click Store, and then click Career Topic Guides) highlights by name companies that have added green initiatives to their business plans. The book *Green to Gold: How Smart Companies Use Environmental Strategy to Innovate, Create Value, and Build Competitive Advantage* lists 50 national and international companies that are incorporating environmental strategies into their business initiatives.

- ✔ **Ratings of companies on green dimensions:** As the green economy develops, more watchdog groups and research organizations are evaluating companies on their green practices. Climate Counts (www.climatecounts.org/scorecard_overview.php) offers a score card on companies in various sectors of the economy. With a simple icon system, you can see whether a company is making strides, just starting out, or stuck when it comes to green initiatives.

See Chapters 18 and 19 for specific tips on researching companies and finding openings online and in your local region.

Staying Motivated and Entertained

Do you ever need an inspirational boost to remind you why you want to help the green movement through your profession? If so, use the following links to find movies and online videos that can snap you out of yourcomplacency:

- ✔ *The Story of Stuff* (www.storyofstuff.com) is an 20-minute online video that shows you where our stuff comes from and where it goes after we throw it away. It will forever change how you look at the stuff you buy and, more important, the stuff you toss.

- ✔ *Who Killed the Electric Car?* (www.whokilledtheelectriccar.com) and the sequel *Revenge of the Electric Car* (www.revengeoftheelectriccar.com) trace the ups and downs and ups of the electric car's journey.

- ***Planet Earth*** (`http://dsc.discovery.com/convergence/planet-earth/planet-earth.html`) is an 11-part miniseries that highlights the Earth's stunning beauty and amazing wildlife.

- ***An Inconvenient Truth*** (`www.climatecrisis.net/aboutthedvd`) provides a summary of the science behind climate change.

If you like to use movies, documentaries, and videos as a source of inspiration and exploration, check out these two green movie lists for more suggestions.

- The GRIST blog (`www.grist.org/article/movies`) provides a list of their top 15 green movie picks.

- Sierra Club blog (`www.sierraclub.typepad.com/greenlife`) has reviewed an extensive list of green movies. Enter **Green Movie Review** in the search box to pull up their entire list.

Finding Current Green Career Trends

If you're interested in discovering more green career tactics and tracking green career trends, take a look at the following blogs and newsletters:

- Green Economy Post (`www.greeneconomypost.com/category/career-development`)

- My Green Education and Career (`www.mygreeneducation.com`)

- Green Career Central's Green Career Tip of the Week (`www.greencareercentral.com/tipoftheweek`)

- Solutions for Green Careers (`www.solutionsforgreencareers.com`)

Chapter 22

Ten Ways to Green Your Current Job

. . . .

In This Chapter

▶ Using your resources wisely

▶ Amping up your energy efficiency

▶ Minimizing your transportation costs

. . . .

Making a green stand with your work doesn't necessarily mean you must change careers immediately. Greening the job you have now is a great place to start. In the process of making your job more sustainable, you deepen your connection with coworkers who share your values and green your resume.

Christine, a Sun Microsystems employee, took it upon herself to volunteer within her company to learn as much as she could about sustainability. The tasks she did outside of her official job helped the company prepare for the launch of their first green server. Volunteering on the green team gave her an opportunity to work with managers who were instrumental in bringing sustainability to the company. When an Eco-Responsibility Marketing Manager position was created, guess where management turned to fill it?

Use the strategies in this chapter to find ways to help your company become more sustainable. Some tips are actions you can take on your own. Others are strategies for stepping into a leadership role in transforming your company.

Minimizing the Paper You Use

How many pages do you print each day? Do you have any idea? Keep track of the amount of office paper (printing, copying, writing) you use for the next week and then estimate the amount of paper you use each year. I suspect you will be startled by the results.

According to GreenPrint (www.printgreener.com/earthday.html), the average U.S. office worker prints 10,000 pages per year. When put together, the amount of paper Americans use each year is enough to build a 10-foot-high wall that's 6,815 miles long. Consumption of global paper products has grown as well, tripling over the past three decades.

To understand the true environmental impact of the paper you use, check out the Paper Calculator by the Environmental Defense Fund (www.edf.org/papercalculator). After inputting the kind of paper and the amount of paper you use, click *calculate* to discover the impact different kinds of paper have on the environment in terms of the amount of wood and energy used to produce it and the amount of greenhouse gases, wastewater, and solid waste that result from its production.

Just to give you some perspective, Conservatree (www.conservatree.org) reports that it takes one tree to make 16.67 reams of copy paper or 8,333 sheets. Ninety percent of printing and writing paper is still made from virgin materials rather than recycled materials.

Here are some strategies to reduce the paper you use in your office:

- ✔ **Don't print.** This is your best option. If you need to share a document, save a copy on a shared drive or send it to people electronically.

- ✔ **Reduce the amount you print.** Instead of printing a copy of a document for everyone in your office, circulate one copy of the materials for review. Encourage centralized filing or online filing so there is no need to print multiple copies for filing.

- ✔ **Use double-sided printing.** If you must print a report, use double-sided printing to halve the number of pages.

- ✔ **Use recycled paper.** Purchasing recycled paper can also make a tremendous difference. See this online brochure for more facts: www.conservatree.com/paper/PaperTypes/RecyBrochure.shtml.

After printed materials are used, dispose of them properly. Reuse the paper to create notepads or packing materials. If reuse isn't feasible, recycle. According to TreeCycle.com (www.treecycle.com) producing recycled paper uses 60–70 percent less energy and 55 percent less water than making paper from virgin pulp. Furthermore, making recycled paper reduces water pollution by 35 percent and reduces air pollution by 74 percent.

Recycling Electronic Waste

According to the Environmental Protection Agency (www.epa.gov/waste/conserve/materials/ecycling/index.htm), the United States disposed of 2.5 million tons of electronic waste in 2007. Only 18 percent of it was recycled.

Electronic waste, or e-waste, is discarded TVs, computers, monitors, printers, scanners, mice, keyboards, and cellphones.

Putting electronic devices into landfill is bad for the following reasons:

✔ **Hazardous materials and chemicals are dangerous**. When electronic equipment ends up in landfill, the lead, mercury, brominated flame retardants, and cadmium get into nearby waterways and soil.

✔ **Precious metals and electronic materials are valuable resources**. When these precious materials go to landfill, we lose access to them. Consider the impact this can have. If we recycled 100 million cellphones, we could recover 3.4 metric tons of gold and avoid disrupting 5.5 million tons of soil, sand, and rock to mine that much new gold.

✔ **Creating brand-new devices uses tremendous amounts of energy.** According to the EPA, if 100 million cellphones were recycled instead of thrown away, we would be able to save enough energy to provide electricity to approximately 19,500 U.S. households for one year.

When you have e-waste to dispose of in your workplace, you have several options. Begin by exploring ways to donate your old equipment to schools or nonprofits in your area. If your equipment is too old or if you have data security concerns, recycling is probably your next best choice. Look into take-back programs and recycling events sponsored by companies that produce electronics. To find an e-waste recycler in your area, check out `www.electronics recycling.org`.

Leading Your Company's Recycling Efforts

If your company doesn't have a recycling program in place, you may have a golden opportunity to take the initiative to implement a program that will save your company money and lighten the load on your local landfill.

The best way to get started is to do a Web search, using the terms **how to start recycling program at work** with the name of your city. The search results will include recycling resources and organizations that are available in your area. You'll likely find effective collateral and recycling programs that are ready to implement in your company. (If you don't find what you're looking for in your search, try the name of your region or state.)

Think it's a little strange to spend your time disposing of other people's waste? Well, if you get the recycling program off the ground at your current employer, you never know how that success will bolster your career path.

Shortly after being hired as a part-time recycling assistant, Cheri Chastain was promoted to full-time Environmental Sustainability Coordinator at Sierra Nevada Brewery (www.sierranevada.com). How did she do it? After tracking the company's recycling efforts as an assistant, she used the data to identify opportunities that would improve the company's environmental impact and bottom line. In 2007 it recycled about 31,000 tons of material — saving $3 million dollars in charges from the waste hauler and the landfill — and earned more than $800,000 from selling excess materials. Cheri now reports to the owner of the company, and her responsibilities extend far beyond recycling; to include tracking greenhouse gas emissions, creating renewable energy sources, setting up composting projects, enhancing energy efficiency, conserving water, and more. (To hear Cheri talk about her green job, visit www.greenbiz.com/podcast/2008/04/14/from-suds-solar-the-greening-sierra-nevada-brewing-co.

Influencing Your Company's Purchasing Policies

Rather than focusing on how to dispose of waste, this greening strategy shifts the emphasis to which products are purchased in the first place. By setting up environmentally preferable purchasing or procurement policies, your company becomes more strategic about what products it buys.

The key purpose of a procurement policy is to minimize the negative impact on the environment by reducing toxicity, conserving energy, materials, and natural resources, increasing the use of recycled content, and maximizing the opportunity to recycle items at the end of their life cycles.

Although they appear straightforward, creating and implementing policies take time and commitment. Familiarize yourself with the following concepts to get a sense of the complexity of this crucial process:

- **Environmentally preferable products and services:** To determine whether a product or service is environmentally preferable, you must consider the raw materials and how they are acquired, the production or manufacturing process, the packaging, the distribution channels, how the product is used and maintained, whether the product is reusable, and how it is disposed of.

- **Life cycle cost:** Considering how much a product costs to purchase isn't the whole story. The life cycle cost must factor in the annual cost of a product, including the cost of installing, operating, maintaining, and disposing of it.

- **Recyclable product:** A product with this designation can be reused as a raw material in the manufacturing process for another product rather than going to landfill.

✔ **Recycled material:** A recycled resource is a material that has been diverted from solid waste and used in place of virgin material in manufacturing a product. This material can be made from post-consumer recycled material, manufacturing waste, industrial scrap, or agricultural waste. Recycled materials cannot, however, contain byproducts generated from an original manufacturing process, which is a sneaky tactic some companies use to claim a product is recycled.

By encouraging the purchase of environmentally preferred products, your company is helping to build a market for products that are recycled, eco-labeled, and environmentally friendly.

Moving toward More Sustainable Promotional Items

Most companies use promotional items to keep the company in front of its target customers. Unfortunately the entire life cycle of your typical promotional tchotchkes isn't very sustainable. From production to distribution, inordinate amounts of energy, raw resources, and fuel are consumed. In the end, most of them end up in the trash.

What do you know about the promotional items your company uses? Use the following questions to evaluate your company's promotional items:

✔ How are the promotional items manufactured? How much energy is used? What energy source is used?

✔ What kind of materials are used in the item? Are any of them hazardous? Are the materials sustainable, organic, recycled, or reused?

✔ How much does it cost to transport the promotional items from the manufacturer to you? What kind of carbon footprint does this transportation create? How about from you to your prospects? Are there any locally produced items you could use to avoid the cost and emissions of transporting items long distance?

✔ Do your prospects really want the promotional items your company offers? Will they keep them or send them straight to landfill?

✔ Are the promotional items recyclable or biodegradable?

Are the items portraying the right image of your company? Perhaps this is an opportunity for you to do some research and find solutions that fit the company budget while enhancing the company's image in your community.

Encouraging Your Company to Do an Energy Audit

Time magazine says that "heating, cooling, and powering office space are responsible for almost 40 percent of carbon dioxide emissions in the U.S. and gobble more than 70 percent of total electricity usage." ("Going Green at the Office," June 7, 2007, www.time.com/time/magazine/article/0,9171,1630552,00.html).

One of the most efficient ways to cut business costs is to do an energy audit. Check with your local utility company to determine whether they offer any auditing services. Often the utility will conduct the audit and produce a report for free. The report will likely tell you which areas of the company use the most energy. You may discover how much the company pays for energy leaks, inefficient lighting, and poor heating and cooling systems. Knowing these numbers makes it much easier to invest in repairs and efficiency upgrades. Calculating the return on investment is usually easy and fast.

During the audit, ask the utility representative about rebates and tax credits available through the utility, your local government, or the federal government. These rebates and tax credits may make energy retrofitting more affordable than you or your managers think is possible.

Persuading Your Company to Turn off Electronic Equipment at Night

Did you know that powering PCs and monitors accounts for 39 percent of the information and telecommunications industry's emissions — equal to a full year of CO_2 emissions from approximately 43.9 million cars? According to the *2009 US PC Energy Report* recently published by 1E (http://www.1e.com/energycampaign/), U.S. companies could save over $2.8 billion by turning off unused PCs overnight.

In the early days of computers it was thought that keeping computers on all the time caused less wear and tear on the systems and prevented costly repairs. Now, however, keeping computers running is just plain costly. If your company wants to cut costs and use less energy, do the math (using this handy calculator: www.1e.com/energycampaign/calculation.aspx) to determine the savings. If the company closes over the holidays, there's another opportunity to save some cash. A solid business case may be all it takes to shift management's view on the situation. If you need a compelling example to include in your report, consider this statement from 1E's *2009 US PC Energy Report*: "If all the world's 1 billion PC's were powered down for just one night it would save enough energy to light up New York City's Empire State Building — inside and out — for more than 30 years."

Traveling Wisely

National Business Travelers Association (www.nbta.org) claims U.S. business travelers rack up 240 billion miles annually. According to Trees for the Future (www.plant-trees.org), a carbon offset company, jets typically emit about one pound of carbon dioxide per passenger mile. Therefore, 240 billion miles of air travel translates into 1.2 billion tons of carbon dioxide in our air (http://www.greenbiz.com/research/report/2002/08/13/environmentally-responsible-business-travel).

Consider one of the following eco-friendly (and time-friendly) alternatives next time you need to book a long-distance flight for a business meeting:

- **Videoconferencing:** If you're the only one traveling to another office location for a meeting, find out about videoconferencing capabilities. You may be able to meet face to face without leaving your office.

- **Webinars:** Another alternative is to set up a webinar. This option can be helpful if you're meeting with people in multiple locations. Sign everyone up for a webinar by using interfaces such as Go to Meeting (www.gotomeeting.com). You can all converse while seeing the presentation or meeting materials on your screens.

- **Skype:** This option is perfect if you work with offices in other parts of the world. Meeting participants can enjoy free video and voice calls, chat, and share files with other Skype users (www.skype.com).

If you absolutely must travel to meet your business goals or attend a conference, pay attention to airlines who are working to green their airplanes (www.seatguru.com/articles/green_aircraft_and_airlines.php) or purchase carbon offsets for your flight.

Commuting Creatively

Business travel is just one part of the work-related transportation equation. Commuting is another. Instead of driving to work alone, consider whether any of the following commute alternatives work for you:

- ✔ **Carpooling:** Can you connect with others who drive to your office or a nearby office each day?

- ✔ **Public transit options:** Depending on where you live, you may be able to take public transit to work. A side benefit is time to read or listen to music, podcasts, or audio books.

- ✔ **Walk or bike:** These alternatives are best if you live close to work or you can combine this method with a transit option. With this option, exercise becomes integrated into your day.

- ✔ **Work from home:** Even if you can't work from home every day, you may be able to negotiate a work-from-home day or two per week.

Rethinking Shipping and Packaging

Moving products and supplies to and from your office has a profound impact on the planet. This carbon calculator can tell you how much carbon is produced by shipping packages: www.fgx.com/tools/carbon-calculator/. As you reevaluate your shipping department standards, consider the following components of the shipping equation:

- ✔ **Packaging:** Whenever possible reuse packing materials such as boxes, bubble wrap, and peanuts. Or use items that are readily available such as newspaper. If you must purchase new packing materials, search for biodegradable or post-consumer recycled packing materials. If your company is willing to spend a bit more, buy packing peanuts made from corn starch that dissolve in water. If you must ship with Styrofoam forms, ask your customers to ship them back to you for reuse.

- ✔ **Choose ground shipping:** Although it requires more planning, shipping by ground costs less and emits eight times less carbon than air travel (http://green.yahoo.com/blog/the_conscious_consumer/18/greener-shipping-options.html).

- ✔ **Shipping route:** Most shipping companies use a hub and spoke system to move packages. Although this strategy creates economies of scale, it's not the most environmentally efficient way to move packages. FGX (www.fgxusa.com), a greener shipping company, sends packages directly to overseas destinations without using out-of-the-way hubs, creating less carbon emissions, more cost savings, and faster deliveries.

Index

● *O* ●

Business/Accounting & Bookkeeping

Bookkeeping For Dummies
978-0-7645-9848-7

eBay Business
All-in-One For Dummies,
2nd Edition
978-0-470-38536-4

Job Interviews
For Dummies,
3rd Edition
978-0-470-17748-8

Resumes For Dummies,
5th Edition
978-0-470-08037-5

Stock Investing
For Dummies,
3rd Edition
978-0-470-40114-9

Successful Time
Management
For Dummies
978-0-470-29034-7

Computer Hardware

BlackBerry For Dummies,
3rd Edition
978-0-470-45762-7

Computers For Seniors
For Dummies
978-0-470-24055-7

iPhone For Dummies,
2nd Edition
978-0-470-42342-4

Laptops For Dummies,
3rd Edition
978-0-470-27759-1

Macs For Dummies,
10th Edition
978-0-470-27817-8

Cooking & Entertaining

Cooking Basics
For Dummies,
3rd Edition
978-0-7645-7206-7

Wine For Dummies,
4th Edition
978-0-470-04579-4

Diet & Nutrition

Dieting For Dummies,
2nd Edition
978-0-7645-4149-0

Nutrition For Dummies,
4th Edition
978-0-471-79868-2

Weight Training
For Dummies,
3rd Edition
978-0-471-76845-6

Digital Photography

Digital Photography
For Dummies,
6th Edition
978-0-470-25074-7

Photoshop Elements 7
For Dummies
978-0-470-39700-8

Gardening

Gardening Basics
For Dummies
978-0-470-03749-2

Organic Gardening
For Dummies,
2nd Edition
978-0-470-43067-5

Green/Sustainable

Green Building
& Remodeling
For Dummies
978-0-470-17559-0

Green Cleaning
For Dummies
978-0-470-39106-8

Green IT For Dummies
978-0-470-38688-0

Health

Diabetes For Dummies,
3rd Edition
978-0-470-27086-8

Food Allergies
For Dummies
978-0-470-09584-3

Living Gluten-Free
For Dummies
978-0-471-77383-2

Hobbies/General

Chess For Dummies,
2nd Edition
978-0-7645-8404-6

Drawing For Dummies
978-0-7645-5476-6

Knitting For Dummies,
2nd Edition
978-0-470-28747-7

Organizing For Dummies
978-0-7645-5300-4

SuDoku For Dummies
978-0-470-01892-7

Home Improvement

Energy Efficient Homes
For Dummies
978-0-470-37602-7

Home Theater
For Dummies,
3rd Edition
978-0-470-41189-6

Living the Country Lifestyle
All-in-One For Dummies
978-0-470-43061-3

Solar Power Your Home
For Dummies
978-0-470-17569-9

Internet

Blogging For Dummies,
2nd Edition
978-0-470-23017-6

eBay For Dummies,
6th Edition
978-0-470-49741-8

Facebook For Dummies
978-0-470-26273-3

Google Blogger
For Dummies
978-0-470-40742-4

Web Marketing
For Dummies,
2nd Edition
978-0-470-37181-7

WordPress For Dummies,
2nd Edition
978-0-470-40296-2

Language & Foreign Language

French For Dummies
978-0-7645-5193-2

Italian Phrases
For Dummies
978-0-7645-7203-6

Spanish For Dummies
978-0-7645-5194-9

Spanish For Dummies,
Audio Set
978-0-470-09585-0

Macintosh

Mac OS X Snow Leopard
For Dummies
978-0-470-43543-4

Math & Science

Algebra I For Dummies
978-0-7645-5325-7

Biology For Dummies
978-0-7645-5326-4

Calculus For Dummies
978-0-7645-2498-1

Chemistry For Dummies
978-0-7645-5430-8

Microsoft Office

Excel 2007 For Dummies
978-0-470-03737-9

Office 2007 All-in-One
Desk Reference
For Dummies
978-0-471-78279-7

Music

Guitar For Dummies,
2nd Edition
978-0-7645-9904-0

iPod & iTunes
For Dummies,
6th Edition
978-0-470-39062-7

Piano Exercises
For Dummies
978-0-470-38765-8

Parenting & Education

Parenting For Dummies,
2nd Edition
978-0-7645-5418-6

Type 1 Diabetes
For Dummies
978-0-470-17811-9

Pets

Cats For Dummies,
2nd Edition
978-0-7645-5275-5

Dog Training For Dummies,
2nd Edition
978-0-7645-8418-3

Puppies For Dummies,
2nd Edition
978-0-470-03717-1

Religion & Inspiration

The Bible For Dummies
978-0-7645-5296-0

Catholicism For Dummies
978-0-7645-5391-2

Women in the Bible
For Dummies
978-0-7645-8475-6

Self-Help & Relationship

Anger Management
For Dummies
978-0-470-03715-7

Overcoming Anxiety
For Dummies
978-0-7645-5447-6

Sports

Baseball For Dummies,
3rd Edition
978-0-7645-7537-2

Basketball For Dummies,
2nd Edition
978-0-7645-5248-9

Golf For Dummies,
3rd Edition
978-0-471-76871-5

Web Development

Web Design All-in-One
For Dummies
978-0-470-41796-6

Windows Vista

Windows Vista
For Dummies
978-0-471-75421-3